THE ULTIMATE GUIDE TO
GRILLING

THE ULTIMATE GUIDE TO
GRILLING

How to Grill Just About Anything

RICK BROWNE

Skyhorse Publishing

Skyhorse Publishing books may be purchased in bulk at special discounts for sales promotion, corporate gifts, fund-raising, or educational purposes. Special editions can also be created to specifications. For details, contact the Special Sales Department, Skyhorse Publishing, 307 West 36th Street, 11th Floor, New York, NY 10018 or info@skyhorsepublishing.com.

Skyhorse and Skyhorse Publishing are registered trademarks of Skyhorse Publishing, Inc., a Delaware corporation.

www.skyhorsepublishing.com

10 9 8 7 6 5 4 3 2 1

Library of Congress Cataloging-in-Publication Data is available on file.
ISBN: 978-1-61608-067-9

Printed in China

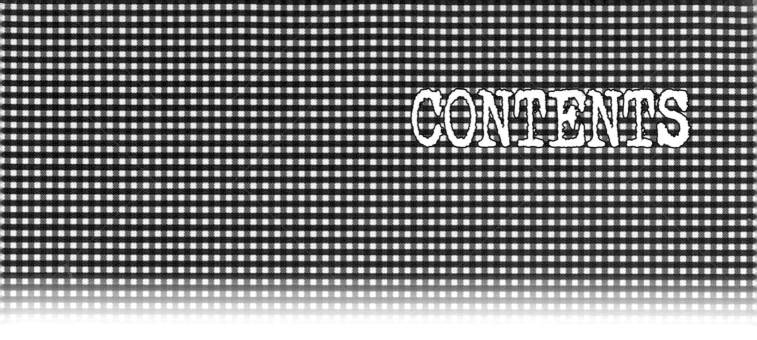

CONTENTS

Introduction   1

CHAPTER 1 Appetizers   4
(Indirect) Grilling America   5

CHAPTER 2 Beef   20
Tenny Lamas, Frickles & Rockies   21

CHAPTER 3 Fish & Shellfish   36
Bbq On The Sammish Slough   37
Got Lobsta?   63

CHAPTER 4 Lamb   68
What's That You're Smokin'?   69

CHAPTER 5 Pork   78
They Make A Village   79
Swine & Dine Team, 2oo2   83

CHAPTER 6 Poultry   104
Plankin' It!   105

CHAPTER 7 Side Dishes   124
Bubba's Got The Mop   125

CHAPTER 8 Sauces, Marinades & Dry Rubs   154
Barbecue's Holy Grail   155

CHAPTER 9 Vegetarian Bbq   180
Name De La Flame   181

CHAPTER 10 Wild Game   196
Smilling & Groking   197
Stopping By Some Woods
On A Barbecue Evening   202

CHAPTER 11 Desserts   216
Que'n At The Ritz   217

Index   245

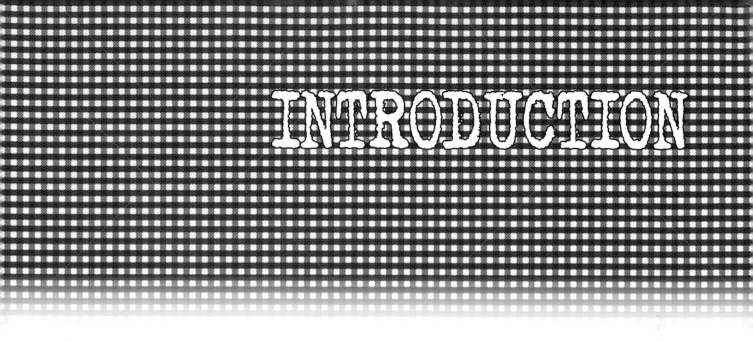

INTRODUCTION

THANKQUE AMERICA

Is it barbecue, or grilling? As he carefully sprays the cinder-black beef brisket which he has been nurturing for 32 straight hours at 220° degrees, Brett says "barbecue can ONLY be defined as the cooking of meat over low heat for long periods of time."

But Andy throws a misshapen burger on a hot grill over a 600° degree fire, sprinkles seasoned salt and steak sauce on it, flips it over once or twice and happily calls that process "barbecue".

And you know what? They're both right.

"Slow and low" purists decry the speed with which grillers sear and serve their meat. "Grillers" don't have time to cook slow nor low. But Andy is just as happy munching his five-minute burger on the back porch as Brett is savoring each bite of his buttery brisket after 1,920 minutes of cooking.

After all, the heating method, fuel, or barbecue equipment we use really don't matter a smidgen. The taste of the finished product, however, matters a whole lot.

And it seems that just about everyone is barbecuing (er, grilling) these days. In fact, in families of four or more in the US a whopping 91% now own outdoor cookers. People cook on gas grills, charcoal kettle cookers, electric grills, pellet and water smokers, deep fryers, and some even still use hardwood logs in their bullet smokers to slow-cook their grub.

Many families have more than one way to cook outdoors—it's estimated that a fifth of all grill owners have BOTH a gas and charcoal unit. And everywhere you look, sales of charcoal grills, gas grills, deep-fat propane-fired fryers, and even electric grills are skyrocketing.

But remember it's not what you cook on. It's **what** you cook, how you cook it, and most importantly, **how the results taste**. Whether you use natural gas, lump charcoal, propane, fruitwood logs, briquettes, grape vines, hardwood pellets, coconut shells, electric heating elements, nut shells, hot oil, or a combination of all of these, outdoor cooking is simply, as the name implies, using some sort of heat source outdoors.

It's no rocket science, Bubba. The same rules apply on the patio as in the kitchen. That $32 butterflied leg of lamb can be done just right inside or incinerated beyond recognition outside. Or vice versa.

You can prepare a soufflé on a gas grill just like you can in your $3,500 gas oven. You can reduce a perfect rib eye steak to charred fibers on your charcoal grill just as easily as you can under the broiler of your old-reliable, never-fail kitchen stove.

What we hope to present here is a way to expand your outdoor grillery beyond hamburgers and hot dogs. And although dogs and burgers, and that good old standby BBQ chicken, are still the mainstays of outdoor cooking, backyard cooks are attempting – and successfully undertaking—more creative culinary endeavors.

We'll show you how to barbecue ice cream. How to do things on your grill that chefs accomplish in fancy restaurants for $30 a plate. How to make your own "custom" BBQ sauce using commercially bottled "generic" sauces as a base. And how to dazzle visitors who come expecting fair backyard fare and instead get grilling great.

But mostly we hope to share with our readers how to have fun creating rhapsodies of smoke, spice, and fire on your lowly backyard barbecue grill.

It was interesting to learn during our travels that at some of the biggest barbecue contests in the country, where the most accomplished BBQ chefs in the world compete for $60,000 in prizes, that $29 hardware-store bullet smokers can hold their own against $30,000 custom-built, stainless-steel, computer-controlled, high-tech smokers that fill 32-foot trailers.

No judge, pitmaster, backyard critic, or even mother-in-law cares how the taste gets into the meat. The trick is to be damn sure it gets there!

For heaven's sakes be bold, broaden your "que" quotient, and get out and experiment. If you live in North Carolina, try a California Tri-tip roast basted in olive oil, garlic, and balsamic vinegar. If you live in Maine, cedar-plank barbecue an Alaska Copper River salmon. And if you live in Vancouver, go ahead cook Owensboro grilled lamb with Kentucky-style black dip.

Missouri grillers need to slop yellow mustard sauce from Georgia on their St. Louis ribs, at the same time that bold pitmasters in Houston should go ahead and commit BBQ heresy by drizzling a Pacific Rim hoisin-soy sauce on their beloved brisket.

With so many regional styles of barbecue available, why cook with the same methods, sauces or rubs that you've used for years? It's time for America to follow a few brave adventurers and break out of the barbecue doldrums. Time to "que" something completely new, or grill something cherished and familiar a brand new way.

INTRODUCTION

Over 2,000 bottled BBQ sauces are commercially available. Literally thousands of kinds of rubs are waiting to enhance anything you wish to rub them on. Once-rare regional food specialties are now readily available coast to coast. And folks just like us spent a whopping $845 million dollars in barbecue restaurants last year. Frankly, it's a sin to isolate, ignore, or deprive educating your BBQ taste buds any longer.

Break free! Go for it! Grab this book, or any one of 100+ BBQ tomes written in the last five years, and boldly go where no man, or woman, has gone before. Bravely close your eyes, open our cookbooks to just about any page, and try whatever is written there. *Youse got nuttin' to lose, Bub.*

We've tried our best to open up the barbecue scene for everyone to enjoy. We've grilled, smoked, BBQ baked, fried, broiled, rotisseried, boiled, and braised whatever came our way. All in an attempt to put great-tasting food on your table. And we think you'll enjoy the process itself, as well as the diversity of tastes, styles, and methods we've set before you.

Grilling America, like its older brother, **Barbecue America**, hopes to freely share the best of the Que we've sampled in five years of travel across America's barbecue heartland. A heartland that has magically expanded to reach from sea to shining sea.

No longer is GREAT BARBECUE indigenous only South of the Mason-Dixon line. World-class pork ribs can be found in Seattle, Syracuse, or Sacramento. Whole hogs, once the exclusive domain of the deep South, today are barbecued in pits from Rockport, Maine, to Rock Port, Missouri, to Rockport, Washington.

Black as a meteorite and mouth-wateringly tender Texas-style brisket can be enjoyed in Dallas (of course) but also in Detroit, Dayton, and Danbury. That's Michigan, Ohio, and Connecticut for the geographically challenged.

And genuine pulled pork shoulder sandwiches topped with crisp mustardy cole slaw are almost as easy to find north, east and west of Dixie as they are in Southern BBQ sanctuaries like Lexington, North Carolina, or Columbus, Georgia.

Barbecue literally is on fire across America.

All we ask is that you make the effort to try a new rub, sauce, and recipe as you join us in fanning the flames.

Rick Browne, Ph. B.
BARBECUE & GRILLING AMERICA

CHAPTER 1

APPETIZERS

007 Martini Oysters   8

Armadillo Eggs   8

CB's Oh-You-Devil Eggs   9

Dixie Watermelon Salsa   10

Frickles Fried Pickles   11

Gilroy Stinking Rose Mushrooms   11

Gouvenor Beach Peanut Salad   12

Kara Beth's Hot Damn Wings   12

Louisiana Fire Pecans   13

Zesty Lemon Butter   13

Mikey's Melbourne Crab Damper   14

Milan's Coconut Babybacks   15

Razorback Patay   16

Scotch-Smoked Trout or Salmon   16

Smoky Wild Mushroom Tart   18

How to Judge BBQ Grill Temps   19

(Indirect) GRILLING AMERICA

The fountain of youth, next week's lottery numbers, and the cure for pattern baldness? Nope! Just the best way to grill just about everything from beer-butt to burgers.

Everyone knows how to grill a hamburger, hot dog or steak. You take the meat, throw it on the hot barbecue grill, turn it once or twice so it doesn't burn (too much anyway), and then slap it on a plate, burger bun or hot dog roll and chow down.

WRONG!

Grilling is actually much more a refined culinary art than that. Sure, you put what you're cooking on a hot grill, but the above method usually guarantees dry, tasteless meat, that almost always has a charred surface hidden somewhere. How many times have you hidden a charred burger or chicken breast with oodles of barbecue sauce, mustard or ketchup?

A better way to grill is to use a combination of "direct grilling," as above, and then "indirect grilling," cooking the food away from the heat source, slowly, thereby keeping it juicy, tender and loaded with taste.

For those who cook with charcoal briquette, mesquite chunk, or hickory logs:

When putting the coals, briquettes or a log into the barbecue, place the combustible materials on ONE SIDE ONLY of the bottom of the barbecue. Leave the other half of the bottom empty (for now) and start your fire as you normally would. Hopefully with an electric firestarter or kindling, NOT flammable chemicals which can then flavor (actually dis-flavor) the food you want to cook.

When the fuel is up to temperature (you know, covered with a thin film of white ash, etc.) take an old metal pan, or a new foil pan, that's about 9" x 12" and using barbecue mitts place the pan on the empty side of the bottom. Using a large pitcher, fill the pan with 1-2" inches of water.

Now place your grill rack into the barbecue over the coals. At this time you should probably clean and oil it, if you haven't done so already.

Some hints here: If you have an expensive copper grill brush for heaven's sakes use it to scrape off the remains of your last BBQ immolation. But if you don't have such fancy gear take a piece of aluminum foil, say a 12" x 12" piece, wad it up loosely into a ball, and, using long tongs, use it to scrape off the grill after it's been over the fire for 2-3 minutes. The foil works wonders on getting the majority of the burned on food off the grill rack, and you just discard it after using. Hot fire will take care of the rest of the remains during the heating period.

Now sit back, close the lid on the barbecue, grab a brew, pull up a lounge chair, and relax until the fire is at the correct temperature for what you're cooking.

At this point you should "oil the grill." A good way to do this is to take a sheet of paper towel and fold it into a 2" x 2" (or similar) square. Again using long tongs, dip the towel into a small bowl of olive, vegetable, or other favorite cooking oil. Then rub it across the grill surface, covering the entire grill rack. You may have to re-dip several times.

You could also keep one barbecue basting brush handy just for this purpose, dipping the brush into the oil, and brushing across the rack. If the bristles are plastic you'll only do this one time however, ending up with a melted mass at the end of the handle. Natural bristles last much longer.

Either the oiled towel, or the brushed-on oil method works fine.

However, some adventurous folks like to use a nonstick spray which they try to spray across the heated grill surface. NOPE! Not a good thing to do unless you really want a wall of flames shooting toward you! The aerosol spray can easily catch fire and, with a dramatic *whoosh* you've succeeded in barbecuing—your face!

Now that the grill is on the barbecue, and is well oiled, you can add the food you wish to Que.

I often start out with the meat, poultry, fish, or veggies placed on the "hot" side of the grill. *Remember the coals, briquettes, etc. are only on one side of the barbecue.* This way I can sear the food with a high heat, keeping the natural juices inside. Depending on the food, it's thickness, and the fire temperature below, I'll cook the food for a short time on each side over the higher heat, 2-3 minutes is an average time.

Then, again depending on the recipe, I'll move the food to the "cool" side of the grill. (Cool is a relative term here: the "hot" side of the grill may be at 600° to 700° degrees, while the "cool" side may be as high as 400° to 500° degrees, or thereabouts.)

The "cool" side of the grill, you remember, is also over the pan of water, which keeps flames from shooting up and engulfing the food, something that often happens when you just "direct grill". Fat drips onto the hot coals, flames up, and you've got fire charring everything on the barbecue.

The water also evaporates during the cooking process and the steam helps keep the food above it moist, juicy and tasty. Note: some folks like to throw herbs, citrus slices, onion peels, etc. into the water to "flavor" the steam. I personally don't think this does anything other than give you a colorful pan of water, but if you wish, give it a try.

Presto, chango! now you're INDIRECT COOKING on charcoal (or whatever).

In a later chapter I'll discuss how to make this set-up into a grill-smoker too, adding fragrant wood smoke to your indirectly grilled vittles.

If you have a gas grill the process is much the same, only different.

Most gas barbecues have at least 2 burners, some have 3, and a few have 4 or more burners. Don't matter, as long as there are 2.

Turn the flame on only one burner. Place your water pan over the unlit burner and Ta-da! you've got your gas grill set up. Because of the height of some burners you may have to put bricks on both sides of the unlit burner to balance the water pan. Easily done.

Clean and oil the rack the same way, and in the same sequence, as the charcoal barbecue and you can cook your heart away. Well, not really, that would hurt a mite. First placing the food on the "hot" side to sear, and then on the "cool" side to cook for the rest of the time. Voila! you're INDIRECT COOKING on gas.

If you've got more burners you can be a bit more creative. With a three burner set-up you can turn on both "outside" burners (to the same temperature please, otherwise you'll cook one side of your grub quicker). Then place the water pan over the middle burner, therefore having even heat on both sides of what you're cookin'. Again, sear on the "hot" side, cook for the duration on the "cool" side.

Using this method you can virtually cook anything on a barbecue that you can cook in your kitchen oven. Remember that a barbecue is just a sort of an "outdoor oven". It has a heat source (gas, briquettes or coals) like an oven (remember Granny's woodstove Bub?), it's an enclosed box like an oven, and you can, somewhat anyway, control the heat like an oven.

Using INDIRECT COOKING I've make soufflé's, baked bread, custards, cakes, and pies, and perfectly cooked what otherwise might have been incinerated over direct heat. And the slower, lower temperature cooking, after the meat has been seared to keep the juices inside, gives just about the best results possible to those expensive cuts of meat that you splurge on for those special occasion barbecues.

As a novice barbecuer I sinned like many of you, making up all the excuses you've uttered yourselves. "That black, crispiness? Oh that's just a new blackened BBQ sauce technique I'm trying, honey." Or, "No, Chris those aren't hockey pucks, they're Daddy's burgers, they'll taste fine, trust me." And of course, "This grill just doesn't work right, everything burns, here I turn my back for just the last quarter of the game, you know the Niner's won, and the steaks look, gulp, burned."

It's okay fellow Bubbaquers, now you can be "cool" and never ever have to scrape the burned flesh from a burger, chicken wing, or T-bone again. Your steaks will be perfect medium-rare, your beer-butt birds golden and juicy, and your burgers . . . well it doesn't get much better!

007 MARTINI OYSTERS

These oysters are perfect when served with lots of ice cold vodka in chilled shot glasses.

1 cup vodka
2 tablespoons finely chopped green olives
1 tablespoons finely chopped shallots
small dash vermouth, optional
12 large oysters on the half shell
fresh black pepper

Put the vodka, olives, and shallots in an 8 oz. plastic container. Add small dash of vermouth if desired. Shake well, do not stir, and put the container in a freezer for at least a day.

Build a hot fire in grill using charcoal, wood or briquettes. Shuck the oysters and put each half-shell containing oyster on grill, saving as much of the natural juices as you can.

Drizzle martini mixture over each oyster, and cook just until the edges curl. Liberally grind fresh black pepper over each oyster.

Remove from grill and serve.

Serves 4-6

ARMADILLO EGGS

I serve with very cold longneck beer.
12 medium size jalapeno peppers

FILLING:

½ cup Velveeta cheese
½ teaspoons garlic salt
¼ teaspoons McCormick Cajun seasoning
¼ teaspoons white or black pepper
1 large egg, beaten
½ pound ground chuck
½ teaspoons onion powder
½ teaspoons dried parsley
pinch tarragon
12 slices smoked bacon

Cut jalapenos in half, seed them and fill with the Velveeta cheese and spice mixture, then put them back together. Mix one beaten egg into the ground beef, add the onion powder, parsley and tarragon. and mold a small amount of the meat around each pepper. Wrap each burger-pepper with a slice of thick bacon, securing with toothpicks.

Cook on smoker grill beside smoking ribs or pork shoulder at approx. 200 ° F for approximately one hour, or until bacon crisps and meat is browned.

Serves 4-6

CB'S OH-YOU-DEVIL EGGS

6 extra large eggs
½ teaspoons salt
⅛ teaspoons pepper
1 teaspoons sugar
1 teaspoons prepared mustard
1 teaspoons cider vinegar
3 tablespoons mayonnaise
paprika

Place the eggs gently into medium sized pan. Add cold water till ½-inch above tops of eggs. Cover with lid and heat slowly to boiling, then immediately turn heat down to very low so water is barely simmering. Cook 20 minutes.

Place pan in sink and run under cold water till cool enough to handle. Remove the eggs tap lightly all over and then peel them under cold running water. Cut each egg in half lengthwise. Remove yolks carefully, putting them in a small glass bowl. With a fork, mash the yolks.

Add the salt, pepper, sugar, mustard, cider vinegar, and mayonnaise. Mix well. Spoon mixture lightly into holes left in the eggs. Sprinkle tops with paprika. Place eggs in a single layer on a platter.

Cover and keep chilled in refrigerator till serving time.

Serves 6

DIXIE WATERMELON SALSA

This salsa is great with steak, roasts, or fish barbecue.

6 cups diced watermelon, seeds removed
1 ½ cup diced onion
4-6 tablespoons jalapeno chilies, seeded and
    finely chopped
3 tablespoons extra virgin olive oil
3 tablespoons red wine vinegar
2 tablespoons fresh lime juice
½ cup finely chopped cilantro salt, to taste

In a large stainless steel or glass mixing bowl, combine all ingredients. Mix well. Chill overnight. Use half watermelon which you've hollowed out as a serving dish, and fill with prepared salsa.

Serves 4-6

PRICKLES—FRIED PICKLES

These deep fried pickles make a great, if quite surprising appetizer, for any barbecue meal. Serve with icy cold beer in frosted mugs.

1 cup flour
1 cup yellow corn meal
1 tablespoons McCormick barbecue seasoning
½ cup mustard
⅛ cup beer
20-30 dill pickle slices

Combine the flour, cornmeal, and BBQ spice mix and place in a medium bowl. Make a slurry of mustard and beer in a separate medium bowl.

Dip pickle slices in mustard mixture and then in flour/cornmeal. Deep fry at 325° F in peanut or Canola oil until batter is browned. Pickles will float to top when done.

Serve as an appetizer with icy cold beer.

Serves 4-8

GILROY STINKING ROSE MUSHROOMS

Have plenty of napkins on hand for these drippy, yummy mushrooms.

2-3 cloves garlic, finely chopped
½ small chopped sweet onion
3 teaspoons fresh chopped parsley
1 cup finely grated Parmesan cheese
4 tablespoons butter, softened
black pepper to taste
sea salt to taste
16 large mushrooms, stems removed

In medium bowl mix all ingredients except mushrooms. Fill each mushroom cap with stuffing, mounding it nicely. Place on grill of barbecue over medium direct heat until mushrooms are lightly browned and cooked soft.

Serves 4-8

GOUVENOR BEACH PEANUT SALAD

We love to present this delicious salad on a plate of radicchio or butter lettuce.

1 small head of cabbage, finely chopped
2 cups finely chopped unsalted peanuts (or pecans or walnuts)
1 teaspoons butter
1 teaspoons mustard
1 teaspoons brown sugar
1 teaspoons whole wheat flour
¾ teaspoons pepper
4 tablespoons apple cider vinegar
2 egg yolks, beaten salt

In a medium bowl mix the chopped cabbage and peanuts together and set aside. Cream the butter, mustard, sugar and flour together until a thick paste, then add the pepper and stir in the vinegar. In a double boiler heat this mixture while stirring, until very thick. Add beaten egg yolks, salt to taste, and mix thoroughly. When mixed and while still warm, pour over nuts and cabbage, toss gently and serve.

Serves 4-6

KARA BETH'S HOT DAMN WINGS

3 to 5 tablespoons Louisiana Hot Sauce

3 tablespoons vegetable oil
1 tablespoons white vinegar
¼ teaspoons garlic powder
2 ½ pound chicken wings—separated

Get a very hot fire going in your barbecue, with glowing coals or the gas turned to high. Be sure to brush the grill with approximately 1 tablespoon of oil to prevent sticking.

In a medium sized mixing bowl combine hot sauce, remaining oil, vinegar, and garlic powder.

After heating grill turn down heat to medium. Grill the wings for 7 minutes on one side before turning them over for another 7 minutes until nicely browned.

Serves 4-6

LOUISIANA FIRE PECANS

½ cup butter

2 tablespoons paprika

2 tablespoons Worcestershire Sauce

2 tablespoons orange juice

½ teaspoons granulated garlic

1 teaspoons mixed dried Italian seasoning

1 ½ teaspoons onion powder

1 ½ teaspoons brown sugar

¼ teaspoons liquid smoke

dash of Louisiana hot sauce

¼ teaspoons red pepper

seasoned salt

1 pound shelled pecan halves

Heat your barbecue grill to very high heat. Turn gas burners to high, or if you're using charcoal or briquettes the grill should be hot enough so your hand can only stay 2-3 inches over it for 1 second .

Mix all ingredients except the nuts in a small saucepan, bringing them to a slow simmer for 5 minutes, or until mixture is well heated through. Take off burner and add the pecans to the pot, stirring well. Drain the pecans slightly and place on a vegetable grill pan (or you can use a cookie sheet) which has been sprayed with non-stick spray.

Place on grill in very hot barbecue for 3-4 minutes until just browned. Sprinkle with salt, to taste.

Serve warm or cold.

Serves 4-6

ZESTY LEMON BUTTER

Juice of one lemon

1 tablespoons finely chopped lemon zest

1 teaspoons finely c hopped fresh parsley

pinch of salt

2 sticks softened butter

sprinkle of paprika

Mix juice, zest, parsley, and salt into softened butter. Mold into small round dish, sprinkle with paprika, and chill.

Serves 8

MIKEY'S MELBOURNE CRAB DAMPER

Michael Coyne, Melbourne, Austalia

A fine chap, who often says "some bread and a piece of cheese would do fine" when asked what he wants for a meal, but is a Tasmanian devil in the kitchen whipping up "down under" culinary wonders.

3 cups buttermilk

1 cup cream

½ teaspoons paprika

1 teaspoons garlic salt

¼ teaspoon pepper

1 cup yellow corn meal

¼ cup melted butter

2 cups crab meat, cooked (Dungeness or other local favorite)

4 eggs, beaten

1 small can green chilies, mild or hot

1 cup cubed Emmenthaler cheese

Combine buttermilk, cream, paprika, salt, pepper in a medium size saucepan. Heat on medium heat until just warm and well mixed, then add corn meal, stirring constantly until smooth and heated through. Reduce heat to low.

Add melted butter, crabmeat, beaten eggs, green chilies, and cheese, stirring over low heat for 3 minutes. Pour the batter into a large greased cast iron pot. As bread will rise make sure you have 2 inches of pot above liquid.

Place in smoker, or kettle type barbecue, on opposite side of grill from coals, gas burners or briquettes, for 40-50 minutes or until surface is golden brown and toothpick inserted into the middle comes out clean.

Cool slightly, take out of cast iron pot and cut into 8 pieces. Serve with butter (see below).

Serves 8

MILAN'S COCONUT BABYBACKS

These are awesome served with garlic mashed potatoes or BBQ sweet potatoes.

The sweet soft potatoes complementing the meaty texture of the ribs.

Milan Chuckovich, Vancouver, WA

A sweet giant of a man who loves to cook, have friends over for lunch or dinner, and watch his son, Ben, play football. The world could do with many more of him.

5 pounds baby back pork ribs

1 cup canned unsweetened coconut milk

½ cup chopped fresh basil

½ cup dark brown sugar

⅓ cup chopped shallots

¼ cup Teriyaki sauce

3 tablespoons chopped garlic

1 tablespoon peeled and finely chopped fresh ginger

lemon peel from two large lemons, finely chopped

1 teaspoon garlic salt

1 cup toasted coconut flakes

Rinse the ribs. Cut them into single ribs using a "Hollywood Cut" (Cut meat close to bone on first rib, then cut meat close to bone on third rib, thereby you have the second rib bone with more meat on each side).

Combine the coconut milk, basil, brown sugar, shallots, teriyaki sauce, garlic, ginger, lemon peel, and salt into a blender or food processor and pulse chop until almost smooth.

Place Hollywood ribs in 1 gallon sealable plastic bag and add marinade, seal bag and refrigerate overnight, turning 2-3 times.

Heat coals or briquettes to medium-high heat. Oil or spray grill with non-stick spray.

Remove ribs from the marinade and pour the liquid into a medium sized pan. Boil for at least 10 minutes but no more than 15 minutes. Cool, add all but 2 tablespoons of the coconut flakes, then use the liquid to baste ribs. Grill ribs until browned and tender, basting often. When ribs are finished place them in a large covered baking dish or on a large piece of heavy duty aluminum foil, brush heavily with marinade, sprinkle with remaining coconut flakes, seal foil, and set away from heat.

Serves 4

RAZORBACK PATAY

Best presented and served with crackers, crisp bread rounds or party rye bread.

12 ounces liverwurst, the cheaper the better
6-8 large finely minced mushroom caps
2 tablespoons onion, finely minced
1 tablespoon Jack Daniel's whiskey
1 tablespoon orange juice, without pulp
1 tablespoon mayonnaise

TOPPING:

2 tablespoons heavy cream
1 tablespoon mayonnaise
¼ teaspoon cumin
¼ teaspoon white pepper, ground
pinch of garlic salt
½ cup cream cheese
Cracked black pepper

Mix the first six ingredients together and mash together well, then put in food processor to blend completely. Spread into a medium sized loaf pan and chill for 2-3 hours.

Thoroughly mix the topping ingredients in a blender or food processor. Spoon over chilled meat mixture and spread evenly to cover mix. Sprinkle with cracked black pepper.

Put medium sized loaf pan back in refrigerator for 2-4 more hours.

Unmold and serve immediately.

Serves 6-8

SCOTCH-SMOKED TROUT OR SALMON

Serve fish with rye or pumpernickel bread with unsalted butter, garnish with small gherkins or *cornishons*. Grant & June Browne, Kimberly, British Columbia

WET BRINE:

3 cups water
1 cup dry white wine
½ cup light brown sugar
20 juniper berries, ground
½ cup pickling spices
4 teaspoons coarse salt
3 tablespoons cracked black pepper
zest of two lemons, finely chopped
whole fish, butterflied or fillet of fish (salmon, trout, shark, halibut, etc.)

Heat the water and wine in a medium sized pan and bring to a boil over high heat, add the brown sugar and quickly reduce heat to medium low and stir until sugar dissolves. Add the berries, pickling spice, salt, pepper and zest. Cover, reduce heat to simmer and cook for one hour. Remove from heat, strain brine through a cheesecloth, discard spices, and cool the brine in the refrigerator.

Lay fillet or whole butterflied fish in a large glass or ceramic dish and cover with cold brine. Cover dish with plastic wrap or aluminum foil and refrigerate overnight. If you don't have that much time following these guidelines for minimum times to brine fish.

Fish thickness	Fat fish	Lean fish
¾″	2 ½ hrs	1 ½ hrs
1″	3 ½ hrs	2 ½ hrs
1 ¼″	4 ¾ hrs	3 ¼ hrs
1 ½″	6 hrs	4 hrs
1 ¾″	7 ¼ hrs	4 ¾ hrs
2″	9 ½ hrs	6 ½ hrs
2 ½″	12 hrs	8 hrs
3″	14 ¼ hrs	9 ½ hrs

These times are just a guide, each variety of fish reacts somewhat differently. When done the flesh will be firm enough for slicing and feel like the lean part of a slab of bacon when pressed with a finger.

Prepare barbecue for smoking, placing a medium sized pan filled with 1″ or so of water under the grill where fish will rest. If using a kettle or small barbecue have coals on one side of barbecue, place fish on side of grill away from the heat, again, completely over water pan.

Remove fish from the brine, pat dry and place it skin side down on the grill. Discard brine. Cover and smoke over aromatic wood smoke for 2 to 2 ½ hours until fish's internal temperature is 140-145°F.

Can be served warm or cold, sliced very thinly.

SMOKY WILD MUSHROOM TART

2 oz. each dried porcini, cepe, oyster, shitake,
  and chanterelles
1 medium red onion
2 tablespoons butter
¼ cup extra virgin olive oil
2 tablespoons dried parsley
1 tablespoon dried savory
1 tablespoon dried sage
½ cup fresh wild mushrooms (from the market)
½ cups portabello mushrooms cut in ¼ inch
  strips
3 tablespoons tomato paste
1 cup beef (or chicken) stock
4 eggs
¾ cup freshly grated Parmesan cheese
2 tablespoons Jack Daniel's
Salt and lemon pepper to taste
1 pre-cooked 10 inch tart pastry shell in
  aluminum foil

Reconstitute the mushrooms in warm water for 20 minutes and set aside.

Chop the onion and sauté in the butter and olive oil until translucent, then add dried herbs and cook for an additional 2 minutes. Add the fresh mushrooms, the reconstituted dried mushrooms, tomato paste, and stock, and simmer for a few minutes until mixture thickens, then remove from heat and let mixture cool completely.

Whip the eggs in a bowl and add to medium sized bowl along with the ½ cup of the cheese, add Jack Daniel's and season with salt and pepper. Stir until well mixed.

Pour the filling into the pre-baked tart shell and bake in a 350°-375° F barbecue grill or smoker for about 25 minutes over indirect heat using hickory, cherry, or alder wood chips for added flavor. Top of tart will be nicely browned and moderately firm to the touch. A knife or toothpick inserted into the filling should come out clean.

Remove from smoker and let the tart firm up while covered for about 10 minutes. Sprinkle the tart with the remaining ½ cup of cheese, slice, and serve warm.

Serves 6-8

HOW TO JUDGE BBQ GRILL TEMPS

Without a Thermometer

Following is a way to estimate grill temperature by holding your hand right over the bbq grill surface. If you can only hold your hand 1-2 inches above the grill for 1 second the temperature of the fire is approximately 600-degrees (or higher), 2 seconds + 500°-650°, etc.

1 Second (or less) = Very Hot Fire—600 degrees or more

2 Seconds = Hot Fire—500 to 650 degrees

3 Seconds = Medium Hot Fire—450 to 550 degrees

4 Seconds = Medium Fire—400 to 500 degrees

5 Seconds = Low Medium Fire—300 to 400 degrees

6 Seconds (or more) = Very Low Fire—300 degrees or less

CHAPTER 2

BEEF

Big Al's Smoked Chili   24

Ceremonial Black Hole Chili   24

Cheesey BBQ'd Roast beef   25

Dan & Ron's Tri-Tip Roast   26

Dr. Pepper Beef Brisket   27

Grilled Huntsman Beef Sandwiches   28

Grilled Shallot-Cognac Steaks   28

Honey-Mustard Grilled Ribeye Steaks   30

Inebriated Top Round   31

Marinated Dinosaur Ribs   32

RB's BBQ Steak Sauce   32

Rodney's Tequila Porterhouse   33

Spats' Grilled Meatballs   34

Tang-y Grill-Roast Prime Rib   35

TENNY LAMAS, FRICKLES & ROCKIES

30th Annual World's Championship Bar-B-Que Contest
Houston, Texas

It's probably the biggest dang barbecue event in America, or in the world for that matter. A competition that spans 45 acres, involves more than 350 teams (some containing as many as 50 members), consumes more than 100,000 pounds of BBQ'd meat, and which last year attracted more than 170,000 people during its three-day life span.

They call it the World's Championship Bar B Que Contest, even though the teams are all from the US, and in fact are almost 100% from the host state itself. Other contests with "International" or "World" in their names actually invite participants from foreign countries. Here the world includes . . . Texas.

But it's a wonderful event nonetheless, and despite humble beginnings three decades ago, it is now one of the biggest events in a big-oriented state. Started as a friendly competition in the driveway beside the Astrodome with a gathering of volunteers, pickup trucks, some coolers and a bunch of backyard barbecue grills, the event has grown into the largest charitable barbecue event in the world, and a vital component of the Houston Stock Show and Rodeo itself.

Last year the proceeds from the barbecue and rodeo, run by an all-volunteer army of more than 13,000, raised just a tad under $10 million dollars for local scholarships, FFA and 4H groups, graduate assistantships, college and university endowments, research programs, and the Rodeo Institute for Teacher Excellence.

And typical of anything Texan they serve BIG amounts of grub there too. The hired cooks grill and dish up thousands of pounds of beef brisket, pork ribs, and of chicken, in addition to wheelbarrow loads of fried pickles, sausages, potato salad, cole slaw, burgers, hams, game hens, beef steaks, hot dogs, guacamole, beans, garlic bread, nachos, tortillas, and other comestibles, which are then served to legions of ten-gallon-hatted guests in the swarming corporate tents. To wash it all down the cowboys n' cowgals quaff an Olympic swimming pool-sized amount of beer and "sodey pop" (over 24,000 cases in all), chilled by a small glacier-sized 300,000 pounds of ice.—all in three days!

Unlike other US Que competitions, which involve either amateur cooks or which have a separate category for the sport's "pros," the Houston BBQ event has a unique format that has corporate teams hiring professional cooks, chefs, and pitmasters to represent and cook up a storm for their team. The cooks compete in three categories: beef brisket (after all this is Texas, where brisket IS barbecue), chicken, and pork ribs, and each team must turn in ten pounds of meat to the judges in one of those three categories. Judging is done on appearance, aroma, tenderness, and (most important) taste.

But, unlike other contests, there is zero prize money. Remember, all proceeds go to scholarships and education funds. The winner receives merely a whole buncha braggin' rights. But again, this is Texas, certainly the inventor and copyright holder of braggin' rights.

Other "competitions" include Most Unique Pit, Most Colorful Team, Best Team Skit, Best Recycling Team, Cleanest Team Area, and last but not least: the Best Butt Contest. No, not the cooked pork shoulder kind of butts. This fiercely battled match is for lithe, and some not-so-lithe, ladies who appear to

delight in showing off their, well . . . assets. Wearing the delightful and very form-fitting regional apparel—Rockies jeans. Which, the manufacturer shyly admits, "have been designed in a style that flatters your hip line and buttocks." Yup it does.

This, by the way, is the only competition at the barbecue championships which have more eager "volunteer judges, " both professional and amateur, in attendance than all the BBQ categories and rodeo competitions put together.

On my visit, I saw another fashion statement traipsing across the sauce-dribbled parking lot, which must have been originated by the likes of Garth Brooks, George Strait, and Alan Jackson: the predominance of black hats. My heavens I thought I was at a convention of Hollywood cowboy badguys, with nary a good-guy white hat to be seen. I reckon the ten-gallon Noir look is IN these days! Roy and Gene and Hopalong are probably all shaking their heads in wonder.

And while we're speaking of fashion, let me mention the "Tenny Lamas" boot, er shoe, er high-top sneakers, tons of folks have a hankerin' fer down here. For these cowpokes and cowpokettes there is now a canvas and rubber substitute so you can achieve that "wrangler look" without putting your tootsies in them hotter' n-the-El-Paso-sun-in-July leather boots.

When not noting the western fashion scene I spent most of my time, other than a few very brief moments at that Best Butt competition, with cook/caterer Carl Triola and his delightful family in the

Damnifino team tent. Its 23 members each paid $500 to help defray the costs of setting up the tent, buying hundreds of pounds of meat, taters and beans, and barrels of adult liquid refreshments for what only seemed like half the population of Houston.

Every evening the "hospitality" flowed, as long as you had the right color bracelet or scarf to let you into the private BBQ parties that is, and hundreds of pounds of barbecued, fried, broiled, baked, and sautéed chow was downed by the truckloads of corporate guests, friends of the team, scattered members of the press, and more than a few stunning Texas damsels (many wearing those durn Rockies) who somehow got past the guards flashing nothing but smiles.

Damnifino's membership list reads like a country club roster. They include real estate brokers, a trucking company owner, electrical contractors, oil field and chemical executives, mortgage brokers, real estate developers, home builders, venture capitalists, business owners, a neuro-surgeon, an oncologist, and (most appropriate for the cholesterol orgy going on in the background) a cardiologist. Luck was with us and no one required his services that night. Pass another fried rib with ranch dressing please.

Not a poor man's sport this. But remember all that money goes to a good purpose. So good in fact that since its inception in 1957 the Rodeo, and the Barbecue competition, which began in 1973, have poured more than $85 million dollars toward education. Since ya gotta eat anyway . . .

Other than expanding our waistline by several magnitudes we learned many things during our three days in Houston. We learned about frickles (fried pickles), we were shown how to do "pitchfork" steaks, we discerned the difference between the "slide" and the "two-step," we watched how to cook up "real" Texas beans, and finally figured out why brisket takes so danged long to cook right. At the same time we decided that Texas hospitality is as friendly and warm as we've ever experienced anywhere. We really felt deep in the heart of Texas.

And, oh yes, we discovered where we can order up a pair o' them Rockies jeans for the missus back home.

BIG AL'S SMOKED CHILI

Serve warm with grilled bread which has been rubbed with garlic and then buttered.

½ pound ground beef
2 cups brown sugar
¼ cup Worcestershire sauce
⅛ cup yellow mustard
1 tablespoon your favorite dry rub
½ medium chopped onion
2–28 OZ cans of Bush's baked beans

Cook ground beef in a cast iron frying pan over medium-high heat for approximately 15 minutes, or until well browned. Add the sugar, Worcestershire sauce, mustard, dry rub and onion, and stir well. Add beans and stir. Cook uncovered in 250°-275° degree smoker for approximately 2 hours, over indirect heat, stirring every 30 minutes, or until desired consistency.

Al Meek
Runnells, Iowa

CEREMONIAL BLACK HOLE CHILI

The Brides of Black Hole Chili team entered their chili in the 1978 Luckenbach Ladies World Championship Chili Cookoff, where it garnered sixth place. The recipe had evolved from the first attempts at the Marble Falls Chili Cookoff some years before, where it was concocted by Flash Bruhweiler and Sonny Day.

25 japone peppers, large red and dried, or other favorite chili pepper
9 + garlic cloves, chopped
1 cup olive oil
7 ½ pounds. tough meat such as chuck, de-fatted & deboned, cut into 1-inch cubes
2 ½ cups water (or beer)
14 chile pequine peppers—smashed with a hammer

SPICES
8 tablespoons ground cumin
6 tablespoons ground oregano
4 tablespoons ground coriander
1 ½ teaspoons cayenne pepper
1 tablespoon Louisiana hot sauce
8 tablespoons or more paprika
4 oz tomato paste
1 teaspoon exotic spice could be added here (Mint? Epizote?)

½ tablespoon masa harina—or less, to thicken the chili if it is too thin. Masa harina is a powdered corn meal used in Mexican cooking.

Start de-seeding the japone peppers (the seeds are too hot) and boil in a few quarts of water until they are soft. Remove from the water, reserving 1/½ cups of the water the chilis have been boiled in. Scrape the inside pulp of the peppers out. Reserve the pulp, discarding the pods.

Combine the oil, garlic and meat and cook over medium heat in a cast iron pot until brown. Add chili pepper pulp to the meat.

Now add 2 ½ cups water or beer, the reserved water you boiled the peppers in, the tomato paste, and the smashed pequine peppers, and simmer slowly in the pot for 80 minutes while you have an egg toss or three-legged race contest, and just generally fall down a lot.

Take chili off heat and let it settle and the grease rise so that you can skim discard it (the grease, not the meat). Add the spices and cook for 10 more minutes. If chili is too thin add the masa harina until it reaches the desired thickness.

Serves 50-60

CHEESEY BBQ'D ROAST BEEF

Don Havranek, Smokin in Montana

4 ½ pound roast beef
Injection:
1 cup water
3 cubes beef bouillon
1" slice of Velveeta cheese (about 2 oz.)
¼ cup butter

RUB:
½ teaspoon granulated garlic
1 teaspoon cayenne
2 teaspoons seasoned salt
cracked black pepper

On low heat in a medium saucepan dissolve all injection ingredients. While still hot place a large bore needle into mixture and, by raising plunger, suck into syringe (you need a large bore needle because of the thick melted cheese). Inject mixture thoroughly into the meat. Rub roast with garlic, cayenne, seasoned salt and cracked black pepper mixture. Cover with plastic wrap and refrigerate for 12 hours or overnight.

Get a good hot fire going on the grill with mesquite briquettes or chunks which have been placed on one side of grill only. Sear roast for 5 to 10 minutes on both sides over the hot side of the grill over the mesquite briquettes. Move meat to cool side of grill to grill indirectly (ideally with a temperature of approximately 300° to 350° degrees) which may take up to an hour.

Take off grill when you have an internal temp of 145°-150° degrees. Cover with aluminum foil and allow to set for 15 minutes before carving.

Serves 6-8

DAN & RON'S TRI-TIP ROAST

Dan Brodsky & Ron Jessen, Scotts Valley, CA

Serve with garlic mashed potatoes or on buttered and grilled Hoagie or Kaiser rolls.

4-5 pound Tri-Tip beef roast
3 tablespoons minced garlic
1 large onion chopped
¼ cup melted clarified butter
¼ cup olive oil
¼ cup A-1 steak sauce
1 teaspoon Louisiana hot sauce 1
    cup teriyaki sauce
1 cup Chianti

Several long rosemary branches tied at one end to form a basting brush

Put roast into a 1-gallon Ziploc bag, add the rest of the ingredients, except rosemary branches, and marinate overnight in refrigerator.

Remove meat from marinade and set aside. Pour reserved marinade into a small sauce pan and bring to boil for at least 10 minutes so it will be safe to use as marinade. Let cool. Use rosemary brushes to baste meat once every half hour during the 1 ½ hour cooking time.

You can leave brush standing in the marinade between basting sessions.

Prepare wood or charcoal fire, piling coals or briquettes on one side of barbecue, or, if using gas, turn on one bank of burners, until you have a medium hot fire (450° to 500° F). Place meat over direct heat for 5 minutes a side, then transfer meat to side of barbecue which is unheated. Cook for 1 to 1 ½ hours until meat is evenly browned and has an internal temperature of 135°-140° degrees.

Seal in foil for 15 minutes and meat's internal temperature should reach 145° F (medium rare) in that time.

Slice thinly.

Serves 8-10

DR. PEPPER BEEF BRISKET

Donald R. Wallace, San Antonio

2 cans Dr. Pepper
2 beef bouillon cubes dissolved in 4 oz. water
4 cloves garlic, minced
1 tablespoon Worcestershire sauce
2 tablespoons lime or lemon juice
12 oz. barbecue sauce, your favorite
McCormick's broiled steak seasoning
Fresh ground pepper
1 10-12 pound brisket

Combine all ingredients in a plastic bag. Marinate brisket for 2 days. Early in the morning of the day you are going to cook, remove brisket from marinade and let sit at room temperature while you get fire ready. Pour remaining marinade into small sauce pan and boil for at least 10 minutes, cool and put in sealable bottle.

Place brisket in smoker, or on indirect heat in a barbecue grill, fat side up, and cook for about 12-14 hours at 225° to 250° degrees. I usually start about 7:00 or 8:00 in the morning and take the meat off the smoker about 10:00 or 11:00 that night. Baste during cooking with marinade (remember it has to be boiled first). After 12 to 14 hours of cooking the brisket should be almost all black and look like you've burned it—you haven't.

Remove brisket from smoker, baste liberally with marinade, and wrap in heavy duty foil. Wrap it a second time. Place brisket in foil in smoker or in the barbecue and let cook overnight at 150° to 160° degrees. About 1:00 or 2:00 the next afternoon, you got the best tasting, juiciest and most tender brisket you have ever had. Internal temperature should be around 160°-170°.

Editor's note: If all else fails and it rains or you can't use a smoker you can put roast (uncovered) in your kitchen oven, set temperature to 220° and cook in a Pyrex pan or roasting pan for 10 hours. Add a pinch of liquid smoke to your BBQ sauce and you'll be amazed at the results.

Serves 10-12

GRILLED HUNTSMAN BEEF SANDWICHES

Serve with shoestring potatoes or barbecued beans.

1 cup crumbled Huntsman cheese
2 tablespoons mayonnaise
1 teaspoon prepared horseradish
8 slices sourdough bread
1 ½ pounds sliced rare roast beef, sliced
1 sweet Walla Walla onion, thinly sliced
1 large Gala apple, thinly sliced
sea salt to taste
cracked pepper to taste
4 tablespoons butter

Mix cheese, mayonnaise and horseradish in small glass bowl until relatively smooth (there will still be lumps of cheese in mixture). Salt and pepper to taste.

Spread mixture thickly on each slice of bread. Top each of 4 bread slices with a quarter of the beef, then onion and apple. Top with remaining slice of bread, cheese/mayonnaise/horseradish side down.

Brush melted butter on top of bread and turn that side down on grill, cook over medium coals (400° to 500°) until golden, about 2 minutes. Butter top slice of bread, then turn over and grill for approximately another 2 minutes.

Serves 4

GRILLED SHALLOT-COGNAC STEAKS

Stuffed with shallots, green onions & shitake mushrooms. Serve with dirty rice, and barbecued vegetables

1 tablespoon extra virgin olive oil
½ cup very finely chopped shallots
½ cup thinly sliced green onions
½ cup chopped shitake mushrooms
⅛ cup cognac
¼ teaspoon salt
¼ teaspoon pepper
2 boneless beef top loin steaks, cut 2-inches
    thick, about 1 pound each
wooden toothpicks, soaked for 20 minutes in hot
    water

In a small non-stick skillet, heat oil over medium heat until hot. Add shallots and mushrooms and cook 4-5 minutes or until tender. Then add green onions and continue cooking and stirring 4-5 minutes or until onions are tender. Remove from heat. Add the salt, pepper, and cognac and cool completely.

Meanwhile, with a sharp knife, make a pocket in each steak by cutting horizontally along one long side to within ½-inch of each of the other 3 sides. Spread half of shallot/onion/mushroom mixture inside each pocket. Secure the pockets with 2 or 3 wooden toothpicks.

Place 2"-inch thick steaks on grill over highest gas setting or white ash-covered coals at 600° to 700°. Grill, covered with BBQ lid. Turn steaks after 6 to 8 minutes (twice per side) cooking according to guidelines below for 2" steaks. At each turning rotate steaks 45° degrees to vary the grill marks. Steaks are cooked to medium rare at 145° internal temperature, medium at 160°, well done (if you really must ruin a good steak) is "ready" at 170°.

Remove wooden toothpicks. Carve steaks crosswise into ½-inch thick slices.

Steak Grilling Guidelines

Thickness	Rare	Medium	Well	Heat
1"	8-10	12-14	16-20	High
1 ½"	10-14	16-20	22-26	High
2	12-16	18-22	24-28	High

These times are total cooking times. Divide in half for each side. Times are approximate and will vary depending on the type of grill, fuel, weather conditions, etc.

Serves 6

HONEY-MUSTARD GRILLED RIBEYE STEAKS

1 cup yellow mustard

2 tablespoons chopped fresh parsley

2 tablespoons crushed rosemary leaves

2 tablespoons crushed thyme

4 tablespoons honey

¼ cup cider vinegar

1 tablespoon Worcestershire sauce

1 cup water

½ teaspoon Louisiana hot sauce

¼ teaspoon coarse black pepper

4 1"-inch thick ribeye steaks

4 pats butter

Mix first 10 ingredients well in large bowl, reserve ½ resulting liquid and put in small bowl, pour remainder of the liquid over ribeye steaks in a 10x12 flat Pyrex dish and marinate for 30 minutes, turning the steaks over several times. Poke steaks several times with fork so the marinade gets into the center of the meat.

Put reserved marinade in small saucepan and boil for 10 minutes, then you can safely use it to brush on steaks.

Turn steaks with tongs, NOT a fork, and cook on hot grill (500° to 600° or higher if using mesquite) or very hot coals for 5-6 minutes a side for medium rare. Brush generously with reserved, boiled marinade once or twice per side.

Drizzle RB's BBQ Steak sauce (see recipe below) on plate, as directed below, place small pat of butter on top of each steak and serve.

Serves 4

INEBRIATED TOP ROUND

½ cup red wine
1 cup Jack Daniels Tennessee sippin' whiskey
¼ cup beer

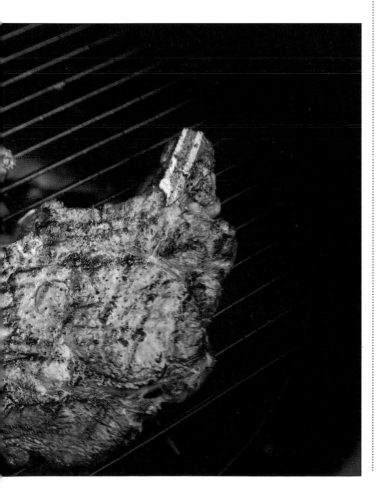

¼ cup Balsamic vinegar
2 tablespoons finely chopped onion
2 teaspoons finely chopped garlic
1 teaspoon tarragon
1 teaspoon rosemary leaves
½ teaspoon pepper
½ cup brown sugar
2 teaspoon sea salt
1 ½-2 pound top round beef steak
A-1 sauce
Pre-heat barbecue to medium high heat.

Mix first 10 ingredients in a large ceramic bowl. Generously salt meat with sea salt and put in a Ziploc bag. Pour marinade into the bag and shake it to coat the meat well. Place sealed bag in large dish (in case plastic leaks) and refrigerate for 24 hours, turning bag over 2-3 times.

Remove steak from refrigerator and let come to room temperature. Pour reserved marinade into medium saucepan and boil for at least 10 minutes. Add dash of A-1 sauce. Cool and put in sealed jar.

When coals reach 400° to 500° place meat on oiled grill 4 inches from medium hot coals and cook for 12-16 total minutes, 6-8 minutes per side or to desired doneness. Baste occasionally with marinade.

Cut steak across grain into thin slices and serve on a very hot platter.

Serves 4

MARINATED DINOSAUR RIBS

2 to 3 racks of beef ribs

2 cups orange juice

½ cup extra virgin olive oil

½ cup balsamic vinegar

½ cup Worcestershire sauce

1 tablespoon garlic salt

1 tablespoon dry mustard

1 teaspoon paprika

1 teaspoon chili powder

1 teaspoon Louisiana Hot Sauce

Pre-heat grill to medium high heat. Pile coals or briquettes on one side of grill only, or, if using gas turn on burners on one side of barbecue only. You will cook meat on side of grill away from heat.

Peel off the membrane on the backside of the rack for more tender ribs using a towel or paper towel to grip the membrane.

Mix together all remaining ingredients, except ribs, in a large bowl. Place the ribs in a dish or Ziploc bag, pour in marinade, and marinate in refrigerator for 4-6 hours. Reserving the marinade, drain ribs and set them aside until they reach room temperature. Put marinade in a medium saucepan and boil for at least 10 minutes. Remove from heat, cool and reserve.

Cook ribs on oiled grill over medium-high fire (450° to 550°) over indirect heat for 1 hour, basting very frequently with the marinade. Remove ribs from grill and place ribs on heavy duty aluminum foil, baste both sides lavishly, seal foil, and set aside for 10-15 minutes to cool and become infused with marinade.

Open foil packages at the table and dig in.

Serves 6-10

RB'S BBQ STEAK SAUCE

1 cup Cattleman's barbecue sauce

3 tablespoons maple syrup

1 teaspoon summer savory

½ teaspoons cayenne pepper

1 tablespoon olive oil

1 tablespoon lime juice

Mix in large bowl and put in plastic squeeze bottle and drizzle over plates before you put steaks on plates. Serve warm in gravy boat or sauce dish along with steaks.

Makes 1 /14 cup

RODNEY'S TEQUILA PORTERHOUSE

Rodney Patten, somewhere over Montana

¼ cup soy sauce

½ cup extra virgin olive oil

4 oz. good quality tequila

2 pound choice porterhouse steak, aged

1 crushed garlic clove

2 tablespoons lime juice

2 tablespoons pineapple juice

¼ cup melted butter

dash of balsamic vinegar

2 teaspoons lemon pepper

2 teaspoons Montreal Steak Seasoning

Mix the soy sauce, olive oil and 2 ounces of the tequila together in a small container and shake until well mixed. Put steak into Ziploc bag, pour in marinade, and marinate at room temperature for 1 hour. Drain the steak discarding the marinade.

Mix the remaining ingredients in a small bowl. Apply to both sides of the meat, rubbing in well with your hands.

Place steak on grill over hot mesquite fire (600° to 700°), and cook until you reach the desired state, approximately 6-8 minutes per side for medium-rare. Place meat on a platter and drizzle the extra tequila over both sides of the steak just before serving.

DO NOT POUR LIQUOR OVER THE MEAT WHILE IT IS OVER OR NEAR AN OPEN FLAME UNLESS YOU WANT TO BE AN IGNITED PART OF THE BARBECUE YOURSELF!!

Serves 4-6

SPATS' GRILLED MEATBALLS

To my best buddy, who always wears a tux and spats.

MEATBALLS

¾ pound ground chuck

¾ pound ground turkey

1 ½ cups fine fresh bread crumbs

1 large egg

¼ cup finely chopped shallots

1 teaspoon granulated garlic

½ teaspoon ground nutmeg

¼ teaspoon cinnamon

1 tablespoon dried basil

½ teaspoon salt

lemon pepper to taste

SAUCE:

⅓ cup honey-Dijon mustard

⅓ cup packed brown sugar

3 tablespoons balsamic vinegar

2 tablespoons extra virgin olive oil

2 tablespoons finely chopped Italian parsley

Pre-heat grill to medium temperature (400°-500°). Soak 12 bamboo skewers in warm water for 30 minutes.

In a large bowl with your hands blend together all meatball ingredients until combined well. Roll mixture into 1 ¼-inch balls and arrange on a platter, cover and chill for at least 30 minutes.

In a bowl whisk all sauce ingredients together until sugar is dissolved. Cover and chill for 30 minutes.

Thread 4-6 meatballs onto each skewer. Prepare grill by heating briquettes or chunks of charcoal so they are glowing (covered with slight white ash covering). If using gas prepare a very hot fire.

Grill kebabs on an oiled rack set 5 to 6 inches over briquettes, charcoal chunks or gas, turning them frequently. Brush meatballs with sauce frequently, turning often until cooked through, about 5-10 minutes.

Serves 6-8

TANG-Y GRILL-ROAST PRIME RIB

12-15 pound prime rib with bone-in, cap off
1 cup kosher salt
1 cup coarse cracked black pepper
½ cup Tang (orange breakfast drink)
¼ cup granulated garlic
5 whole garlic cloves sliced thinly

Rub the prime rib all over with salt, pepper, Tang and granulated garlic.

With a sharp knife cut slits in meat and insert slices of garlic in each slit.

In a large kettle grill, mound charcoal well over to one side, place an aluminum 9x12 pan on other side of coal bed filled with 1-2 inches of water. Place grill above coals. When the coals are glowing, at approximately 350° to 400°, place the prime rib on the grill on the side opposite the coals, being careful that no part of the rib is directly over the coals. Put the lid on the kettle with the vents ¼ open. Cook for approximately 2 hours, adding a handful of fresh charcoal every 30 minutes or so. If using a gas grill turn gas jets on medium high on side away from meat.

At the 2-hour point, check the rib with a meat thermometer to determine doneness; remove from the fire at 130° F for rare, 140° F for medium rare, 160° for medium, and so on, adding 4° F for each degree of doneness.

Remove from heat, seal in foil, and allow to rest for 30 minutes before slicing.

Serves 8-10

CHAPTER 3
FISH & SHELLFISH

Aunt Lilly's Sizzling Lobster   40

Car Dogs' Award Winning Salmon   41

Catfish with Tangy Orange Sauce   42

Chris & Colette's Venetian Stuffed Calamari   43

Pineapple Salsa   44

Cedar Plank Swordfish with Pineapple Salsa   45

Crumbly BBQ Rainbow Trout   46

Dungeness Crab Cakes with Basil Mayonnaise   48

Grilled Mussels With Spicy Fish Sauce   50

Honeydew Grilled Ahi   50

Honey, Do-That-Shrimp-Thing-Again!   51

Just for the Halibut   52

Ol' Jeremiah's Grilled Oysters with Butter Sauce   52

Les Burden's Awesome Shrimp & Scallops   54

Mozambique Fire Shrimp with Pili Pili Sauce   56

John Davis' Oregon Cedar Salmon   58

Scottsdale Spicy Smoked Tuna Steaks   60

Zesty Smoked Oysters   62

BBQ ON THE SAMMISH SLOUGH

Pacific Northwest Regional Barbecue Championships
Red Hook Ale Brewery, Woodinville, Washington

In one of the most idyllic settings we visited on our entire barbecue pilgrimage across the fruited plains of the US, we delighted in the quiet, calm, and peaceful setting of the Pacific Northwest's biggest barbecue event in the tiny town of Woodinville, about 30 minutes north of Seattle.

Held in the park-like setting of the Red Hook Ale Brewery, in a rural area scattered with upscale wineries and rolling vineyards, sits the venue for what proved to be a delightfully calm, cool, and collected event. Forget the madness of Houston, the frenzy of Memphis, or the bustle of Kansas City's American Royal. The PNWBA Championships were almost lethargic in tone, but delightfully slow, not boring.

Until the meat went on the barbecues that is. Then serious cooks and serious-er judges took over and the reverence put on properly cooked meat, poultry, and fish matched the largest contests in the land. Barbecuing may be fun, but it's also a serious business, even among the neighborly folks of the Pacific NW.

Under Kansas City Barbecue Society contest rules (KCBS sanctions more than 500 contests across the country) the teams compete in brisket, chicken, pork ribs, pork shoulder and, yes we are close to the Pacific, salmon. And not just any salmon mind you. Here they cook up the premier variety of this species. The Mercedes Benz, Cartier or Gucci of salmon: Copper River Sockeye from the Gulf of Alaska.

If you've ever shopped at a market for this famed variety of fish you've missed a grate, I mean GREAT, culinary barbecue treat. The cold rushing waters of the Copper River produce some of the richest, most naturally succulent salmon in the world. Wild Copper River Chinook (King), Sockeye (Red) and Coho (Silver) salmon—with their rich color, firm texture, and wonderful flavor—are renowned throughout the world. And lucky are the folks who live in the Pacific Northwest where the Spring brings these luscious fish to our markets.

The Copper River terminates in the Gulf and is one of the most pristine river systems in the world. Because of its 300 mile length and the challenges of its hundreds of rapids, the salmon that originate here are noted for their firm, bright red flesh, nutty flavor, and the extra oils and fat that they carry to fuel them on their migration to their spawning grounds. The King and Red salmon, arriving in early May, are the first salmon of the season to return to the rivers and streams of Alaska. Fortunately for those of us who appreciate their rich flavor and firm texture, the fats and Omega-3 oils are the kinds that your cardiologist would recommend. Fatty fish, yes, but a good fat that!

Red Salmon are the second most abundant species of salmon in Alaska. Red Salmon spend one to four years in the Pacific Ocean and reach sizes of 4- 7 pounds. Red Salmon range far and wide in the nutrient-rich waters of the North Pacific feeding on natural plankton and fishes before returning to fresh water to spawn. King Salmon may migrate to the marine environment the spring after they hatch or can spend up to two years in the riparian environment prior to migrating out to sea. King Salmon spend five years or more in the ocean, reaching sizes of up to 60 pounds before returning to spawn.

The Car Dog team, which consists of the dynamic duo of Jack Rogers and Jim Minion, took us under their wing, or rather, fin, and acted not only as our hosts, explaining the inner-workings of this particular contest, but fed us until we near burst, provided liquid refreshment on an unusually tepid Pacific Northwest day, and even shared some of their award-winning recipes with us.

Jack demonstrated how to remove the pin bones from a filet (use strong tweezers or needle-nose pliers) and Jim shared their double-rub method of cooking salmon, which won a recent Canadian championship in a British Columbia barbecue competition, and which placed second at the Red Hook event. We also share it with readers in the recipe section of this chapter.

We watched as filets were rubbed, marinated, salted, peppered, fruited, smoked, grilled, sauced, drizzled with butter or lemon or bourbon, and gobbled up in seconds once the judges had their portion delivered to their lofty perch in a room atop the brewery.

Simply put, what we tasted was the best salmon any of us had ever wrapped out teeth around. Consider the quality of the fish itself, its freshness; 24 hours out of the Gulf of Alaska, or as Jack put it, "one day from brine to broiler." Put the filets in the hands of some of America's best barbecue cooks (who've won categories in the major national BBQ contests: Jack Daniel's, Memphis in May, and the American Royal), and you have the best of the best cooking the best.

Not to demean the pork butts, ribs, beef briskets or chicken samples we were offered and hungrily gobbled. The deep south and America's BBQ heartland aside, the quality of barbecue, especially competitive barbecue, has almost leveled off. That means that nowadays incredible taste of a good rib, a slice of beer-can chicken, or hunk of brisket is as good North of Seattle as it is South of the Mason Dixon line.

We saw North Carolina vinegar sauce dribbled on pork butt, Georgia mustard sauce glazing baby back ribs, Pacific Rim-style teriyaki-hoisin marinades used on Texas brisket, and hot curry rubs inspired by Tandoori barbecue used on salmon fillets which were one day earlier swimming in the Gulf of Alaska.

Thanks to fervent barbecuers like the folks smoking on the banks of the Sammish Slough, BBQ has spread across the country like wildfire, and finally people are trying other regional rubs, sauces, meats, and cooking styles and discarding their old provincial "we don't do it that way here" disdain of "que" practiced in other places.

First it was the South, then it moved West, then to the shores of the Atlantic, and to the middle of America, and now good, no, GREAT barbecue is being done from coast to coast. America is pretty much BBQued up.

Now it's time to Que the world!

AUNT LILLY'S SIZZLING LOBSTER

Richard Westhaver, Norwell, Massachusetts

Aunt Lilly, who was from a fourth generation of Gloucester fishermen, could grill up some great lobsters. She swears this is the exact recipe she uses, I'm not sure about that but it's close enough for me and an excellent recipe either way.

4 cloves garlic, mashed
2 shallots, minced
1 pound salted butter
¼ cup chopped fresh parsley
⅔ cup fresh lemon juice
Juice of ½ medium orange
2 tablespoons fresh tarragon
salt & pepper to taste
4 two-pound Maine lobsters, live
fresh lemon wedges

Sauté the shallots and garlic in medium saucepan for five minutes or until soft. Add rest of ingredients except lobster and lemon wedges, and heat until butter is melted. Lower heat to lowest setting and keep butter warm, stirring occasionally.

Line grill with aluminum foil, prepare a medium hot fire (450° to 500°).

Split lobsters by placing on its back, sever the spinal cord by inserting a sharp knife between tail and body, then split lobster in half lengthwise. Remove stoach and intestinal vein. Paint lobster with melted butter mixture and place on grill flesh side down, cooking until there is a light char on the meat. Turn, baste with butter and grill until meat is firm.

Remove lobster from grill and paint with melted butter. Remove claws from lobster and place claws back on grill for 5-6 minutes more, wrap remaining lobster, including tail, in foil. Remove claws from grill, unwrap lobster and serve with the melted butter.

CAR DOGS' AWARD WINNING SALMON

Jim Minion and Jack Rogers hail from Washington state and compete as the Car Dogs Barbecue Team. In 2002 they won 3rd overall, and placed 2nd in Salmon (with this recipe) at the Pacific Northwest Regional Championships at the Red Hook Brewery in Woodinville, WA. In 1999 they won a Reserve Champion ribbon at the Canadian BBQ Championship at New Westminister, British Columbia with this salmon recipe.

3 pounds fresh filet of salmon , (preferably Sockeye or King) boned

1ST RUB:

1 cup light brown or turbinado sugar

½ cup non-iodized salt

6 tablespoons garlic salt

6 tablespoons onion salt

1 tablespoon dill weed

1 tablespoon summer savory

2 teaspoons tarragon

2ND RUB:

¼ cup light brown or turbinado sugar

1 tablespoon granulated garlic

1 tablespoon granulated onion

1 teaspoon summer savory

1 teaspoon tarragon

Bone the filet using tweezers or needle nose pliers. Do not remove the skin. Place in a glass or stainless steel pan.

Mix all the 1st rub ingredients in a small bowl and pack on the flesh side of the filet. DO NOT RUB IN. Let the filet rest for 3 hours. You will see how rub has drawn out liquid from the filet. Rinse the filet in cool clean water to remove the dry rub and pat dry. Allow to dry for about 30 minutes, until the flesh becomes tacky.

Mix up second rub in small bowl and set aside.

Heat your barbecue grill to medium or medium-high (300° to 400°). On a charcoal grill sprinkle wood chips on coals just before you put fish on grill. If using gas you can put foil packet containing fruit wood, in which you've poked holes, on burners to add smoke flavor to the grilled fish.

Sprinkle finishing rub on both sides of the filet (twice what you would use as if you were heavily salting and peppering). Place on well-oiled grill and cook with the BBQ lid closed until the temperature in the thickest part of the filet reaches 155° F (about 10 minutes).

Serves 4

CATFISH WITH TANGY ORANGE SAUCE

The Catfish Institute

Where young catfish study hard day and night, working on their manners, trying to attain great taste, and who hope to one day be invited for a splendid meal hosted by the person who is reading this book. Southern law says you have to serve these with hush puppies and coleslaw.

2 pounds catfish fillets (4-6 filets)

MARINADE:

¼ cup orange (or pineapple) juice
2 tablespoons vegetable oil
2 tablespoons light soy sauce
⅛ teaspoon pepper
1 tablespoon lemon juice
1 clove garlic, minced
dash Louisiana Hot Sauce

Combine all marinade/sauce ingredients in a bowl or Ziploc bag and add the fish. Marinate for 20 minutes. Drain fish and pour liquid into small saucepan and boil for 10 minutes. Cool and set aside.

Meanwhile place fish on lightly-oiled grill over medium heat (300° to 400°) for 5 minutes, brushing frequently with marinade. Turn and grill 5 minutes longer or until fish flakes when tested with a fork.

Serves 8.

CHRIS & COLETTE'S VENETIAN STUFFED CALAMARI

Chris Browne and Colette LeGrand

Picked up on a trip to Venice, Italy, by these young travelers during a summer of travel around Europe on a budget, and prepared superbly by the young chefs for "the parents" who weren't able to travel.

1 pound calamari, approximately 8 medium
    squid
1 tablespoon salt
1 tablespoon olive oil

STUFFING

4 tablespoons extra-virgin olive oil
4 garlic cloves, finely chopped
½ cup finely chopped sun-dried tomatoes
1 cup toasted bread crumbs
1 teaspoon dried thyme
1 teaspoon dried oregano
1 teaspoon dried summer savory
4 green onions, chopped
¼ cup chopped fresh basil leaves
Salt and pepper
Extra-virgin olive oil

Clean the calamari (squid) removing the tentacles, leaving the bodies whole. Place the calamari tubes and tentacles in large pot and cover with water. Add 1 tablespoon salt and 1 tablespoon olive oil to water and bring to a boil over high heat. Cook squid until quite tender, approximately 1 hour. Drain and cool.

Heat the 4 tablespoons of olive oil in a medium sauté pan over medium-high heat until just beginning to smoke and then add garlic and tomatoes and cook until garlic is golden brown, about 30 seconds. Do not overcook or garlic will be bitter. Lower heat to medium. Add the bread crumbs, thyme, oregano, savory, green onions, and basil leaves and continue cooking until well mixed and heated through.

Place oiled grill over medium-hot (450° to 500°) charcoal, gas, or briquette coals.

Stuff the cooled calamari bodies with the bread crumb-herb mixture, brush the stuffed calamari and tentacles with olive oil, season with salt and pepper, and grill until nicely charred, about 5 minutes per side (less time for the tentacles).

Serves 4

PINEAPPLE SALSA

½ cup chopped fresh pineapple

¼ cup finely chopped red bell pepper

1 green onion, thinly sliced

2 tablespoons lime juice

½ jalapeño pepper, seeded and minced

1 tablespoon chopped fresh cilantro or fresh basil

Place all ingredients in bowl and blend well. Serve salsa at room temperature.

CEDAR PLANK SWORDFISH WITH PINEAPPLE SALSA

Harry Aldrich, Portland, Oregon

President of Outdoor Gourmet, makers of the Oregon Cedar Grill Cedar planks, which are available through their website: www.outdoorgourmet.com

Cedar planks (from food or seafood stores, or the internet, NOT your local lumberyard). One plank will hold and cook two large sized steaks or filets.

1 tablespoon lime juice
2 cloves garlic, minced
4 swordfish steaks
½ teaspoon chili powder or ground black pepper
Soak cedar plank(s) in warm water for 20 minutes.

Prepare coals for grilling. Grill should be at 450° to 500° degrees. Combine lime juice and garlic in large Pyrex dish. Dip swordfish in mixture, let marinate for 12 minutes (6 mins. per side). Sprinkle with chili powder. Drain and gently brush plank with olive oil. Place fish on planks and place planks on grill over coals, briquettes or low flame. Grill until just opaque in center and still very moist, about 20 minutes. Do not turn fish on plank.

Planks may start to smolder, but that is okay. But in case they flame up have a spray bottle of water handy to discourage the open flames. Bottom of plank will be charred after cooking. Throw planks away after using, as there is no safe way to thoroughly clean them for re-use.

Serve steaks with pineapple salsa (recipe below).

Serves 4

CRUMBLY BBQ RAINBOW TROUT

3 pound rainbow trout, or other local fresh
    variety
1 cup heavy cream
2 egg yolks
1 cup bread crumbs
1 cup corn meal
1 teaspoon plus a pinch of garlic powder
1 teaspoon plus a dash of summer savory
1 teaspoon ground basil
1 teaspoon ground marjoram
2-3 small pats of butter (2 tablespoons)
sea salt to taste
lemon pepper to taste
6-8 lemon quarters
¼ cup melted butter

Clean and pat whole trout dry. Mix cream and egg yolks together and soak fish in mixture for 5 minutes. Mix the bread crumbs, corn meal, 1 tsp. garlic powder, 1 tsp. savory, basil and marjoram. Remove fish from cream mixture, drain slightly and roll in bread crumb-corn meal-herb mixture in a flat Pyrex dish.

Carefully put breaded fish back in cream and repeat soaking for an additional 5 minutes. Remove and gently roll fish in dry ingredients again, pressing mixture into fish. Place butter inside cavity sin 2-3 pieces. Sprinkle with summer savory, and a pinch of garlic powder

Place fish on very hot grill (450° to 500°) which has been oiled or sprayed with nonstick spray. Salt and pepper liberally. Cook for 3-4 minutes or until fish flakes easily, then using two spatulas (NOT tongs) gently turn fish over and grill for same time on second side. (If using a smoker put in hottest part of smoker and cook for 5-6 minutes per side, or until fish flakes easily)

Remove fish from grill and place on a cutting board. Cut down back of fish with a very sharp knife and gently separate halves, pulling backbone and rib bones away from bottom layer. Divide each half. Serve with fresh lemon quarters and melted butter.

Serves 4

DUNGENESS CRAB CAKES WITH BASIL MAYONNAISE

Serve with chilled basil-mayonnaise, sprinkled with red paprika.

MAYONNAISE:

1 bunch cleaned basil leaves

1 ½ cups mayonnaise

2 teaspoons yellow mustard (or Dijon)

2 teaspoons fresh lemon juice

pinch of Cayenne pepper

CRAB CAKES:

2 tablespoons olive oil

2 stalks celery; finely minced

⅔ cup sweet onion, finely chopped

1 pound fresh Dungenesss crabmeat (or local variety)

2 ⅔ cups dry bread crumbs, fresh if possible

¼ cup chopped chives

2 tablespoons chopped parsley

Salt and pepper to taste

6 tablespoons flour

3 large eggs

2 tablespoons extra virgin olive oil

Finely chop basil leaves and mix into 1 cup mayonnaise, then add mustard, lemon juice, and cayenne. Refrigerate.

Heat olive oil in large cast iron skillet over hot (400° to 500°) grill. Add celery and onion and sauté until tender, about 10 minutes.

Place crabmeat into large bowl. Add ⅔ cup breadcrumbs, chives, parsley, remaining ½ cup mayonnaise. Salt and pepper to taste. Form into twelve 2 ½″ cakes using ⅓ cup crab mixture for each.

Place flour in a small bowl. Whisk eggs in another bowl. Place remaining 2 cups breadcrumbs in a third bowl. Dip each cake in flour, then eggs, then breadcrumbs, patting crumbs softly so they are well adhered.

Heat the olive oil in cast iron skillet over medium hot grill (450° to 500°). Cook crab cakes until golden on each side, adding more oil as required.

Serves 6

GRILLED MUSSELS WITH SPICY FISH SAUCE

2 pounds fresh mussels

2 cloves garlic, finely minced

½ teaspoon red pepper flakes

3 tablespoons lemon juice

1 teaspoon lemon zest granules

3 tablespoons Thai fish sauce

2 teaspoons brown sugar

3 tablespoons water

Clean and scrub the mussels, drain very well.

While mussels are draining, blend garlic and pepper flakes into a paste and add lemon juice, lemon zest granules, fish sauce, sugar, and water.

Preheat BBQ grill to high heat (500° to 600°). Place clean, dry mussels in a single layer on hot grill. Grill mussels just until they are all open and aromatic.

Remove from grill with long tongs and serve. Spoon 1 tsp. of sauce into each open mussel, serving remaining sauce as dip.

Serves 4-6

HONEYDEW GRILLED AHI

6 tuna steaks, 1-inch thick each

¼ cup olive oil

2 tablespoons garlic powder

2 teaspoons granulated sugar

2 teaspoons ground black pepper

HONEYDEW ONION RELISH

¾ cup finely chopped honeydew melon

¼ cup minced sweet onion

2 tablespoons chopped green onions, top ½ of onions (green section only)

2 tablespoons extra virgin olive oil

1 teaspoon finely chopped lemon zest

1 tablespoon finely chopped mint leaves

1 tablespoon lime juice

2 tablespoons finely minced red and yellow bell peppers

Salt and pepper to taste

Brush steaks with olive oil. Mix together the garlic, sugar and pepper then season the steaks with the mixture. Dry marinate the steaks for an hour.

Put steaks on heated (400° to 450°) and oiled grill, cooking for 5 minutes per side. Red tuna turns very white when cooked. Inside should still be red/pink, and should be very moist.

Combine all relish ingredients in small bowl. Gently warm in small saucepan over low heat and until mixture reaches approximately 120° degrees. Spoon warmed relish over tuna steaks or serve on the side of each plate.

Serves 6

HONEY, DO-THAT-SHRIMP-THING-AGAIN!

2 pounds 16-20 count shrimp, shelled and
  deveined
Marinade:
2 tablespoons finely chopped fresh ginger root
2 cloves garlic, finely chopped
4 tablespoons sesame oil
½ cup Japanese rice wine
1 tablespoon clover or orange honey
2 tablespoons molasses
4 green onions, chopped
1 teaspoon blackened seasoning (see below)
¼ teaspoon dry mustard
1 tablespoon butter

BLACKENING SPICES:

4 teaspoons paprika
1 teaspoon ground oregano
1 teaspoon ground thyme
1 teaspoon cayenne powder (or more to taste)
½ teaspoon black pepper
½ teaspoon finely ground white pepper
½ teaspoon garlic powder

Soak 4-6 bamboo skewers in hot water for 20 minutes.

Mix marinade ingredients in small bowl, then pour into Ziploc bag and add shrimp. Drain and bring shrimp to room temperature. Boil remaining marinade for 10 minutes, adding 1 tablespoon butter, then cool and set aside.

Mix blackening spices in small bowl.

Preheat grill to medium hot (450° to 500°). Put 4-5 shrimp on each skewer. Sprinkle both sides with blackening spices. Grill shrimp for 1-2 minutes on each side, turning once.

Serve with cooled marinade as a dip or pouring sauce.

Serves 6-8

JUST FOR THE HALIBUT

BASTE MIXTURE:

¼ cup butter

2 tablespoons rich maple syrup

1 tablespoon minced garlic

2 tablespoons lemon juice

2 tablespoons soy sauce

dash Worcestershire sauce

4 ½ pound halibut steaks

grind or two of fresh black pepper

Combine butter, maple syrup, garlic, lemon juice, soy sauce and Worcestershire in a small saucepan over medium heat. Stir ingredients until well mixed. Remove from heat.

Generously brush the halibut with the baste mixture. Place the steaks on a grill that is heated to medium high (450° to 500°) and cook for 5 minutes on EACH side, basting liberally and often on both sides, until the fish is nicely marked and golden.

Serve on very hot platter.

Serves 4

OL' JEREMIAH'S GRILLED OYSTERS WITH BUTTER SAUCE

1 tablespoon finely chopped fresh chives

6 shallots, minced

¾ cup dry white wine

1 pound unsalted butter, cut into 1-inch thick
    pieces

Salt and pepper to taste

24 Hood River oysters (or your favorite local,
    fresh, variety)

Hungarian paprika

Combine chives, shallots, and wine in saucepan over medium heat and cook until reduced by half. Remove from heat and cool slightly. Whisk in the butter, 1 piece at a time, until sauce is smooth. Season to taste with salt and pepper, and keep warm over double boiler of warm (not boiling) water.

Place the oysters on the grill of a very hot charcoal, gas or briquette fire (550° to 650°), and close lid. Cook until the shells open, approximately 15-20 minutes. Remove oysters to a serving platter, being careful not to spill natural juices. With an oyster knife take off top shell and spoon one teaspoon of the sauce over each oyster. Sprinkle lightly with paprika.

Serves 6

(or just Jerry and me on a cold Washington Winter day)

LES BURDEN'S AWESOME SHRIMP & SCALLOPS

Les Burden, California

This marinade gets rave reviews from everyone tasting it. It started with a recipe from Hawaiian restaurateur Sam Choy. It was good, but nothing earth shattering, so Les altered the amounts of ginger, garlic and pepper flakes; added green onions and vinegar and left out the sugar. Those slight changes made all the difference in the world. Les is the former host of a TV grilling show, writes a column about barbecue, and is a consultant to an on-line barbecue company.

The seafood can be served over a bed of rice or mixed in with grilled onion and bell peppers. Allow one yellow onion and one pepper per pound of shrimp.

¼ cup Canola oil

3 tablespoons rice wine vinegar

3 tablespoons soy sauce

4 tablespoons peeled and minced fresh ginger

3 tablespoons chopped fresh cilantro

3 tablespoons minced fresh garlic

3 green onions, sliced very thinly, only use top (green) half of onion

½ teaspoon red pepper flakes (more if you like it really hot)

2 pounds 16-20 count shrimp, shelled and deveined

2 pounds 20 count scallops

Mix all ingredients except shrimp and scallops together. Pour mixture over shrimp and scallops in a shallow dish and refrigerate at least 30 minutes, no more than 4 hours. Pre-heat grill and barbecue griddle plate on grill for about 2 minutes over high temperature (500° to 600°) to heat it up. Pour off excess marinade from seafood and discard. Dump shrimp and scallop mixture onto hot griddle plate.

Stir constantly and remove from grill when shrimp have just turned pink. With the scallops, watch closer as they won't change color, but will go from being fairly translucent to being opaque. Take them off immediately.

MOZAMBIQUE FIRE SHRIMP WITH PILI PILI SAUCE

Serve shrimp with dirty rice and garlic butter, garnished with fresh parsley sprigs and quartered fresh lemons and limes.

1 ½ pounds fresh shrimp, 16-20 count, shelled and cleaned

PILI PILI SAUCE

4 tablespoons lemon juice, fresh squeezed
Juice of 1 lime
4 tablespoons extra virgin olive oil
4 tablespoons red pepper flakes
¼ teaspoon ground Cayenne pepper
1 tablespoon sea salt
1 teaspoon granulated garlic

MARINADE:

¼ cup lemon juice
juice of 1 lime
½ cup extra virgin olive oil
3 cloves garlic, crushed
½ teaspoon pili pili sauce (below)
1 tablespoon fresh cilantro
salt and pepper to taste

GARLIC BUTTER:

½ cup butter
1 tablespoon chopped fresh garlic
1 tablespoon chopped fresh parsley
½ teaspoon pili pili sauce (see above)
sea salt to taste
cracked black pepper to taste
pinch of dark brown sugar

Prepare Pili Pili Sauce in a small bowl mixing all ingredients together and stirring well until blended.

Mix together the marinade ingredients in a medium size bowl. Put cleaned and deveined shrimp into a Ziploc bag, and pour over shrimp, refrigerate for 2-3 hours.

Prepare garlic butter by mixing ingredients in small saucepan cooking for 15 minutes until well blended. Set aside.

Remove shrimp from marinade, and discard marinade. Bring shrimp to room temperature and grill over medium hot grill (350° to 400°), basting with garlic-butter until shrimp are cooked.

Serves 6

JOHN DAVIS' OREGON CEDAR SALMON

BASTE:

1 tablespoon balsamic vinegar

1 tablespoon ground ginger

1 tablespoon granulated garlic

2 tablespoons brown sugar

2 tablespoons chopped green onions (green end only)

1 untreated cedar plank *

2 ½-poundsssssssss fresh salmon fillet, boned with skin on

4 tablespoon extra virgin olive oil

3-4 fresh rosemary sprigs (optional)

Coarse sea salt to taste

Black pepper to taste

fresh raspberries

1 cup water

1 teaspoon balsamic vinegar

1 teaspoon sugar

Soak the plank for at least an hour in warm water, weighing it down with water-filled glasses to keep it fully submerged. During this hour mix baste ingredients in a small bowl and pour over salmon which you've placed in a glass pan, turn the fish once or twice during the hour. Heat your smoker or kettle grill to very hot (550° to 600°).

Remove salmon from marinade and drain fish, reserving marinade. Remove the plank from the water, brush with olive oil, and (if you like) spread the rosemary sprigs on top. Place the salmon skin side down on the cedar plank (or bed of rosemary), sprinkle with salt and pepper, and place plank on the grill.

Cover and grill for 20-30 minutes, or until the fish is cooked and the center is still just a little bit rare. Baste quickly with the marinade once or twice during the cooking time. You want salmon just pink in the center, sort of medium-rare. Nothing is worse than overcooked salmon. Nothing.

The board will probably smolder and smoke, that's what's supposed to happen. If it catches fire, douse it with a spray bottle filled with water.

Remove the whole plank from barbecue and place on serving tray over hot pads on the table for a superb presentation. Divide into sections and serve from the plank. If you are careful the skin will stay on the plank as you scoop up the filet.

Marinate fresh raspberries in 1 cup water and 1 teaspoon balsamic vinegar, with 1 teaspoon sugar for 20 -30 minutes. Sprinkle on top of fish on planks and serve fish.

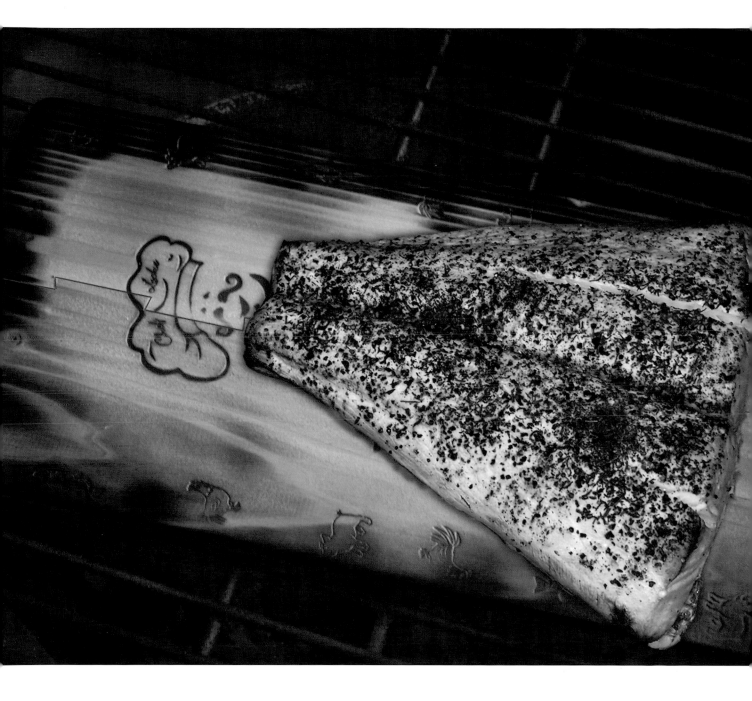

SCOTTSDALE SPICY SMOKED TUNA STEAKS

Bob and Marti Browne, Scottsdale, Arizona
Garnish with lime wedges and fresh cilantro

RUB:

1 teaspoon ground chipotle peppers (1-2 dried peppers, seeds removed)

1 teaspoon fresh ground black pepper

¼ teaspoon New Mexico chili powder

¼ teaspoon ancho chili powder

3 cloves garlic, finely minced

¼ cup fresh cilantro

1 teaspoon dried oregano

1 teaspoon dried cumin powder

Juice and zest of 1 lime

2 tbs. tequila

¼ cup corn oil

4 tuna steaks (preferably sashimi quality), 1-inch thick

2 cups coarse kosher salt

Puree all the rub ingredients thoroughly in a blender or food processor until you have a paste. Coat all surfaces of the tuna thoroughly with the paste, wrap the coated steaks in plastic wrap, and refrigerate at least 2-4 hours but preferably overnight.

Prepare the smoker or grill by heating to 225° to 250° using liberal amounts of mesquite chips that have been pre-soaked. You can also use a kettle or gas grill and the indirect cooking method. Put soaked wood chips in aluminum foil, poke a few holes in package with a pencil and place packet on coals or gas jets. Just watch the temperature closely. Wood chips will smoke very quickly.

Heat a skillet over high heat, add the kosher salt covering the bottom of the pan, and briefly sear the tuna steaks on both sides, about 1 minute.

Transfer the tuna steaks to the barbecue smoker or grill and cook only until they are medium rare, about 15-20 minutes. The center of the tuna steaks should be moist and pink. Do not overcook as overcooking destroys the flavor and texture of tuna.

Serve immediately while still hot.

Serves 4

ZESTY SMOKED OYSTERS

Jennifer Lyons & Stephen Brennan, New York, NY

Serve with lemon wedges, Louisiana Hot Sauce, and black pepper. Please, please do not serve these with "cocktail sauce"—you'll love the wonderful marinade flavors!

MARINADE/MOP:

1 cup fish stock or bottled clam juice

6 garlic cloves, minced

Several liberal dashes of Louisiana Hot Sauce

1 cup fresh lemon juice

fresh ground black pepper to taste

¼ cup extra virgin olive oil

¼ cup fresh chopped parsley

2 tbs. dry vermouth (or lemon or orange vodka)

2 dozen fresh oysters in their shells

5 pounds of crushed ice

Mix all the marinade ingredients thoroughly. Shuck the oysters and separately retain the oyster liquor and shells. Place the oysters in a Ziploc bag, add the marinade, and refrigerate mixture for 1-2 hours.

Heat the smoker or grill to a temperature of 300° to 350° degrees. If using kettle smoker and briquettes put them on both sides of kettle, leaving open space in the center of the grill. Place soaked wood pellets in an aluminum foil pan on bottom grill between beds of hot coals. Try alder or cherry wood for smoke flavor.

Place the marinade and the retained oyster liquor in a small saucepan and bring to a boil for 10 minutes. Remove from heat and allow the mixture to cool.

Take several baking pans (sufficient to hold all oysters in a single layer), and put 1-inch of crushed ice in the bottom of each pan. Place each oyster in a shell on the ice. The ice keeps the oysters from over-cooking while they are smoked. Place pans in the smoker or on grill away from the fire and smoke for 35-40 minutes.

Mop oysters with the marinade several times during the smoking. Fully cooked oysters are slightly firm, but still moist and juicy.

Serves 4

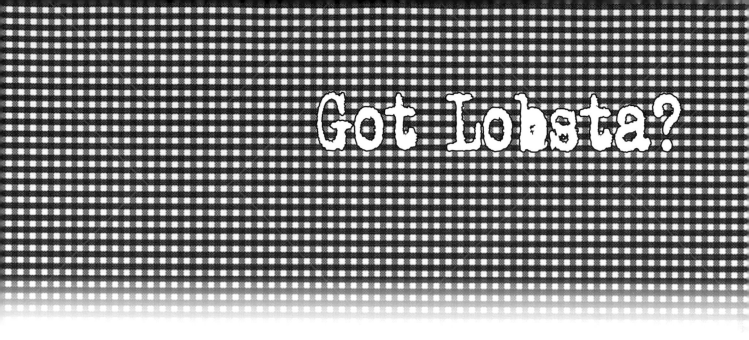

Got Lobsta?

The delicious triplets Homarus Americanus

That's what the bumper sticker said. "Got Lobsta?" We were driving through Freeport, Maine, home of L. L. Bean and just about every other factory outlet in the world, when we spotted the bumper sticker. A New England version of the ad campaign for that white dairy liquid, the folks around *heah* are poking fun at themselves and the white mustached crowd.

But if there's a mustache with their campaign it's bright yellow. Butter yellow to be exact. As in bowls of another dairy product, melted and infused with fresh lemon, that are used to wash down a local sea creature. It seems Mother Nature smiled Down East and sprinkled its waters with literally millions of lobsters.

Hence the lure to the two of us, and about 98,998 others, as we visited Rockland's Lobster Festival one August weekend. Over and above tourists, factory outlets, and speed traps this part of Maine has one thing aplenty: Lobster.

And we're not just talking food here Bub. There are lobster dolls, platters, cups & saucers, salt & pepper shakers, bumper stickers ("Got Lobsta?"), tattoos, puzzles, hats, shirts, underwear, oil and watercolor paintings, pencil sharpeners, erasers, gummy candy, hats, balloons, kites, and jewelry ("A 14-karat lobster claw charm for the lady, sir? That'll be $89.95 with tax.").

But let us not forget the lobster Christmas ornaments, charm bracelets, life-sized carvings, man-sized statues, decorated lobster traps and floats, toys, commemorative posters and note cards, golf socks, needlepoint and even glow-in-the-dark lobster neckties.

Then there's the lobster they want us to eat.

First you have your lobster stew, an arterial firming mixture of cream (or perhaps only half & half), and butter filled with Rhode Island-sized chunks of the colorful red crustacean itself. Then there are lobster rolls which consist of up to a pound of lobster meat, mixed with mayonnaise, butter, and a dash of lemon, all crammed into buttered and grilled buns. We mustn't forget, however, the lobster fritattas, enchiladas, fajitas, lobster Caesar salads, fried lobster cakes, lobster tail scrambles, lobster cocktails, patés and etouffeés, and the fiery tableside presentation of flambeéd lobster.

They grill 'em down heah. They fry 'em. They poach and barbecue. They boil and bake them. They stuff them with crab and shrimp, they make omelets that ooze lobster meat, they cook them in puff pastry and dabble on pernod sauce, they sauté them with marsala and cream, and they put chunks of lobster in buttered and brandied ramekins and call it Thermador.

They really, really like lobster, (sorry, lobsta) down heah!

To show what extremes they go to we discovered an ice cream shoppe (why do they always call them shoppes when they sell ice cream?) in Bar Harbor hopefully offering up "lobster ice cream," and a peek in the case showed bits of red lobstery-looking bits of flesh surrounded by otherwise ordinary vanilla ice cream. I ordered the fudge ripple.

But perhaps the most common way locals facilitate the eating of these armored seaside denizens is when they boil them a bright red, and then serve the scarlet seafood with corn on the cob, fresh baked rolls, bags of crisp potato chips and, you guessed it, bowls of melted butter.

In other parts of the country this feast would result in very expensive dinners and long notes explaining expensive expense account dinners to the accounting department. But *heah*, in Maine, in August, during the festival, lobster is as cheap as you'll ever find anywhere.

A scant week before our journey to Lobster Never-Never Land, my lovely wife and I visited a posh Seattle harborside restaurant and just for sport I asked the price of a whole lobster. I was sort of hoping to begin spring training for the following week's lobster festival by getting a head start on the gluttony I wanted to practice on Maine's crustacean-enriched coastline.

"The current market price is $39.00," the waiter gaily replied. "$39 American dollars?" I asked peckishly. "Yes sir, but it's a 1 ¼ pound lobster," he extolled.

I ordered the grilled Pacific Northwest salmon.

But in Rockland at Maine's main event, the Lobster Festival, all fears of having to mortgage my house for a butter-infused lobster tail, or a tasty claw, or even a tad of tomalley, vanished into the briny waters.

Reverse sticker shock struck when I tip-toed up to the food tent to peruse the menu. It read: "1 ¼ -pound Lobster Dinner—$9.95." $9.95? Are you kidding me here? A breakfast in New York City the day before cost me $11.00 for a bagel, one overcooked egg, and a small glass of watered down orange juice!

The gentle sign continued.

"Twin Lobster Dinner—$15.95" Twins, like in a toothsome twosome, as in a double play of deliciousness, like two helpings of yummyness! Wow! Ain't America, at least Homerus Americanus, wonderful?

But then my heart stopped as I read the third listing.

"Triple Lobster Dinner— $22.95" $23 bucks for THREE lobsters! Well this triple hit a home run in my gustatory heart. A dream come true, a life-enriching experience (for me anyway—the lobsters weren't quite so lucky), a culinary and glutinous milepost was within three paper plates of being achieved.

Triumphantly I carried my prizes to the picnic table, laying out my instruments before me like a surgeon; the napkins, the wet wipes, the knife, the fork, and the lobster pick. The baked rolls placed here, the cobs of fresh corn there, the trio of fire engine red lobsters aligned from left to right. Time seemed to stop. A yellow haze descended on the crowd, or was it a bit of lemon that mis-squirted onto my already steamed-up glasses instead of into the waiting butter dish.

I began with a controlled frenzy, ripping the soft shells apart with my bare hands, and sometimes front incisors, as I dug out the precious flesh, bathed the tender fragments in rich unguents of butter and citrus, and relished each morsel as it touched my tongue. In a flash I had sucked out all the juices, gnawed out all the tender flesh, and picked out any tiny remnants of edible meat from the discarded shells. I was a Master culinary artist and the table was my canvas.

Now let me tell you, I really like lobster. I mean to me it's perhaps the best thing the Lord ever intended us to eat. And when it comes to eating I can pretty well hold my own against anybody. But as the final remnants of the second lobster were gliding butterly down my craw I began to have . . . doubts.

Lobster is, after all, a very rich meat. (I know it's not meat but that's what *they* call it here, and, after all it is *their* lobsta). And dipped in bowls of lemony melted butta one can only speculate what cholesterol damage one is doing. But by then I threw away all cares, along with a handful of butter-soaked napkins.

But I must say for a moment there lobsta number three gave me pause. I didn't give up mind you. No lobster wimp heah. And even though I did have second, and third, thoughts, I looked up to see two little old ladies from Hackensack, New Jersey, ripping up their trio of lobstas like lions snacking on Christians, and their fervor firmed my resolve.

Rip, crunch, dip, gurgle, chew, slurp, swallow, wipe. It was done. A crimson array of several dozen dozen gnawed pieces of lobster shells sat in a woeful pile at my side. A deliciously disgraceful testimony to my ravenous plunder. Evidence of a triple homarus-cide.

A triple! My, oh my, oh my! I did a triple! Now forever when others brag about their eating prowess I could stand tall, and a bit wide too, among 'em. I ate three whole lobsters at one sitting. In the end there wasn't enough flesh left on any of the shells to feed a microbe. Not to mention a matched set of corn on the cobs, and a duo of freshly baked rolls that had magically disappeared into the deepest recesses of my being. Burp.

But because I am a professional, a skilled master of the culinary arts and sciences, and in deference to my waistline, I have to tell you that I passed on those tempting but caloric-ridden, cholesterol-laden, waistline-expandin' bags of potato chips.

I wouldn't want people to think I had no self control.

WE CAME FOR THE LOBSTER—AND FOUND GREAT BBQ TOO

The Maine Lobster Festival began 56 years ago and today ranks as one of the top ten food festivals in America. In 2002 over 100,000 people came to Rockland and happily consumed 23,200 pounds of lobster. That's enough lobster that if you placed them end to end they would be 12 times taller than the Empire State Building. Ravenous visitors also chowed down on thousands of pounds of fresh scallops, mussels and shrimp, as well as several truckloads of hot dogs, hamburgers, pizza, corn on the cob and ice cream, which disappeared during the five days of the festival.

In addition to the food tent and the hordes of people devouring thousands of lobsters and other seafoods, the festival features a lobster cooking contest, a children's parade, pancake breakfasts, lobster crate races, lobster eating contests, jug, steel, polka and accordion bands, several tents featuring local handicrafts, a 10K race, carnival rides and a midway, a wonderful three-hour long parade down Rockland's Main Street, and evening entertainment under the stars by headliners from the pop and country music worlds.

*Two special discoveries merit your attention. On the outskirts of Rockland, on the way to Camden, do not miss **Lil Piggy's Barbecue**. Barbecue pork ribs, chopped pork shoulder and smoked turkey as good as we've had anywhere in the country, and at very reasonable prices. They feature six different homemade barbecue sauces inspired by regional recipes from around the country, and all of them are wonderful.*

*The other discovery was the **Maine Luau & BBQ Pit**, an incredible merging of the best parts of a lobster pound and a barbecue pit, located just outside Bar Harbor. Their lobster is top notch, their ribs as good as they get, and their Maine-style red hot dogs out of this world.*

CHAPTER 4

LAMB

Assyrian Grilled Leg Of Lamb
with Pomegranate Sauce   70

Aussie BBQ Lamb Leg   71

Denver Mint-ed Lamb Ribs   72

Grilled Lamb Loin with Zinfandel-Sage-Morel
Sauce   73

Herbed Crown Roast of Lamb   74

Maple Smoked Lamb Shanks
with Whiskey Onion Marmalade   75

Patty Browne's Browned Patties   76

Tailor-Made Lamb Chops   77

Thai Lamb Kabobs   77

WHAT'S THAT YOU'RE SMOKIN' ?

ASSYRIAN GRILLED LEG OF LAMB WITH POMEGRANATE SAUCE

1 4 pound leg of lamb, butterflied

MARINADE:

3 whole Spanish onions, sliced
32 oz. pomegranate juice (available in health
    food section)
4 garlic cloves, chopped
1 cup olive oil
2 lemons, juiced
2 teaspoons fresh rosemary, if possible (if not
    then used 1 tablespoon dried rosemary)
1 teaspoon marjoram
1 teaspoon oregano
1 teaspoon summer savory
1 teaspoon coarse grind black pepper
2 teaspoons salt

POMEGRANATE SAUCE:

2 tablespoons butter
1 tablespoon brown sugar
1 tablespoon fresh rosemary, or ½ tablespoon
    dried
seeds of one medium pomegranate
Pre-heat grill to 500° to 600°.

Combine all marinade ingredients in a large glass, enamel, stainless, or plastic container and whip with a whisk until completely mixed. Pour marinade into a large plastic bag (a garbage bag does fine) and put this inside another similar bag. Add the lamb, turning it to make sure it is coated on all sides.

Marinate for TWO TO THREE DAYS in refrigerator. No kidding, 2-3 days! It's well worth the wait. Turn bag over 2-3 times a day.

Drain leg of lamb, reserving marinade which you will then strain and put in saucepan to boil for at least 10 minutes. Remove from heat, cool and set aside ½ of the liquid to baste meat, leave other half of liquid in saucepan.

Place lamb on hot charcoal or briquette fire (500°-600°), 8 inches from the flame, for 12-15 minutes on each side, brushing occasionally with the marinade.

Heat saucepan containing remaining half of marinade over medium heat. Add 2 tablespoons butter, 1 tablespoon brown sugar, and 1 tablespoon rosemary, and stir until mixed and sugar dissolves, about 4-5 minutes. Just before removing from heat add pomegranate seeds, stir quickly, take pan away from heat, and pour warm sauce into a serving dish to pass at the table.

Serve sliced, with the warmed pomegranate seed sauce.

Serves 10

AUSSIE BBQ LAMB LEG

Judith Vincent–Sydney, Australia

2-3 pound leg of lamb–

3-4 garlic cloves, sliced thinly

3 lemons, seeded

3 small oranges

1 cup olive oil

1 cup white or red wine

1 large sweet onion

1 lime, seeded

black pepper to taste

Sea salt to taste

5-6 fresh rosemary sprigs

Bone out and butterfly the leg of lamb (lie flat and insert 2-3 skewers all the way through horizontally to keep flat). Take small sharp knife and cut slits into lamb, on both sides. Insert thin slices of garlic. Break up 1-2 large sprigs of rosemary into 2-3 smaller lengths and insert in meat as well. Salt and pepper the meat.

Squeeze juice out of 3 lemons and 2 oranges. Remove peel of third orange and reserve, discarding the rest of the orange. Add ½ cup olive oil and ½ cup white or red wine. Cut up onion into thin slices, and chop one seeded lemon, one seeded lime and one orange peel into small pieces and add to liquid.

Put lamb in flat Pyrex glass dish and pour marinade over. Cover it with plastic wrap and marinate 6-8 hours or overnight. Take out of refrigerator in the morning, remove plastic wrap, and let meat come to room temperature.

Place lamb on very hot barbecue grill (500° to 600°), then just as you place meat on grill, adjust heat (turning down gas or adjusting vents on charcoal) to lower it to medium(400° to 500°). Cook for ½ to ¾ hour, turning only once. Keep an eye on the lamb to make sure it does not burn. If you like tender lamb cook for a little under 35 minutes for a slightly pink center, or 45 minutes if you like it cooked a little more. Lamb can become dry and tasteless if overdone so watch your times carefully. Take off barbecue and let the meat rest, covered, for 10 minutes. Slice and arrange on platter with fresh rosemary sprigs for garnish.

Serves 4-8

DENVER MINT-ED LAMB RIBS

3 slabs lamb ribs, Denver cut

MARINADE:

1 tablespoon sea salt
1 tablespoon coarse ground black pepper
1 tablespoon teriyaki sauce
1 teaspoon olive oil

SAUCE:

1 cup mint jelly
½ cup English style mint sauce
¼ cup finely julienned mint leaves
1 tablespoon granulated garlic
1 tablespoon dark corn syrup
1 tablespoon butter

Mix marinade ingredients in small glass or stainless steel bowl, then rub into slabs of ribs and let sit covered with plastic for 1 hour at room temperature.

Bring smoker up to 225°-250° degrees, oil grill, add ribs and cook for 3 ½-4 hours. Making sure ribs are not over direct heat. If using barbecue grill, use indirect heat method, placing ribs over the side of the grill that has no coals or briquettes under it.

Mix sauce ingredients and heat in a small saucepan on low heat until ingredients are well warmed. Keep the sauce on low temperature while the lamb cooks.

After ribs have been grilling approximately 2 ½ hours brush them liberally on both sides with the sauce. Repeat once or twice more before they are ready to be taken off grill. Remove ribs from heat and place on double thickness of heavy duty foil and brush generously with sauce, then seal foil and set ribs aside off heat for 5 minutes to let meat juices move back into center of meat. Internal temperature of ribs should be 145° for medium rare, or 160° for medium.

Serve ribs with the remaining warmed sauce in a sauce pitcher.

Serves 6

GRILLED LAMB LOIN WITH ZINFANDEL-SAGE-MOREL SAUCE

Matt Pinsonneult, Amador Foothill Winery
16 oz. lamb loin

MARINADE:

2 tablespoons olive oil
1 tablespoon fresh minced rosemary

1 tablespoon sage
1 teaspoon chopped garlic

SAUCE:

6 oz. fresh morels, thinly sliced (you can also use shitake mushrooms)
2 cups Amador Foothill Zinfandel, or you can also use a good Pinot
2 teaspoons minced fresh sage
1 teaspoon minced fresh rosemary
2 teaspoons black pepper
4 tablespoons sweet butter

Mix marinade and pour over lamb loin in large flat glass dish. Marinate for 2 hours at room temperature.

Heat ½ tablespoon olive oil in frying pan on high. When pan is hot add lamb loin and sear loin quickly, browning on all sides, about 10 minutes. Remove from pan and transfer to smoker. If using barbecue grill mound charcoal or briquettes on one side of the barbecue, put pan of water on other side. If using smoker make sure there is a water pan in the smoker to keep meat moist. Cook the meat to an internal temperature of 140° to 150° degrees, about 3 to 3 ½ hours at 225° to 250° degrees.

In a small saucepan, combine morels, wine, sage, rosemary, and black pepper and cook over medium heat, reducing the sauce volume by one-third, about 30 minutes. Add butter, whisk into mixture and simmer until sauce thickens, stirring constantly, about 3 minutes.

Slice the lamb thinly and serve over a bed of the sauce.

Serves 4

HERBED CROWN ROAST OF LAMB

5-6 pound prepared crown roast of lamb, chine
    bone removed

RUB:

2 tablespoons crushed dried mint

1 tablespoon crushed dried rosemary

1 tablespoon crushed dried oregano

1 ½ teaspoons onion salt

1 ½ teaspoons lemon pepper

1 ½ teaspoons granulated garlic

Bring roast to room temperature and spray with olive oil. Spray all surfaces of the meat, as this will help the rub stay in place.

Mix dry ingredients in a small bowl and rub well into crown lamb roast. Put lamb and remaining rub in plastic bag and marinate overnight in refrigerator.

Prepare the smoker or barbecue, about 225°-250° degrees. If using barbecue use indirect heating method, mounding charcoal or briquettes on one side of the barbecue, putting a pan of water on other side. If using a smoker, make sure there is a water pan in the smoker to keep meat moist.

Place roast on the grill. Close the lid. Check the temperature. Maintain between 225° to 250° degrees. Meat is ready when internal temperature reaches 140° degrees, in about 1 ¼ to 1 ½ hours. Medium rare is the ONLY way to serve lamb.

Remove and allow to set, covered, for 5 minutes before carving. Serve on heated plates.

Serves 8-10

MAPLE SMOKED LAMB SHANKS WITH WHISKEY ONION MARMALADE

I A good Cabernet Sauvignon or Pinot Noir goes well with this dish.

ingredients **Method**

12 medium lamb shanks

MARINADE:

4 oz. whiskey

16 oz. red wine

1 tablespoon garlic

¼ cup orange juice

2 tablespoons rosemary

1 tablespoon black pepper

2 tablespoons sea salt

Whiskey Onion Marmalade:

3 pound sliced onions, sweet onions like Walla
    Walla, Maui, or Vidalia work best

1/4 cup butter

1/2 cup whiskey

2 tablespoons black pepper

pinch of red pepper

salt to taste

Combine marinade ingredients in large bowl. Place meat in Ziploc bag, pour in marinade, and marinate lamb shanks overnight in refrigerator.

Smoke shanks on oiled grill with hickory, alder, or pecan chips or pellets at 220° to 225° degrees for 4 hours, or until tender. You can use a barbecue grill or smoker. If using barbecue mound charcoal or briquettes on one side of the barbecue, put pan of water on other side. If using smoker make sure there is a water pan in the smoker to keep the meat moist.

In a cast iron frying pan sauté the onions in butter until soft. Add whiskey of your choice, black and red pepper, add salt to taste, and simmer for 15-20 minutes. Remove from heat and let rest at room temperature until ready to serve lamb.

Serve the lamb shanks on a very hot platter with small ramekins of the marmalade at each place setting.

Serves 4-6

PATTY BROWNE'S BROWNED PATTIES

Lamb Burgers in Pita with Feta-Yogurt Topping
Patty Browne Anderson, Vancouver Island,
British Columbia

PITA TOPPING:

1 teaspoon lemon juice
½ cup yogurt
¼ cup crumbled feta cheese

PATTY MIXTURE:

¼ cup olive oil
⅓ cup pine nuts
1 ¼ pounds ground lamb
1 teaspoon finely minced garlic
¼ teaspoon salt
¼ teaspoon freshly ground black pepper
1/3 cup crumbled Roquefort cheese
¼ cup sour cream
4 pita breads

Using a medium bowl mix lemon juice, yogurt and feta cheese and refrigerate covered with plastic wrap.

Prepare a medium hot fire (450° to 550°) in the grill making sure the grill rack is oiled or sprayed with nonstick spray. An easy way to oil is to take a paper towel which has been folded into a 2-inch square and using tongs dip the towel into olive or vegetable oil and then using tongs rub the towel over the entire grill surface.

In a small, heavy skillet, over medium-high heat toast the pine nuts over the grill until golden, about 10 minutes. Remove from the pan to cool.

In a large bowl combine the lamb, garlic, salt and pepper, and gently mix together. In a small bowl, combine the Roquefort and the sour cream, loosely mixing until just combined. Add pine nuts.

On waxed paper, divide the lamb mixture into 8 equal portions. Gently flatten each portion into a thin patty, and spread ¼ of the cheese mixture over the center of each of four patties, leaving a ½ inch border. Place the remaining four patties over the tops and seal the edges firmly. Press down gently to flatten the burgers. Brush patties with just enough olive oil to make them glisten, 2 tablespoons should be enough for all of the patties.

Place on grill and cook until done, 4-5 minutes per side for medium.

Place each patty into pita bread and top with a generous dollop of the lemon-cheese-yogurt mix, about 2 tablespoons.

Serves 4

TAILOR-MADE LAMB CHOPS

Ralph Tailor, World Barbecue Associations
8 lamb loin or rib chops (or 4 shoulder chops)

Sauce:
¼ cup extra virgin oil
2 tablespoons honey
2 tablespoons soy sauce
2 tablespoons dry white wine
2 tablespoons minced onion
¼ teaspoon ground ginger
¼ teaspoon dry mustard
½ teaspoon salt
⅛ teaspoon ground pepper

In small bowl mix together all sauce ingredients. Brush lamb chops generously with sauce and let stand one hour at room temperature.

Grill chops six to seven inches from hot coals (500° to 650°) for 6-8 minutes per side (or until desired doneness), brushing frequently and generously with sauce.

Serve chops with remaining sauce.

Serves 4

THAI LAMB KABOBS

John Baker, Powderpuff Barbecue, *The Kansas City Barbeque Society Cookbook*. Serve over Dirty Rice or Garlic Mashed potatoes.

1 ½ pounds lamb, cut into 2-inch cubes
2 lg. Spanish onions, cut into 2-inch pieces
1 green bell pepper, cut into 2-inch squares
1 yellow bell pepper, cut into 2-inch squares
1 red bell pepper, cut into 2-inch squares

MARINADE:
½ cup olive oil
⅓ cup coconut milk, unsweetened
¼ cup lime juice
2 tablespoons minced fresh cilantro
2 teaspoons crushed red pepper
1 teaspoon ground cumin
1 teaspoon sea salt
1 clove of garlic, crushed

Thread lamb, onions, peppers alternately onto skewers. Place in large Ziploc bag. Mix together the olive oil, coconut milk, lime juice, cilantro, crushed red pepper, cumin, sea salt and garlic, and pour into bag over lamb skewers; seal bag. Marinate in refrigerator for 4-6 hours, turning occasionally; remove meat and drain. Reserve marinade and place in large saucepan and boil for 10 minutes. Remove from heat and cool. Grill lamb kabobs over medium-hot coals (450° to 550°) for 5-7 minutes per side, for medium-rare or until kabobs are done to taste. Baste liberally with marinade while grilling.

CHAPTER 5

PORK

Bacon-Wrapped Smoked Pork Tenderloin   85

Huckleberry Mountain Porterhouse Pork Chops   86

Carolina-Style Pulled Pork Shoulder   87

Mt. Adams Huckleberry Sauce   88

Grilled Loin of Wild Boar with Sour Cherry Sauce   88

Cedar-Planked Sugar Cane Canadian Peameal Bacon, Eh?   89

Grilled Pork Chops with Peach Chutney   90

Peach Chutney   92

Grilled Pork Shoulder   94

Selecting the Pig   95

North Carolina Style Whole Hog   95

Building the Barbecue Pit   95

Building the Fire   96

Pecan-Walnut Crusted Pork Loin   97

Roast Suckling Pig   98

Sherried Pork Spareribs   100

Smoked BBQ Sausage Roll   102

Southern Sugared Ribs   102

Terry's Sweet and Sour Riblets   103

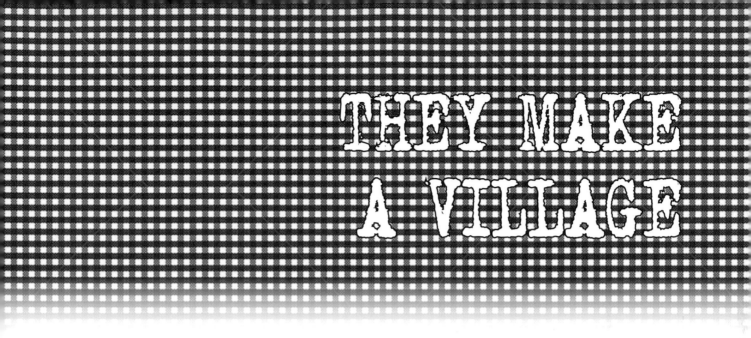

THEY MAKE A VILLAGE

26th Annual World Championship Barbecue Cooking Contest
Memphis, Tennessee
Saturday, May 11th
8am

The mile-and-a-half strip of green grass lines the Memphis side of the mighty Mississippi. A couple quietly walks hand in hand across the grass enjoying a park where they are the sole occupants.

The only things moving about are the puffy white clouds, and the river. And it is unusually muddy and murky and fast due to heavy spring rains in Arkansas, Missouri and Illinois up North. Huge tree stumps, logs as big as telephone poles, and branches pointing gaunt limbs into the gray skies, silently and swiftly pass by. Another peaceful and sleepy day along the banks of America's most storied river.

10am

The peaceful calm is disturbed by a truck and flatbed trailer driving across the emerald lawn. Then a twin appears and parks beside the first truck. Almost immediately hordes of people appear and begin unloading the trailers. Huge wood-framed pieces, looking almost like Hollywood sets, are taken off by hand, set into place, and assembled together.

Swine & Dine building committee directors Jim Massey and Jim Fields supervise the mass of 2x4's, eight-foot-long ³/₄" plywood sheets, prefab walls and floor sections, and they unload and begin to construct the Swine & Dine "home."

2pm

At this moment you can still easily walk from one end of the park to the other in less than 15 minutes. By the weekend it will take upwards of an hour or more to walk through huge crowds, and past hundreds of booths, to traverse the entire 1 ½ miles of the contest grounds. The framework is beginning to resemble a small house as team members swarm on the Swine & Dine compound.

4pm

More vans and RV's begin to appear, thus beginning the arrival of the hundreds of BBQ teams, some with upwards of 80 members, who will smoke and sing and cook and carouse along the banks of the Mississippi in the annual frolic known as the Memphis in May World Championship Barbecue Contest.

It takes a full day but now Swine & Dine has the exterior of their two-story structure sitting overlooking the river. All around, other buildings are being put together in a similar manner. Some are two-story, others single-story, some fancy, some Spartanly bare, but by 6pm the bee-hive of construction has slowed. The work crews begin to disperse with only a few dedicated souls still hammering and nailing and constructing. The exterior walls are now up, the kitchen and interiors will have to wait until tomorrow.

8pm

As the last volunteers head off for the evening, the sun dips beyond the Mighty Mississippi and twilight creeps over the roofs of the 350 new "homes" that have sprung up on its banks. There are a few smokers already cooking up a hearty dinner for the construction crews but otherwise the grounds are quiet. The "village" has begun to take shape.

Sunday, May 12th

8am

Another truck and flatbed drive up, accompanied by two RV's with trailers. Within minutes the flatbed trailer has unloaded a mobile kitchen complete with 3 large coolers, a 4x12 foot cabinet for dry foods, a double stainless steel sink, a stainless steel prep table, and two large butcher block tables, all covered by a huge white tent canopy.

The smaller trailers move up and are unloaded to reveal three large barbecue smokers, one big enough to cook a whole pig (indeed that's what they often do). Twin black smokestacks soar above a cavernous interior that is filled with bags of charcoal, BBQ tools, two boxes of barbecue sauces, dozens of multi-colored spice containers, and 15-20 large stainless steel pans. Team members busily unpack the grills and contents and arrange everything on the shelving units that have been set up in the kitchen.

10:30am

Other crew members, the contingent numbering 45-50 now, are unloading sections of flooring for the patio and the kitchen, both of which measure 16x30 feet, bolting each new section into place, while other volunteers arrange the kitchen shelving, tables, sinks and coolers. Much of the equipment looks, and is, professional, having been purchased at auction from local restaurant supply outlets over the years.

As the crew continues putting together their mobile kitchen another RV can be seen coming across the park towing a barbecue smoker on a simple open trailer. Seconds later, yet another RV drives over the grass and parks next to another set-up kitchen, where it deposits a brick red smoker, this one shaped like a huge squatting pig.

12noon

A long caravan of cookers tied onto trailers stretches from the park as far as the eye can see up a nearby hill. Dozens of RV's and trailers ready to deposit every kind of BBQ smoker and grill that is known to man, continue to appear on the rapidly diminishing greenspace.

Smokers are unloaded from huge trailers, or the sides of expensive rigs are removed, revealing trailers with built in smokers, grills, stainless steel kitchen sinks and counters, and walk-in refrigerators the envy of some small restaurants. Awnings are raised, chairs are set out, tables are unfolded and groceries are unpacked and either put in the huge refrigerators, or standard picnic sized coolers, to be chilled with bags of ice.

Tens of thousands of dollars will be spent by hundreds of teams to construct colorful two-story themed shelters, complete with bathrooms, full kitchens and bars, carpeting, chandeliers, mirrored disco balls and ceiling fans, expensive DVD sound systems, and tables set with crystal, sterling silver and elaborate floral bouquets. Swine & Dine's budget for 2002 was $25,000, collected as dues from its 85 members, winnings from other BBQ contests, and sales of their colorful team T-shirts.

To save money S & D re-constructs their two-story unit. It's built, torn down and re-built every year. Their "booth" includes a covered deck on the top level, and two stairways to that upper level where "night shift" team members are allowed to sleep late above the fray below while the morning crews noisily begin preparing the food in the ground level kitchen.

1pm

After the walls are finished, the floors installed, and the kitchen has been completed, the facade of the booth begins to take shape, a huge American flag is drawn and then painted across the entire front, and a 20-foot papier maché Statue of Liberty is hoisted to the top of the structure as part of S&D's "Americana" theme.

Team members Drew and Jayme Armstrong spent over 100 hours making the statue and it now sits proudly high above the festival. "It made us feel real good to see people stop in the middle of the festival to take pictures of our booth and the statue," Drew confessed.

Below Liberty, under the 35-foot painted American flag, are stacked bags of charcoal, hickory logs, 25-pound bags of ice and cases of beer—critical supplies for the long weekend ahead.

What began as a small weekend barbecue event in 1976 which had 20-30 teams has now become a five-day marathon of cooking, celebrating, carousing and culinary excess for thousands of the world's most dedicated carnivores. But aside from contest cooking, Swine & Dine, like most teams, spends a considerable amount of their funds feeding friends, sponsors and their families, and anyone they care to invite into the private parties they hold nightly.

They'll cook up 300 pounds of chicken, 500 pounds of pork ribs and over 2,500 pounds of pork shoulder to feed the several hundred hungry visitors who gleefully invade their area each evening. The food is washed down with 180 cases of beer and 28 fountain canisters of varied sodas. And the Jell-O Shooter Committee has dutifully made up 4,000 lime, orange, cherry and grape "shooters," for the adventurous.

But right now the traditional "baloney bullet" is being prepared for the grill. Two 13-pound rolls of bologna are cut into smaller segments, grilled for 30-40 minutes, slathered with their own barbecue sauce, and served as the traditional start of the cooking phase of the contest for the Swine & Diners. The village is up. On with the barbecue!

8pm

Tom Lee Park is now filled with fragrant clouds of smoke as other teams fire up their grills, smokers and deep fryers. The grounds are no longer quiet or peaceful, and will not be that way for five more days, when the last of the combatants folds up their trailers, dump the ashes from their barbecues, put away unused sauces and spices, and resolutely head off for the next Que contest somewhere down the road.

Oblivious to it all, the Mighty Mississippi river just keeps rolling along.

SWINE & DINE TEAM, 2002

Swine & Dine is one of Memphis in May's largest teams, and has competed in 24 of the contest's 26 years. Their 85 members are teachers, wrestling coaches, network television executives, cooks, bartenders, restaurant managers, oil company and advertising executives, nurses, real estate and stock brokers, engineers, and furniture sales people. Before coming to Memphis we picked their name out of a hat, and found 85 wonderful, friendly, generous, and hospitable folks—who cook up a mean pork shoulder, luscious ribs, and oh! that BBQ baloney!.

Committees:

Building
Jim Fields
Jim Massey

UP
Greg Shepard
Craig Campany

Decorating
Toni Sterns

Cooking
Jerry Crain
Robert McIvor
James Prescott

Beer
Chip Armstrong
Paul Schully
Pat Cavenaugh

Special Events
Sherry Zinn
Toni Sterns

Judge Serving
Kellie Prescott
Carl Pfeiffer

Serving
Jayme Armstrong
Kelli Polatty

Joan Hermann
Security
Drew Armstrong
Bobby Allen
Clean Up
Barry Poole
Jell-O Shooters
Vic Vescovo
Chip Armstrong & Arta Meredith
Drew & Jayme Armstrong
Guy & Cathy Armstrong
Mike & Linda Armstong
Craig & Sandy Campany
John & Sandy Carls
Pat Cavanaugh & Jim McKinney
Richard Crawford & Vickie Karnes
Jim Fields & Sherry Zinn
Sarah & Jim Gamage
Gary & Joan Hermann
Tony & Jeanne Herrera
Greg & Susan Hyde
Gary & Mary Pantlik
John & Sherry Perry
Toni Petersen & Bill Sterns
Kelli & Mills Polatty
Barry & Debbie Poole
James & Kellie Prescott
Greg & Felicia Shepard
Paul & Linda Schully
John & Donna Uitendaal
Phillip & Leslie Webster

Steve & Christine Wigley
Gary & Lynn Wilkerson
Bobby Allen
Ralph Beard
Tim Bethany
Danny Botto
Michelle Burnell
Cindy Cockrill
Jerry Crain
Larry Dalgo
Rick Dietze
Missy Delk
Angie Garrison
Wesley Loflin
Rick O'Leary
Sean O'Leary
Jim Massey
Bobby McIvor
Tom Mitnick
Beth Moye
Carl Pfeiffer
Mark Puchalla
Lindsey Rogers
Guy Roth
Sandy Rousseau
Steve Schully
Susan Smith
Vic Vescovo
Amber West
Mark Wilson
Brooks Wolfe

BACON-WRAPPED SMOKED PORK TENDERLOIN

Donny Teel, Buffalo's BBQ Sauce and Competition Team
   Sperry, OK

¼ cup yellow mustard

2 small pork tenderloins

RUB:

1 teaspoon garlic powder

1 teaspoon paprika

1 teaspoon Mexene chili powder

1 teaspoon sugar

½ teaspoon ground black pepper

12-16 smoked bacon slices, very thick

1-1 ½ cups favorite BBQ sauce

In medium bowl combine garlic, paprika, chili powder, sugar and pepper and mix well. Set aside.

Massage yellow mustard into entire tenderloin covering every surface. Sprinkle the rub onto the meat. Wrap bacon slices around the meat completely, using several toothpicks to hold bacon in place.

Let loins absorb mustard and herbs, marinating in a covered pan for 2 hrs. in the refrigerator. Heat grill to 400° to 450° degrees, to cook using indirect method mound charcoal or briquettes on one side of the barbecue. Put a pan of water on the other side.

Cook meat on oiled grill above water pan for 1 to 1 ½ hours, then remove and immediately wrap loins in foil, put back on the grill, again on indirect heat, and cook until meat reaches an internal temperature of 155° degrees.

Open foil, lavishly baste tenderloin with BBQ sauce and set on coolest part of grill for 15-20 minutes, at which time temperature should have risen to 160° degrees.

Take meat off grill and keep sealed in foil until ready to serve.

Serves 6-8

HUCKLEBERRY MOUNTAIN PORTERHOUSE PORK CHOPS

RUB:

1 teaspoon dried sage

½ teaspoon salt

½ teaspoon sugar

¼ teaspoon paprika

1 tablespoon garlic powder

MEAT:

¼ cup honey mustard

4 porterhouse pork chops, 16 oz. each

5-6 sprigs fresh rosemary or sage

Mix rub ingredients in small bowl. Massage mustard into chops with your hands and then sprinkle rub over chops, coating evenly.

Put on a plate, cover with plastic wrap and refrigerate for 4 to 24 hours.

Grill chops on oiled grill rack set 5 to 6 inches over glowing coals, or hot gas fire (400°-450°) for 10 to 12 minutes on each side, or until a meat thermometer diagonally inserted 2 inches into centers registers 155° degrees. Remove from heat, seal chops in heavy duty foil and let them stand 5 minutes before serving.

Serve with blackberry sauce (see below) and garnish chops with sprigs of fresh rosemary or sage.

CAROLINA-STYLE PULLED PORK SHOULDER

Serve on hamburger buns or hard rolls with a scoop of cole slaw on top of meat. National Pork Producers Council

RUB:

2 tablespoons salt

2 tablespoons paprika

1 tablespoon garlic powder

1 tablespoon black pepper

2 teaspoons cayenne

1 five-pound boneless pork butt (shoulder)

BASTE:

½ cup bourbon

2 tablespoons molasses

1-½ cups cider vinegar

1 cup water

2 chopped chipotle peppers, rehydrated

2 tablespoons salt

1 tablespoon crushed red pepper

1 tablespoon black pepper

2 tablespoons cayenne pepper

Mix rub ingredients in medium bowl. Rub pork shoulder on all surfaces with the mixture; cover and refrigerate up to 24 hours. Prepare a medium fire in covered grill with coals banked to one side of barbecue.

Smoke pork shoulder adding more charcoal and wood chips to maintain a medium-low heat of between 300° of 400° degrees throughout the cooking time. Smoke/grill until internal temperature of pork shoulder is 160° degrees, about 5-6 hours. Use hickory, pecan or cherry wood for smoke flavor.

Mix together the ingredients for the basting sauce in a small saucepan.

Baste the shoulder quickly every 30 minutes during the last couple of hours of cooking, remembering you can lose 15 minutes of cooking time each time you open the lid of the smoker.

Boil any leftover basting sauce for 10 minutes then cool.

Shred ("pull") the meat, add sauce and stir well.

Serves 12

MT. ADAMS HUCKLEBERRY SAUCE

Kathy Browne, Ridgefield, Washington

After a long day in the cold rain, picking fresh huckleberries on the side of Mt. Adams, we vowed that the day would not be wasted and developed this recipe to go with game, pork, and turkey. Very hard to get, the huckleberry is worth the trouble, as its strong flavor, crisp bite, and luxuriant color enhances even the plainest meat dish.

1/4 cup fresh huckleberries (or lingonberries or blueberries)
1-1/2 cups burgundy
2 cups beef stock
1/2 cup sugar
1 rosemary sprig
1 bay leaf
1/2 cup cold butter chunks
1/2 teaspoon cracked black pepper

Heat the wine and beef stock in a medium saucepan, over high heat, until it starts to bubble, add the huckleberries, sugar, rosemary, bay leaf, and pepper, stirring frequently, and simmer until the mixture is reduced by half, about 15-20 minutes. Remove the bay leaf and whisk in the butter, one chunk at a time, until the sauce is smooth and creamy, except for a few lumps of huckleberry that is.

Remove from heat, and allow it to cool and serve warm over pork, poultry or game.

Serves 4

GRILLED LOIN OF WILD BOAR WITH SOUR CHERRY SAUCE

1 2 1/4–3 pound loin of wild boar
1 teaspoon salt
1 teaspoon pepper
2 teaspoons paprika
4 oz. bacon slices
10 cloves
1 cup water
1 cup olive oil
1 tablespoon all purpose flour
1 cup cherry-cranberry juice
1 cup stock
6 tablespoons sour cherry preserves

In small bowl mix salt, pepper and paprika and set aside. Heat grill to 500° to 600° degrees.

Trim the meat. Rub with olive oil and then sprinkle with the salt, pepper and paprika rub. Wrap bacon slices around the meat and stick with cloves. Using indirect cooking method place loin on hot grill above water pan to which you've added 1 cup water, and cook for 1 to 1 1/2 hours, or until internal temperature is 160° degrees.

Remove the excess fat from the pan and stir in flour. Cook over medium burner for 1-2 minutes, stirring, until mixture thickens. Gradually stir in the cherry-cranberry juice and stock. Bring to a boil, stirring, and cook for 3-4 minutes until thickened slightly. Stir in the cherry preserves and seasonings and cook an additional 1-2 minutes. Remove from heat, and let sauce come to room temperature. Serve warm with wild boar loin.

Slice meat thinly and ladle sauce over slices on each plate.

Serves 6

CEDAR-PLANKED SUGAR CANE CANADIAN PEAMEAL BACON, EH?

1 2 to 3 pound Canadian peameal bacon roast, split in half horizontally *

2 tablespoons granulated garlic

2 tablespoons chopped fresh rosemary

¼ cup Steen's Cane syrup (or maple syrup)

2 tablespoons French's mustard

2 tablespoons brown sugar

¼ teaspoon nutmeg

¼ teaspoon allspice

¼ teaspoon ground cloves

2 tablespoons cracked black pepper

2 teaspoons coarse salt

apple juice in spray bottle

3-4 fresh rosemary sprigs

* An incredible cut of meat. A Canadian favorite you will love when you try. Try at your local butcher shop, but also available online through the wonderful folks at Real Canadian Bacon Company, at www.realcanadianbacon.com. Meat comes in 2-3, or 5-pound roasts. They also sell the world's best Canadian Maple Syrup.

Soak 1 cedar (or maple) plank for 6 hours in water. These are specially treated cedar planks you get from grocery, barbecue or gourmet food stores or the internet, NOT from the lumberyard.

Preheat barbecue to high (600° to 750°). If using coals make sure your hand can only stay over coals 1-2 seconds, if using gas turn on all jets to high.

Score the top of the pork roast about ½-inch deep in diamond pattern with a sharp knife. In small bowl, mix garlic, rosemary, cane syrup, mustard, and brown sugar and combine well. Rub paste into meat and set aside for at least 1 hour to dry marinate.

Place pork roast on soaked plank. Put directly on grill over high heat for 15 minutes, then reduce heat to medium (approximately 350° degrees) by opening air vents or turning down gas. Continue plank-roasting for 1 hour. After 45 minutes spray tenderloin with apple cider, cover with foil, shiny side down, for last 15 minutes of cooking. Internal temperature of meat should be 160° degrees on a meat thermometer. Remove pork from barbecue, spray once again, seal in foil, and then let it rest for 10 to 15 minutes before carving. Slice into ¼" inch slices and serve on the cedar plank, garnished with fresh rosemary sprigs.

Serves 6-8

GRILLED PORK CHOPS WITH PEACH CHUTNEY

4 Pork loin chops, 2 inches thick

MARINADE:

½ cup soy sauce

¼ cup sake

¼ cup apricot brandy

The day before serving, mix together the marinade ingredients, pour the marinade over the pork chops in a shallow glass dish, cover with plastic wrap and refrigerate overnight.

When ready to cook the pork chops, prepare a charcoal or briquette fire and wait till coals are tinged with white ash (500° to 650°). Remove the chops from the marinade, reserving the marinade and boiling it in a small pan for 10 minutes.

Grill the chops for 5 minutes on each side, brushing with the marinade, until browned and flecked with brown. Internal temperature should be 160°. Remove the chops to a hot serving platter, and serve immediately, topped with chutney, (see below).

Serves 4

PEACH CHUTNEY

2 cups peaches, 2-3 firm and ripe

¼ cup vinegar

⅛ cup fresh lemon juice

½ cup seedless golden raisins

⅛ cup slivered preserved ginger

¼ cup finely chopped onion

½ tablespoon salt

½ teaspoon ground allspice

¼ teaspoon ground cloves

¼ teaspoon ground ginger

¼ teaspoon each ground cinnamon, cloves, and
    ginger

2 cups granulated white sugar

½ cup firmly packed light brown sugar

½ box fruit pectin

In a large saucepan over high heat combine all ingredients except brown and white sugar, stir to combine. Bring mixture to a full boil for 5 minutes, stirring, then add brown and white sugar and bring back to a boil. Boil for 2-3 minutes more, then remove pan from heat, skim surface of liquid, and let cool for 20 minutes. Pour into glass container and store tightly covered. Serve chilled or at room temperature.

GRILLED PORK SHOULDER

* It's Really Spam, But Don't Tell Your Wife/ Husband Cause She/He Wouldn't Like It, Until She/He Tastes It, Then She'll/He'll Say It's One Of The Best Things You've Ever Cooked!

RB & KB one rainy Saturday afternoon

Serve with baked beans, corn on the cob, potato salad and lots of cold adult beverage. After several adult beverages it'll taste like crown roast of pork.

Two 12 oz. cans of SPAM
½ cup prepared yellow mustard
3 tablespoon brown sugar
¼ teaspoon ground cloves
¼ teaspoon ground ginger
¼ teaspoon black pepper
1 tablespoon chopped green onion

Open both cans of SPAM and cut into ½-inch slices, you should get 12 slices from two cans, or 6 slices from one can, or 198 slices from 33 cans. (Multiply other ingredients if you do 33 cans however!).

In separate bowl mix remaining ingredients until a thick paste is formed. Reserve at room temperature.

Put slices on very hot grill (500° to 600°) until bottom is charred with grill marks and browned, approximately 3 minutes. Turn meat slices over and carefully spoon one tablespoon of mustard-sugar paste onto the cooked side of each slice, taking care not to spill onto the coals or gas flame.

After 2-3 minutes meat is ready to remove to a heated platter for serving.

Serves 4-6

SELECTING THE PIG

Select a pork carcass that will weigh from 60 to 100 pounds. A live pig weighing 90 to 130 pounds will dress out as a carcass of approximately the desired weight. The carcass should be lean without too much fat. Excessive fat may cause a flare-up during cooking. The pig should be slaughtered, cleaned and the carcass properly chilled before cooking.

The carcass should be opened butterfly-fashion for cooking. To do this, saw or cut through the backbone, but not through the meat or skin.

The yield of cooked meat is approximately 35 percent of the carcass weight. Plan on at least 1.5 pounds of meat per person for a generous serving. A 100 to 120 pound pig will serve 65 to 80 people.

NORTH CAROLINA STYLE WHOLE HOG

North Carolina Pork Producer's Association
Pig pickin' has become a favorite pastime for many North Carolinians. Barbecuing pork on the open grill and serving the delicacy from the grill is known as a pig pickin'. Any month or season of the year is good for pig pickin' in North Carolina.

BUILDING THE BARBECUE PIT

The pit should be constructed 12 to 24 inches from the fire to the grill. The advantage of this distance is that it provides more even heat distribution. An easy way to build a pit is using concrete blocks (8 inch) and laying the blocks two high. Build the pit 3 to 4 feet wide (inside measurements) and as long as needed. Lay metal rods across the cement blocks and place a suitable wire or screen over the rods.

BUILDING THE FIRE

The traditional source of heat is coals from burning oak or hickory wood, however some pitmasters use charcoal briquettes. If charcoal is used it will take approximately 60 pounds to cook a 100-pound pig. Start with 20 pounds of briquettes and allow them to burn outside the pit until gray before spreading in the pit. The heat should be distributed so that the hams and shoulders get more heat and the center of the pig gets less. This will allow the pig to cook uniformly. Additional briquettes started outside the pit or coals from the hard wood are added to maintain the proper grill temperature as listed below.

Cooking Schedule	Approximate Temperature
8:00 am–12:00 noon	100–125 deg. F
12:00–1:00 pm	135–145 deg. F
1:00–2:00 pm	150–160 deg. F
2:00–4:00 pm	170–175 deg. F
4:00 pm	Turn carcass
4:00–4:30 pm	150–160 deg. F
4:30–6:00 pm	170–200 deg. F

Place the pig on the grill lean side down (skin side up) for 4 to 8 hours (depending on weight of carcass), then turn pig over. Be careful in turning since the pig may disjoint at this time. Cook with skin side down for an additional 1 to 2 hours. Be sure to use a meat thermometer and get the internal temperature of the hams to 170° degrees to be sure the carcass is completely cooked throughout. Remember, do not cook too fast!

After turning, the carcass can be basted with a sauce of your choosing. A typical mopping sauce consists of 2 quarts of vinegar, ¼ to 1 cup crushed red pepper (depending on the degree of spiciness desired), and 1 cup sugar, and salt to taste. Use a new mop to baste the meat.

Last, but not least, when you plan a pig pickin' select a congenial group that likes good food and lots of fellowship and you'll have a successful pig pickin'.

Serves 40-80

PECAN-WALNUT CRUSTED PORK LOIN

5-6 pound boneless loin of pork

MARINADE PASTE:

2 teaspoons chopped fresh rosemary leaves
¼ teaspoon thyme
⅛ teaspoon ground cloves
2 teaspoons minced garlic
¼ cup olive oil
3 tablespoons dark brown sugar, packed
Salt and pepper to taste
Nut coating:
¼ pound finely chopped pecan halves
¼ cup finely chopped walnut halves

MANGO SALSA:

2 ripe mangos, peeled and chopped
½ cup finely chopped red onion
¼ cup coarsely chopped cilantro
1-2 jalapeno peppers, diced and seeds removed
1 tablespoon balsamic vinegar
pinch of salt

Mix rosemary, thyme, cloves, garlic, salt, pepper, 1 tablespoon olive oil and the brown sugar in a food processor and pulse until you have a thick paste. Work the paste into the pork loin, covering completely, then wrap with plastic and refrigerate overnight.

In a medium bowl make up salsa, blending ingredients well with a spoon, and store in refrigerator in covered bowl or container.

Mist the pork loin with the remaining olive oil from a sprayer, being careful to not disturb the marinating paste and then roll the loin in the chopped pecan-walnut mixture.

Prepare water smoker or barbecue grill for smoke cooking at 200° to 250°.

If not using a smoker either use metal smoker box or place wood chips in aluminum foil package and pierce with a fork, place on or near hot charcoal or briquettes.

Place meat, fat side up, on the grill. If using barbecue grill mound coals or briquettes on one side, place water pan under grill on other side, and place meat on grill over water pan away from heat. Cover and smoke/grill for 3 to 6 hours, maintaining the grill temperature by adding briquettes or wood, and adjusting vents on smoker or grill. Add water as needed. Meat is done when internal temperature reaches 160° -170° degrees.

Remove meat to a large platter or cutting board, and let tenderloin rest and cover with foil. Let rest for 15 minutes before slicing. Serve room temperature with cooled, but not cold, salsa on the side.

Serves 6-8

ROAST SUCKLING PIG

1 young suckling pig, 20-25 pounds

2 ½ cups white vinegar

5 gallons water, approximate amount to cover
   pig

STUFFING:

3 cups bread crumbs

2 cups chopped onions

1 cup chopped celery

1 ½ cups chopped apples

1 cup chopped apricots

¼ cup ground sage

¼ cup salt

⅛ cup pepper

BASTING SAUCE:

1 cup honey

1 cup soy sauce

1 cup orange juice

2 limes, cut in slices

2 lemons, cut in slices

1 tablespoon salt

2 cups chicken stock

1 cup dry white wine

Wash pig inside and out and soak it in very cold water with vinegar for a few hours (½ cup vinegar to 1 gallon of water). Weigh pig down and cover completely with vinegar water. This freshens and whitens the meat.

Place stuffing ingredients in large bowl and hand toss to mix thoroughly. Firmly fill stomach cavity with stuffing and seasoned with ground sage, salt and pepper. This not only adds a tasty side dish but keeps the pig from collapsing in on itself during cooking.

The easiest way to close the opening in the pig is to use an ice pick or an upholstery needle to punch rows of holes about an inch apart on both sides of the stomach flaps. Then lace it up with thick string just as you would a shoe. You may also use skewers and string as you would for a turkey, or just thread a long skewer from side to side closing the opening.

Because protein firms as it cooks, the pig will stay in whatever position you place it. It should resemble a dog resting on its haunches. Place the pig on the grill. If it is too large it may have to be placed diagonally. Tuck the hind legs close to the stomach on either side; tie them together with string under the stomach if needed. The forelegs should be pointing straight ahead (also tied together so they won't spread out) with the head resting between them.

Mix basting sauce in large pan over medium high and heat until well mixed, about 5 minutes.

Tear off small bits of aluminum foil and fit tin foil caps over the ears, snout and tail to avoid burning. These caps should be removed about 1/2 hour before the barbecue is completed to obtain a uniform baking color. Place a wooden block or round stone in the pig's mouth, so that a red apple, or other fruit, can be inserted when the barbecue is completed.

Briquettes are placed only on the sides of the charcoal grill and separate from the suckling pig by the walls of the foil drip pan. To make this drip pan, use 3 sheets of heavy aluminum foil molded slightly larger than the pig to collect the rich drippings. Place the cooking grill over the foil drip pan. This will allow you to add more briquettes as needed, and to collect the basting fluids. All cooking is done by reflected heat, not by direct flame.

Place about 35 briquettes on each side of the foil drip pan and ignite. It will take about 25 to 30 minutes for the briquettes to be ready for the cooking to begin. Place a meat thermometer in the pig, being careful not to hit the bone, which would reflect an incorrect reading. Approximate cooking time will be 10 minutes per pound of body weight. For a pig of 30 pounds this is about five hours. The thermometer will read 160° to 170° degrees when the suckling pig is done. During cooking, baste the pig with a long mop or brush about once an hour.

The barbecue should be operating with all dampers wide open, and the addition of approximately 12 briquettes to each side every 1 ½ hours will be necessary. About 1/2 hour before the suck-

ling pig is done, baste generously with the basting sauce and remove foil from ears, snout, and tail.

Remove the pig from the grill to a cutting board and wrap in foil, letting meat sit for 20 minutes so juices can retreat back into meat.

Make a sauce by skimming the fat off the juices in the roasting pan and discarding. Place the roasting pan and remaining liquid over 2 burners, add the stock and the wine and bring to the simmer. Stir to dissolve all the roasting juices coagulated on the bottom and continue cooking about 10 minutes. You can add wine, orange juice, coca cola, or other flavored liquid. If you wish to thicken the sauce, whisk in 2 tablespoons of flour that have been blended with 2 tablespoons of butter. Bring the sauce back to a boil for 2 minutes, stirring constantly.

To serve the barbecued pig, slice the skin from the base of the tail to the back of the neck and peel the skin down the sides. Carve the small hams first, slice the rib sections next, and carve the front shoulders and jowl last.

Serves 8-10

SHERRIED PORK SPARERIBS

Denise M. Doyle
1997-98 COOKSHACK SMOKED FOODS RECIPE SWEEPSTAKES FIRST PLACE WINNER

MARINADE:

1 cup water
1 cup vegetable oil
½ cup soy sauce
¼ cup apple cider vinegar
2 cloves garlic, crushed

PEPPER GLAZE:

1 cup apple jelly
1 teaspoon finely chopped, seeded jalapeño
    pepper
¼ cup dry sherry
1 tablespoon of honey
4 pounds pork spare ribs

Mix all marinade ingredients in medium bowl and set aside.

Combine jelly and chopped pepper in a small sauce pan and cook over low heat until jelly is melted, about 3 minutes. Continue to cook for 1 minute. Remove from heat and stir in sherry and honey. Set aside.

Place ribs in a large baking pan and pour marinade over them. Cover and refrigerate for 2-4 hours, turning ribs once. Prepare grill to 300° to 400° degrees. Remove ribs from marinade, drain and place on grill cooking on indirect heat for approximately 4 hours. Try placing apple or other fruit wood chunks directly on the coals or briquettes.

Remove the ribs from the grill to a platter or cutting board. Brush all sides with Pepper Glaze and seal in foil, return to cool side of grill for 15 to 20 minutes. Remove from oven and serve.

SMOKED BBQ SAUSAGE ROLL

*D*onny Teel, Sperry, OK—This is something that is easy to prepare and is great for munchies before the main meal. I came up with this recipe when some unexpected guest showed up for dinner one night. I was scrambling through the refrigerator to find something else to put on the smoker that would be done the same time everything else would. I saw the sausage, so I sprinkled some rub on it and put some sauce on it also, it turned out great. Now the family asks "is the sausage on?"

1 pound roll of pork sausage
8 oz. of your favorite BBQ sauce

RUB:
1 teaspoon granulated garlic
1 teaspoon ground paprika
1 teaspoon brown sugar
⅛ teaspoon black pepper

Preheat your grill to 230° to 250° degrees for indirect cooking, mounding charcoal on one side of barbecue.

Mix rub ingredients in small bowl with a spoon. Set aside.

Take the roll of sausage, generously sprinkle the rub on and roll it around, set the sausage log on some foil, cut a valley about ¼"–½" deep down the middle of the log, spread sides, and fill with BBQ sauce. Place sausage on opposite side of grill away from heat. DO NOT TURN sausage or BBQ sauce will leak out and flame. Cook sausage to 160° degrees internal temperature, about 1 hour.

Serve 8-10

SOUTHERN SUGARED RIBS

Carl Triola, Houston, Texas
These are perhaps the simplest and most delicious ribs I have ever tasted.

salt and pepper to taste
2 racks of pork ribs, membrane removed
1 cup dark brown sugar
cayenne pepper to taste

Salt and pepper ribs and put on oiled grill rack in smoker for 4 hours at 165° degrees. Or you can use indirect method of heat on a grill by putting coals on one side of barbecue, placing a water pan on other side of the barbecue. Place ribs on cool side of grill rack above water pan.

When cooked, remove from smoker or grill, place on aluminum foil, and generously rub both sides with brown sugar mix. Sprinkle small amount of cayenne pepper on each side.

Completely seal ribs in double thickness of heavy duty foil, sealing each layer separately, and put foiled ribs back in smoker or on indirect heat for 1-2 hours.

Cut the ribs apart and serve.

Serves 4-6

TERRY'S SWEET AND SOUR RIBLETS

Terry Browne, Vancouver Island, British Columbia

2 tablespoons olive oil
1 large sweet onion, chopped
2 cloves garlic, crushed
1 tablespoon grated fresh ginger
1 cup soy sauce
¼ cup cider vinegar
¼ cup balsamic vinegar
1 cup dry sherry or rice wine
1 tablespoon red pepper flakes
2 tablespoons dark cane syrup
2 tablespoons dark honey
2 tablespoons molasses
1 teaspoon sea salt
Rack of pork ribs, separated
12 trays ice cubes, placed in ice water

Heat the oil in a large saucepan, add the onion and cook until soft, stirring often. Add the garlic and ginger and cook until garlic just begins to turn golden brown. Add all remaining ingredients except the ribs and bring to a rolling boil over high heat, then add the ribs and immediately reduce to simmer for 1 hour.

Remove pan from heat and cool the entire pan quickly by sitting in a larger bowl or pan half filled with ice-cubes and ice water. When cool, drain ribs, then seal in package of double strength aluminum foil which must be refrigerated for at least 12 hours.

Next day bring the ribs to room temperature and grill for 2-3 minutes per side over medium hot grill (450° to 500°). Some of the sugar mixture might burn but this gives the charred ribs character and adds to the caramel flavor.

Serves 4-6

CHAPTER 6

POULTRY

BBQ Peking Duck with Cold Duck-Hoisin
Sauce   108

Beer Butt Chicken   110

Beer Butt Turkey   112

BoBo's BBQ Boid   114

Brooklyn Jerk Wings (or Thighs)   114

Carl's Smoked Quail   115

Grilled Turkey Breast with
Hawaiian Fruit Salsa   116

Hawaiian Salsa   116

Leroy Brown's Thai BBQ Chicken   116

De-Dip De-Dip Sauce   117

Lexington #1 Pulled Chicken   118

North Carolina Barbecued Turkey   118

Smoky Mountain Cornish Hens with Wild
Rice   120

Spit BBQued Duck   122

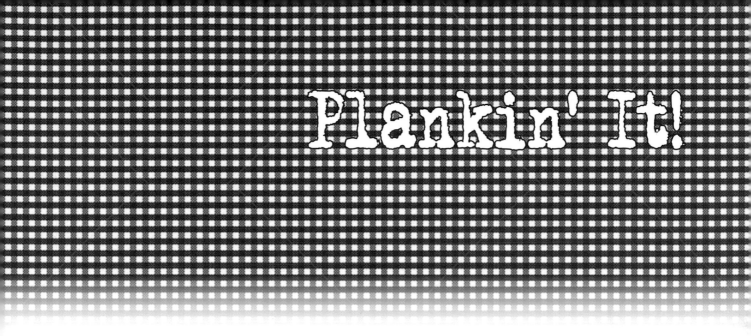

Plankin' It!

Charbroiling steaks, poultry ,and seafood on a wooden board

Okay, so you wanta impress your next barbecue party? Wanna watch their mouths drop open and stay there when you serve up your barbecue dinner?

Then grab a board and head to the grill—we're plankin' tonight.

Wood-plank cooking. This technique, probably copied from the Native American way of cooking salmon and other fish, has suddenly become very popular with barbecuers from coast to coast and is not only a dramatic way to cook, but it also keeps the food moist, adds a wonderful flavor, and is just a plain fun way to present dinner to your guests.

Not only does the wood add a seasoned and unique taste and fragrance to the food, but it imbues it with a smoky flavor, doesn't take a long time, and keeps the food stays juicy right up until it's put onto plates.

First you need a plank (wood board). The best wood to use is western cedar. Alder, hickory, maple, cherry, pecan and oak are also popular. AVOID pine or other resinous woods as the sap is acrid and bitter and will impart those tastes to the food.

In California, or other wine-producing areas of the country, people have been using oak staves from discarded wine barrels when available. Wood that has contained red wine offers up the best chance of any flavor being imparted to the food.

If you don't want to visit a barbecue store or a supermarket, or don't like to shop on the web, all is not lost. Just visit your local lumber yard ask for "construction grade, untreated wood" and have them cut planks 8"x12" or so (to fit easily on your grill) that are ½"-⅝" inch thick.

Or if you do like to surf the internet there are several companies which sell wood planks for cooking. My favorite is Oregon Cedar Grills at: www.outdoorgourmet.com. That site not only offers the planks, in sets of 3, but also shares some fun and delicious recipes.

Their planks are inexpensive and the "use once and throw away" kind, but there are several other companies who sell re-usable planks as well, substantially more expensive but you can use them again and again. The only negative factor is that you MUST pre-heat the re-usable planks on a hot grill for at least ten minutes at 350° degrees to kill all bacteria remaining after the last cooking.

But be forewarned: wherever you get your plank, and whether you use it once or many times, make sure it's "untreated" wood. Wood that's treated has been soaked in chemicals which don't go well with food, and may in fact be poisonous.

What to cook?

Okay, you've got the right kind of plank . . . now what do you cook? The answer: just about anything you can grill. But remember the plank imparts a fairly heavy smoky taste so you don't want to cook delicate foods on it that will be overpowered by the smoky flavor.

The best bets are salmon or other firm-fleshed fish, shrimp, clams & oysters, lobster, pork (tenderloin, chops, and ribs), beef ribs or steaks, lamb, or chicken and turkey breasts or legs. Again just about anything you'd grill over an open flame.

Since the plank can catch fire, or at least smolder heavily during cooking, I don't recommend items that require long cooking times (brisket, large roasts, etc.), as the food you're cooking may well burn up along with the plank. Stick to filets, steaks, chops, tenderloins or other smaller cuts of meat, poultry, and fish.

How to use your plank.

If you try plankin' without pre-soaking the wood, you'll be doing another kind of cooking: incineration, as the planks ignite and burn up that $20 rib eye or $40 salmon. *(Remember if you're using a re-usable plank you MUST pre-heat it at 350 degrees for at least 10 minutes BEFORE you soak it.)*

Put your plank in a large tub and completely cover it with hot water. Since wood floats, the last time we looked anyway, you must weigh it down so it stays underwater. If possible soak the plank for 5-6 hours to make sure it's real soggy and well moistened. We use large, unopened cans of vegetables or a large pitcher filled with water to weight them down. In an emergency you can soak a plank for as little as an hour, just be careful and check it more often while it's cooking to see that it doesn't flame up.

Some people soak the plank in apple juice, beer, or other flavored adult beverage. I personally think that's a waste and would rather drink the apple juice, beer, or adult beverage. *(I like my martinis very dry!)* I would hazard a somewhat educated guess that using any soak other than water does nothing to enhance the flavor of the food you're cooking, in fact if you're using a sugary liquid like apple juice the sugar may catch fire easier than just the plain wood itself.

When the plank is thoroughly soaked, remove it from the water and rub the top surface (the one you're going to put your food on) with olive or vegetable oil (or spray with cooking spray) so the food won't stick. Especially if you're using one of the more expensive re-usable planks.

Prepare a very hot bed of coals or charcoal, or a gas grill with all burners on HIGH. Pre-heat the grill for 10-15 minutes so it's hot. I actually think a gas grill is the best way as the gas flames generate a continuous and constant high heat that will cook your food evenly. In charcoal or briquette fires there are often uneven hot or cold spots which can over- or undercook foods.

Place the food on the plank and sprinkle it with seasonings if you haven't used a marinade or rub. Place the plank in the center of the grill. Close the lid and note the time you began cooking the food.

Keep a bottle filled with water beside the grill in case the plank begins to flame, although if you've soaked it properly and you're not cooking something for a long time the plank should not catch on fire. Smolder, yes; on fire, no!

As the plank heats up and the food begins to bake/broil in the hot grill several things happen. First the aromatic wood sends delightful aromas into the food, and anywhere within ½ mile of the grill. Cedar is particularly wonderful for this, and that's why cedar plank salmon is probably the most popular plankin' dish.

The second thing is that the natural fats, oils, and juices within the food begin to boil and self-baste it from within, creating tender, moist, and very flavorful meat, fish, or poultry.

In most cases, you can go the entire time without lifting the lid to check the food and plank. In fact this is highly recommended, as each time you lift the lid, you lose precious minutes of cooking time. And when you're only cooking for short periods this can cause havoc with your food.

The plank will eventually begin to smolder, and that's okay. The wet wood should smoke a lot and that smoke, plus the fragrance of the wood itself, is what plankin' is all about. But if you peek and flames are starting, douse the plank with your spray bottle of water.

Cooking times vary but the three items we've listed in this book: Cedar Plank Swordfish (page 45), Oregon Cedar Salmon (page 58), and Cedar-Planked Sugar Cane Pork Tenderloin (page 93), come out wonderfully on a plank in under an hour.

In these days of hurry-up and bustle it's nice to fall back on an ancient (some say, slow but sure) way of doing something. Pull up a chair, grab a book and "set a spell" on your deck or porch while the plank merrily does its job. It'll be cracklin' and charrin' and smokin' the way we learned from the first Native Americans, sending up 20th century smoke signals that'll tell everyone—"Hey everyone, we're plankin' again!"

BBQ PEKING DUCK WITH COLD DUCK-HOISIN SAUCE

MARINADE:

1 cup Cold Duck sparkling wine

1 cup honey

½ cup Chinese hoisin sauce

1 teaspoon garlic powder

1 tablespoon powdered ginger

¼ teaspoon salt

1 5-6 pound duck

apple juice

hoisin sauce, to serve with duck

1 package Mandarin pancakes

1 bunch green onions

Mix marinade in large bowl and set aside. Wash and dry bird then place duck in Ziploc bag and add marinade, seal bag and refrigerate overnight. Next morning, take duck out of bag, drain off marinade and reserve, putting it in covered container and either freezing or refrigerating. Using twine or butcher string make a loop through both wings and hang duck from a cabinet, ceiling fixture or pot rack so bird is suspended over pan in kitchen. Let dry for one day.

Put reserved marinade in saucepan and boil for 10 minutes. Set aside.

Place duck on an upright opened can of apple juice. Juice boils and steams duck from inside, and fat under the skin melts and drips away as the skin has pulled away from the meat due to the action of the marinade drying the skin surface.

Heat grill to medium temperature (400° to 500°) degrees putting coals or briquettes on one side on bottom of grill, water pan on other side. Place duck on grill over water pan so dripping fat does not fall on hot charcoal or briquettes and flame up. Use marinade to baste duck once an hour during the 2 to 2 ½ hours it takes to cook the bird.

When duck reaches an internal temperature of 160° degrees take it off barbecue. Keep on can of apple juice, baste once more with thick coat of marinade/basting sauce, wrap loosely in foil. Remove can and let duck cool to a temperature you can handle comfortably.

Cut duck skin and meat into bite sized pieces and serve with hoisin sauce, scallion brushes and mandarin pancakes (available in packages at most oriental food stores). To make scallion brushes take green onions (scallions) and using sharp knife (after trimming away root)cut into 2-inch long pieces, then cut vertically into onion about 1 inch, then making a cross do again so that onion is quartered into four segmented "brush."

Use brush to spread hoisin sauce on pancakes, add a piece of duck skin and a piece of duck meat, wrap or fold up and eat. Voila BBQ Peking Duck!

Serves 4

BEER BUTT CHICKEN

The original "Beer-Butt Chicken" recipe demonstrated for the first time ever on network television by the author on the *Regis & Kathie Lee Show* in 1999, and about a thousand times thereafter. There is nothing like this recipe for cooking up a bronze-colored, moist, and incredibly-flavorful chicken. Not to mention the awe-inspiring way it's cooked and presented. If you worry about the stability of the chicken, as directed below, you can purchase a wonderful device called a "Chickcan" which allows the beer can to sit in a stainless steel device, over which you place the chicken, guaranteeing that the chicken won't fall over. You can find it at www.chickcan.com.

DRY RUB:

1 teaspoon brown sugar

1 teaspoon garlic powder

1 teaspoon onion powder

1 teaspoon summer savory

¼ teaspoon cayenne pepper

1 teaspoon paprika

1 teaspoon dry yellow mustard

1 tablespoon sea salt (ground fine)

BASTING SPRAY:

1 cup apple cider

2 tablespoons olive oil

2 tablespoon balsamic vinegar

1 cup warm beer

Steaming liquid:

1 12 oz. can of your favorite beer, fruit juice, wine or soda can be substituted

1 large chicken

Mix the rub in a small bowl until it's well incropoated. Wash, dry and season the chicken generously inside and out with the rub. Work the mixture well into the skin and under the skin wherever possible. Place in medium bowl, cover and set aside at room temperature for 20 to 30 minutes.

Pour half the can of beer into a spray bottle, add the cider, olive oil, and balsamic vinegar and set aside.

Take the beer can in one hand and insert it vertically into the bottom end of the chicken while keeping the bird vertical as well. Place the chicken on the grill over indirect heat and use the legs, and the can itself, to form a tripod to hold the chicken upright. This positioning does two things: first it helps drain off the fat as the chicken cooks, second the beer steams the inside of the chicken, while the outside is cooked by the BBQ heat, making it the most moist bird you've ever laid yer eyes, or gums, on. Some people put a small potato or carrot in the neck opening of the chicken to keep the steam inside, I prefer to let it pass through.

Smoke for 2 to 2 ½ hours. During the cooking time spray the chicken all around with the basting spray several times. The chicken is done when the internal temperature reaches 180°. Carefully remove the bird, still perched on the can, and place it on heatproof counter top. After your guests have reacted appropriately, remove the chicken from the beer can with tongs while holding the can with an oven mitt (careful! that aluminum can is very hot).

Give the chicken one more spritz of the basting spray and then carve and serve.

Serves 2 to 4

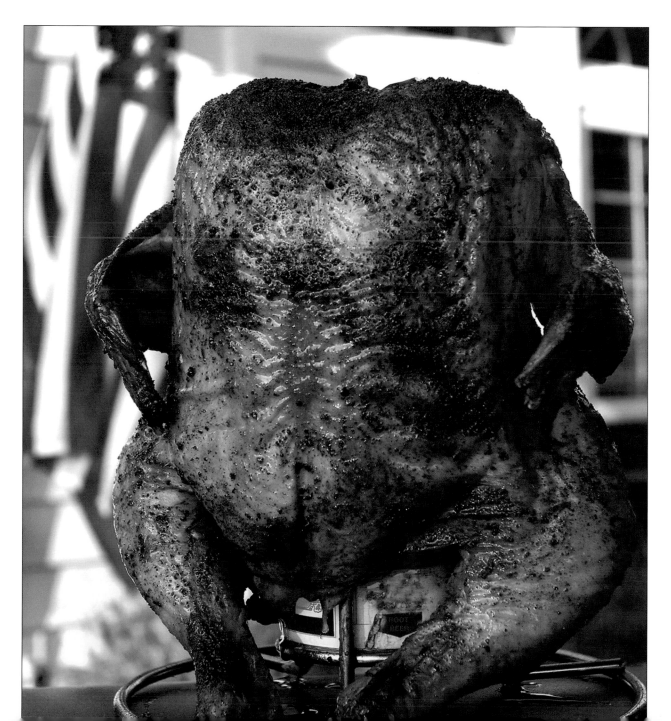

BEER BUTT TURKEY

BASTING SPRAY:

1 cup cider vinegar

1 tablespoon soy sauce

2 tablespoonsolive oil

1 tablespoon balsamic vinegar

1 cup beer

10-12 pound turkey

¼ cup olive or vegetable oil

HERB RUB:

1 teaspoon garlic powder

1 teaspoon poultry seasoning

1 teaspoon chopped rosemary

1 teaspoon black pepper

1 tablespoon ground ginger

1 large (24 or 32 oz.) beer can

Mix Spray ingredients in large bowl and then pour into plastic spray bottle and set aside. Mix herb rub in medium bowl and set aside.

Rinse the turkey in cold water, pat dry, rub with 2 Tbs. olive or vegetable oil, then massage in herb rub, making sure you get some in cavity, and also work rub under the skin as much as you can. Set aside and let bird dry-marinate for 30 minutes.

Get a 32 oz. can of beer, drink half, and add 8 oz. cider vinegar.

Set up BBQ smoker using a water pan under turkey if possible, if not place pan of water beside turkey on grill rack and heat to 200° to 220° degrees. Place bird on grill rack in the classic beer-butt posture (see previous recipe), standing upright with legs helping to support and balance bird, and can inserted into tail end of turkey, and smoke for about 6 hours, checking coals and water periodically.

If instead of a smoker, you are using a barbecue grill, mound charcoal or briquettes on one side of the barbecue, put pan of water on other side under bird, replace grill and put bon heated grill rack above pan. Heat grill to low heat (300° to 400°) as you'll be cooking turkey for about 4 hours and you don't want a very hot fire.

Spray turkey periodically with spray bottle to keep moist.

For both methods (smoker and grill) when bird reaches 160° internal temperature it is done. Carefully lift the lid so your guests can see the clever way you've cooked this particular bird, and when the laughter subsides you can take bird off the can, let it rest for 15 minutes covered in foil on a cutting board or platter, then carve and enjoy.

Serves 6-8

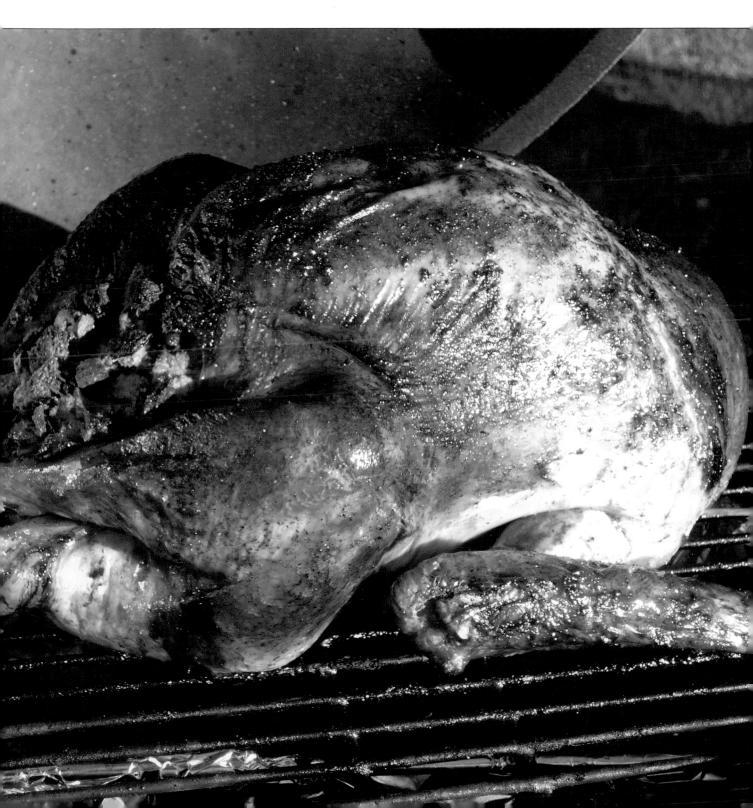

BOBO'S BBQ BOID

BASTE SAUCE:

½ cup bottled Italian dressing

½ cup bottled chili sauce

1 tablespoon blackstrap molasses

3 pounds chicken pieces, skinless

¼ cup olive oil

garlic salt to taste

garlic pepper to taste

In small saucepan combine the Italian dressing, the chili sauce and molasses, and bring to a boil, then immediately reduce heat to low and simmer for 10 minutes.

Brush the skinless chicken with olive oil, then generously salt and pepper.

Grill the chicken over medium coals or flames, 5 minutes on each side, then after 15 minutes, brush with the baste sauce and continue to grill, turning and brushing two or three more times, until chicken is tender, juices run clear and meat is no longer pink, approximately 10 minutes more. Internal temperature should be 170° for breasts, 180° for thighs. Serve on heated platter.

Serves 4-6

BROOKLYN JERK WINGS (OR THIGHS)

24 chicken wings, skin removed

or 24 chicken thighs, skin removed

1 onion, chopped

2/3 cup chopped green onion

6 tablespoons dried onion flakes

2 tablespoons ground allspice

2 tablespoons fresh ground black pepper

2 tablespoons cayenne pepper

2 tablespoons sugar

4 ½ teaspoons dried thyme

4 ½ teaspoons ground cinnamon

1 ½ teaspoon ground nutmeg

¼ teaspoon dried ground habanero chile *

1 tablespoon soy sauce

5-8 drops Louisiana hot sauce

¼ cup vegetable oil

16 ounces of your favorite ranch dressing

Place all ingredients except chicken in food processor and blend until smooth.

Place chicken in large, heavy Ziploc bag. Pour marinade over chicken. Do not let marinade touch your skin, if it does wash immediately. Seal bag, refrigerate for two days, turning bag over occasionally.

* You can use jalapeno chili peppers instead of habanero, but jerk isn't jerk without this fiery Jamaican pepper—even if it's 1,000 times hotter than the jalapeno pepper.

Remove chicken from marinade with **tongs** (not fingers!). Grill on a hot grill (500° to 600°) until cooked through and golden brown, approximately 10 to 15 minutes. Turn frequently to avoid charring.

Serve with creamy ranch dressing.

Serves 4-6

CARL'S SMOKED QUAIL

*Carl Triola, Damnifino Team
Houston, Texas*

6 whole or boneless quail

RUB

2 tablespoons paprika
2 tablespoons garlic salt
2 tablespoons brown sugar
2 tablespoons oregano
1 teaspoon cinnamon
1 teaspoon ground cumin
pinch of cayenne pepper

Butterfly quail. Mix the rub ingredients together in a medium bowl and rub on and under skin, and let birds sit at room temperature for about one hour.

Lay birds on smoker at 200° to 250°, and smoke for around 1½ to 2 hours depending on the heat from your firebox. Or, if you're using a grill, mound briquettes or charcoal on one side of bottom, place water pan on other side, and place birds on the side of the grill away from heat. Grill at 300° to 350° degrees for 30 to 35 minutes.

Remove from barbecue and put several birds at a time on large sheet of extra strength aluminum foil. Fold to seal birds inside foil envelope. Place back on cool end of barbecue and leave for 30-45 minutes. Birds will be juicy and moist when foil is removed.

If you can get boneless quail they are easier to cook, and much easier to eat.

Serves 6

GRILLED TURKEY BREAST WITH HAWAIIAN FRUIT SALSA

3 pound boneless breast of young turkey, thawed
2 tablespoons olive oil
1 teaspoon garlic salt
1 teaspoon chili powder

Lightly spray or oil grill rack with nonstick cooking spray, and prepare grill for medium indirect heat cooking. Temperature should be 400°-500° degrees. Make sure you have a water pan under the "cool" side of the grill.

Remove wrapper from turkey but do not remove the string netting. Brush surface of turkey lightly with the olive oil, and with your hands massage garlic salt and chili powder into turkey. Place the turkey on grill over drip pan, cover grill, cook for 1-1 ¼ hours or until internal temperature of turkey is 160° degrees.

Remove from grill, let sit for 5 minutes sealed in foil, then slice and serve with tropical fruit salsa (see below).

Serves 6-8

HAWAIIAN SALSA

1 papaya, seeded, diced
1 mango, pit removed, diced
2 oranges
1 lime
1 red bell pepper, finely minced
1 small red onion, finely minced
2 large orange habanero chiles, seeded, finely minced
½ cup chopped cilantro leaves
¼ teaspoon salt
1 teaspoon sugar

Placed the papaya and mango in a medium glass or stainless steel bowl. Cut the oranges and lime in half and squeeze juice over the fruit in the bowl, removing any seeds which drop onto fruit.

Add minced pepper, onion, chiles, and cilantro to the bowl. Sprinkle with salt and sugar, mix well with a spoon, and let marinate for 30 minutes. Put in chilled serving bowl to pass at the table.

LEROY BROWN'S THAI BBQ CHICKEN

Inspired by a dish I had in a now-closed Thai restaurant on the South side of Chicago on a college trip there in the 1960's. Best chicken I'd ever had.

1 can (14 oz) unsweetened coconut milk
2 tablespoon yellow curry paste (or 1 tablespoon curry powder)
2 tablespoon Thai fish sauce
6 cloves garlic, roughly chopped
1/3 cup loosely packed chopped cilantro
2 ½ tablespoons golden brown sugar
½ tablespoon white pepper
2 frying chickens, about 3 ½ pounds each, split in half

Combine the coconut milk, curry paste, fish sauce, garlic, cilantro, sugar, and pepper in a blender. Blend until smooth. Put chicken pieces in Ziploc bag and pour the marinade over the chicken halves. Marinate in the refrigerator for at least 5 hours or, better yet, overnight. Turn occasionally to coat each half.

Build a hot charcoal fire or preheat a gas grill to high (500° to 600°). Drain chicken, then arrange halves on the grill and cook for about 30 minutes or until the juices run clear when you pierce the leg joint (160° internal temperature). Turn chicken halves several times during cooking, basting often with the marinade.

Transfer the chicken to a cutting board and cut into serving pieces. Arrange the chicken on a heated platter and serve with the De-Dip De-Dip dipping sauce (see below).

Serves 4-6

DE-DIP DE-DIP SAUCE

½ cup distilled white vinegar
1 cup sugar
½ Tsp. salt
1 tablespoon Chinese-style chili-garlic sauce

In a saucepan, combine the vinegar and ½ of the sugar, bringing pan to a low boil over medium-high heat, stirring occasionally for 10 minutes, or until mixture thickens slightly. Lower the heat to medium and stir in the rest of the sugar.

Cook for 3 minutes, stirring frequently as liquid comes to a boil. Reduce the heat to low and add salt, then simmer for 4 minutes, stirring occasionally, adding all the chili-garlic sauce and cook an additional minute. Remove from the heat, cool and serve at room temperature.

LEXINGTON #1 PULLED CHICKEN

Vicky Bryant, Hendersonville, Kentucky

Serve piled atop French rolls, which have been buttered and grilled.

BBQ Sauce:

1-½ sticks butter

¼ cup distilled vinegar

crushed red pepper to taste

cayenne pepper to taste

1 tablespoon sugar

1 5 to 6 pound chicken

salt and pepper to taste

Melt sauce ingredients together in a small saucepan at medium and heat, but DO NOT BOIL the sauce.

Rub olive oil on chicken and salt and pepper to taste.

Cook chicken on grill or in smoker. Grill over medium heat (400° to 500°) for 1 ½ to 2 hours until skin is brown, juices run clear when thigh is punctured, and internal temperature is 160° degrees.

When chicken is done, pull off skin and remove meat from the bones. Feed skin to your pet alligator, save bones for necklace for next Halloween.

In a large bowl chop up and pull meat like you would pork shoulder, pour the BBQ sauce mix into the bowl and mix well.

Serves 4-6

NORTH CAROLINA BARBECUED TURKEY

Albert Farmer

Bible Baptist Church, Wilson, North Carolina

As the birthplace of barbecue, the Carolinas embrace many rich and flavorful traditions. Many area churches host Sunday afternoon get-togethers. Seeking healthier options to serve these generally large crowds, many have turned to turkey. This is Albert Farmers' original recipe from the Bible Baptist Church Sunday get-togethers. For additional information contact John Scroggins at (800) 545-4087, ext. 5118, or visit www.eatturkey.com.

1 10 to 12 pound whole turkey, fresh or thawed

½ cup peanut, olive or Canola oil

1 ½ pounds bacon, or, if turkey is more than 12 pounds, bacon substitute

salt and pepper, to taste

1 tablespoon crushed red pepper flakes

2 cups apple cider vinegar

1 cup water

Cut turkey in half lengthwise, removing back from both sides, and rub with oil. Wrap with bacon (if turkey is more than 12 pounds, use bacon substitute, as a large amount of real bacon can cause a fire hazard as the grease drips onto fire).

Prepare grill for medium indirect heat cooking (400° to 500°). For gas grills, place a drip pan under one half of the rack then spray the rack with nonstick cooking spray, turn on the heat on the other half of the grill. For charcoal grills, place the coals around the outside edges of the grill, a drip pan in the center, spray the rack with non-stick spray and light the charcoal.

Place turkey, breast side up, on grill rack over drip pan. Cover and grill turkey 2 ½-3 hours or until meat thermometer inserted into deepest portion of thigh reaches 180° F and leg bone will turn and separate from meat. Turkey should be golden brown.

Allow turkey to cool. Remove turkey from bones, remove skin and chop meat. Add salt and pepper to taste. Sprinkle with red pepper flakes and mix well. In small bowl mix vinegar and water and sprinkle over meat. Stir gently into chopped turkey. Add more water if vinegar mixture is too strong.

Serves 8-10

SMOKY MOUNTAIN CORNISH HENS WITH WILD RICE

John Angood, Saratoga, California

A great, innovative, and creative cook, John has had a tough time this year with back surgery. But slowly he's getting back to rare form, cookin' up a storm for wife Kathy, and their precious cats.

2 Cornish game hens

salt to taste

pepper to taste

¼ cup chopped green onions

1 medium shallot, chopped

3 tablespoons butter

1 cup cooked wild rice

¼ cup chopped pecans or walnuts

¼ cup craisins (dried cranberries)

½ cup marmalade

¼ cup orange juice

Rinse hens, pat dry and season cavity with salt and pepper.

In medium saucepan over high heat, sauté onions and shallots in 1 tablespoon butter, add rice, chopped nuts, and craisins. After mix is heated through, remove from heat and set aside until cool.

Fill hens with rice stuffing and secure opening with twine or turkey lacers.

Prepare glaze by melting remaining 2 tablespoons butter in a saucepan, adding marmalade and orange juice, stir and cook over medium-low heat until smooth.

Brush hens with glaze and place on grill.

Smoke 2 to 2 ½ hours at 225° to 250° degrees. Can also be done in charcoal or gas barbecue by setting bird on side of grill away from heat, and putting a water pan under birds. Time may be less, approximately 1 ½ to 2 hours, check internal temperature and when it reads 160° degrees the hens are cooked. Brush with glaze before serving.

Serves 4

SPIT BBQUED DUCK

2 ducklings, 4 pounds each
salt and pepper to taste

STUFFING:

½ cup each shitake and chanterelle mushrooms
½ cup chopped onion
½ cup chopped celery
1 apple, chopped
1 teaspoon poultry seasoning

BASTING SAUCE

½ cup Sherry wine
½ cup soy sauce
1 teaspoon ground ginger
8 tablespoon pineapple-orange juice

Preheat hot coals, smoker or briquettes to medium heat (450° to 550°). Season ducklings with salt and pepper. Mix stuffing ingredients in small bowl and fill the duck cavities with mushroom, onion, celery and apple mix. Run spit through birds lengthwise, catching the bird in the fork of the wishbone, tying legs and wings close to birds with twine. Cook on a rotisserie over grill until tender, about 2 hours for barbecues, 3-4 hours in smoker.

Mix together basting sauce ingredients. , Reserve ½ of it to use on cooked duck, ½ to baste birds with during cooking. Brush birds with basting mixture during the last half-hour of cooking. Have remainder of sauce heating in a small saucepan at medium temperature, so it's warm and ready to put in gravy boat on the table.

When internal temperature is 160° degrees, ducks are done. Remove from spit, let sit for 15 minutes covered in foil. Scoop out stuffing and place in serving bowl, carve ducks and serve.

Serves 4-6

CHAPTER 7

SIDE DISHES

Asparagus with Lemon Marinade   127

Aw Shucks Grilled Corn   128

Bar-B-Q Polenta Cakes & Tomato Sauce   130

Blazin' Saddles Fireside Beans   131

Cape Cod Cottage Cabbage   132

CB's Saturday Nite Grilled Veggies   132

Charcoal Grilled Shiitakes   134

Grandma Leah's Grape Salad   136

Grilled Wild Mushroom Sausage   136

Morel Mushroom Gravy   137

Onion-Fired Steaks   138

Oz Onion Pudding   138

Qued Glazed Squash   139

Snow Goose Beans   140

Tongue Tangy Coleslaw   141

Aunt Rhoda's Dirty Rice   142

Chiang Mai Saffron-Raisin Rice   144

Smoked Tomato-Basilica Rice   145

Curses . . . Foiled Agin' Taters   146

Tug Boat Annie's Sweet Potato Salad
with Marjoram Honey Vinaigrette   147

Dorothy's Sweet Potatoes   148

Grilled Onion & Potato Skewers   149

New Potatoes in Garlic-Lemon Butter   150

RBq's Smoke-Baked potatoes   151

Uncle John's Beer & Potato Salad   152

Bubba's Got the Mop

by Baxter B. B. Chicken

The outlook wasn't hopeful,
for Baxter's team that day,
His ribs were dry, his brisket charred,
with one more bird to spray.
And then when one Judge gave a six,
and one other did the same,
A darkened silence fell on the team,
who'd sadly share the blame.
A few got up and choked good-bye;
our Carolyn stayed and prayed.
They knew Bubba had entered chicken,
he'd win a prize for that.
For sure he'll come out a winner,
with a ribbon for his hat.
But the Baron had won brisket,
a victory far from small.
And Ol' Willingham said he'd be surprised,
to see Bubba win at all.
And when the smoke had lifted,

and all saw what occurred,
here was Ardie with a second,
while Smokey grabbed a third.
Then from the grilled assemblage,
there rose a hearty yell;
it rumbled through the stockyards,
it really sounded swell,
it bounced off KC stadium,
and off the Stockyard top,
for Bubba, sweaty Bubba,
was picking up the mop.
There was style in Bubba's manner
as he stepped up to the grill,
he had a regal bearing
and a smile remembered still.
And then he fast responded
by raising up his gimmie hat,
the hungry folks around there
saw our Bubba grease his rack.
A thousand Judges watched him

as he rubbed away the dirt,
Four hundred of them with sauce spilled
up and down their judges shirts.
Then while his rivals rubbed their rubs,
and stirred up yet more dips,
the challenge burned in Bubba's eyes,
a snarl spread 'cross his lips..
And now the beer-butt chicken,
came outta the hot air,
he smiled and quickly carved it
with tender loving care.
"Too salty" said one virgin Judge.
While from the crowd who waited,
there came an anguished roar,
like the sound of Oscar losers,
as they creep on out the door.
"Grill him! Grill that first-timer!"
yelled someone from the stands,
and it's certain they'd have grilled him
had not Bubba raised his hands.
He glanced over at the Judges,
one dressed in baby blue,
but Bubba just ignored her,
as she mumbled, "hard to chew."
"It's tender," cried his sponsors,
and others called out "Jerk!"

But one gentle look from Bubba,
sent the Judges go back to work.
The team saw his brow get furrowed,
they saw his shirt get stained,
and they all knew now for certain,
he'd be Royal Champ again.
The frown has gone from Bubba's lips,
he knows it's not too late,
He sprays the bird with practiced hands,
fair Kathy wipes the plate.
And now the bird is on the green,
with clear juices pouring fro,
but the Judges are all heaving,
It's not a pretty show.
Oh somewhere in this flavored land
the chicken tastes "jest right."
Ferlin Husky's playing somewhere,
and somewhere gas grills light.
And somewhere smokers bellow,
and hungry eaters shout,
But there is no joy for Bubba,
his beer-butt chicken has lost out.

In tribute to Carolyn Wells, Paul Kirk, Ardie Davis, Smokey Hale and John Willingham, true giants of barbecue lore, and with humble apologies to Ernest L. Thayer's Casey at the Bat.

ASPARAGUS WITH LEMON MARINADE

1 pound fresh asparagus, Choose bright green
    spears with tightly closed tips
½ cup melted butter
2 teaspoons olive oil
2 tablespoons honey
¾ teaspoon freshly ground black pepper
pinch of sea salt
juice of 1 lemon
non stick cooking spray
Preheat the grill to medium high (450° to
    500°).

Wash the asparagus thoroughly and peel off the bottom end of stems with a hand peeler if they seem woody. Using sharp knife cut an "X" vertically from the bottom to about 1/3 of the way up the stalk.

Place asparagus in a flat Pyrex pan. Whisk the butter, oil, honey, pepper, salt and lemon juice in a small bowl. Pour this mixture over the asparagus and allow stalks to marinate for 15 minutes, then drain and reserve marinade.

Coat the grill with cooking spray and place the asparagus crosswise on the grill. Grill until lightly browned and tender, about 4 minutes, turning once with tongs.

Transfer the asparagus to a heated serving platter and drizzle the remaining lemon marinade over them. Serve at once.

Serves 4

AW SHUCKS GRILLED CORN

Try this with sweet white corn and you'll never want yellow again! If you want to speed things up, remove the husks and place the corn directly on the grill for 5-7 minutes, turning several times.

6 corn on the cob, unshucked
1 cup melted butter or olive oil
1 teaspoon dried dill
½ teaspoon garlic powder
fresh ground pepper
1 teaspoon brown sugar

We usually soak the corn in salt water for several hours to get the shucks moist. (Use 2 tablespoons of salt for every gallon of water.) At the same time throw twin into same container and soak.

Place butter or oil in small glass dish and add spices and sugar. Whisk to thoroughly mix in the flavors.

Peel the corn shucks back, one at a time, until most of the corn is exposed and then remove and discard the silk. Do not remove shucks,; they should remain attached. With a pastry brush lavishly coat the corn with the spiced butter or oil mixture using about half. Reserve the rest.

Carefully close the shucks around the seasoned corn, sealing the end with a piece of the soaked twine. Grill the corn over hot coals or high gas burners (500° to 600°) on the grill, turning frequently, until done, about 30 minutes. The shucks will often turn dark/black but will protect the corn. Carefully peel off the shucks and pass the corn around at the table. Use the remaining melted butter available to brush on corn with a pastry brush.

Serves 6

BAR-B-Q POLENTA CAKES & TOMATO SAUCE

For a shortcut you can buy prepared polenta at your local market (usually in the natural foods section) in rolls you can cut into slices. There are several flavors available.

1 ½ cups polenta mix
1 ½ cups chicken broth

SAUCE:

6 medium ripe tomatoes
2 tablespoons extra virgin olive oil
2 sweet onions, chopped finely
2 cloves garlic, minced
½ teaspoon sea salt
¼ teaspoon pepper
¼ teaspoon oregano
¼ teaspoon ground basil
¼ teaspoon minced fresh rosemary leaves
2 oz. extra virgin olive oil
1 tablespoon finely chopped fresh basil
1 tablespoon finely chopped fresh sage
¼ cup Grated parmesiano-reggiano cheese
3-4 tablespoons fresh parsley, chopped

Using a long-handled spoon, gradually stir polenta mixture into boiling broth, it will thicken and spatter. Reduce the heat to low and continue stirring for 5 more minutes until smooth and thick. Remove from the heat and at once spoon the polenta into a 4"x8" loaf pan which has been sprayed with non stick olive oil spray. Spread evenly with a spatula or knife. Let it stand for 30 minutes to firm and cool (or let it cool in the loaf pan, then cover and refrigerate for up to 3 days). Run a knife around the pan and turn the polenta out onto a board. Chill.

To make the sauce place the tomatoes on a barbecue grill over medium-hot coals or gas at approximately 450° to 550° degrees and cook until skin is charred in spots. Remove the tomatoes to a medium bowl and cool slightly. Cut tomatoes in half and scrape out and discard seeds, then chop the tomatoes in large chunks. In large cast iron pan on the grill, over high heat, add the olive oil, onions, garlic, and tomatoes and bring to a boil stirring constantly. Reduce heat to low. Sprinkle with salt, pepper, oregano, basil, and rosemary, and simmer (covered) for 4-6 minutes.

In a small bowl, mix the oil, basil, and thyme. Cut chilled or store-bought prepared polenta, into 2-inch thick slices. Brush both sides with oil-herb mixture. Grill the polenta slices on an oiled or sprayed grill over medium-hot coals (or gas) for 5-7 minutes, or till the bottom is golden brown. Brush the top side with the oil-herb mixture and flip, cooking the slices until golden brown.

Arrange the polenta on a hot serving platter; remove the chunky tomato sauce from the heat and ladle over top. Sprinkle with freshly grated parmesiano-reggiano cheese and fresh parsley and serve immediately

Serves 4

BLAZIN' SADDLES FIRESIDE BEANS

John Davis, Vancouver, WA. John's a big fan of baked beans and this is one of his favorite recipes. It's great served with beer-butt chicken, fresh corn bread, and a Corona beer. Addition of celery stalks to cooking beans aids in digestion, and it also can help reduce the effects so vividly portrayed in the movie Blazing Saddles.

14 oz can kidney beans

16 oz can butter beans

16 oz can black beans

3 16-oz cans baked beans

10 slices bacon, chopped in ¼ inch pieces

1 large sweet onion, chopped

½ cup dark brown sugar

1 cup chili sauce

1 tablespoon Mexene chili powder

dash of Louisiana hot sauce

2 tablespoons prepared mustard

2 tablespoons cider vinegar

three whole stalks of celery

¼ pineapple rum (optional

Drain kidney, black, and butter beans; combine with baked beans in a large pot. Cook over medium heat, on your grill (350° to 400°) or on a stovetop, for 15 minutes, stirring often until beans are thoroughly heated and beginning to bubble.

In a cast iron deep pot, over medium heat (grill or stovetop), fry cut-up bacon with the onion, until bacon is beginning to crisp and onions are beginning to brown, then add contents of the skillet, including grease, to pot of beans. Add the sugar, chili sauce, chili powder, hot sauce, mustard, and cider vinegar. Stir until well mixed.

Bury the celery stalks in the mixture with tongs and move the pot into the barbecue or smoker, 300° to 350° degrees, and bake the beans for one hour, stirring two or three times.

Remove celery stalks with tongs and discard. Just before beans are taken off the heat you might want to add the pineapple rum for extra flavor and a nice punch. Remove from the heat, and serve beans with fresh homemade cornbread or garlic bread.

Serves 6

CAPE COD COTTAGE CABBAGE

In loving memory of Dennis Welch, who could cook up a storm and loved his cooked cabbage while staying on Cape Cod with his wife and daughters many summers ago.

1 head of cabbage, quartered and cored
2 strips raw bacon, cut in small pieces
1 small onion, chopped
1 tablespoon sugar
¼ teaspoon sea salt
¼ teaspoon white pepper
½ stick butter, cut in pieces

Spray a large cooking bag with non stick spray. Place cabbage, bacon, onion, and butter in the bag. Salt and pepper to taste.

Seal the bag and place it on a grill over low flame (250°-300°). Turn the bag over periodically, every 5 -7 minutes to avoid burning the contents. The cabbage is done when it's soft, about 20-25 minutes.

Serves 4

CB'S SATURDAY NITE GRILLED VEGGIES

"Ready when you are CB!" rang the words on the set of many a C.B. DeMille movie, and a young member of the next generation of world class movie directors is waiting on side stage, soon to walk in his footsteps. Chris Browne, "CB" to many of those who love him. He apparently learned to cook from Ma and Pa.

¼ cup soy sauce
½ cup balsamic vinegar
2 teaspoons dried oregano
1 teaspoon dried thyme
2 cloves garlic, minced
2 teaspoons olive oil
½ teaspoon black pepper
½ teaspoon sea salt
2 bunches green onions, use bottom inches including white root
2 small sweet red peppers, cut into small bite-size pieces*
2 small sweet golden peppers, cut into small bite-size pieces*
4 small zucchini, cut in quarters lengthwise*
2 small eggplants, sliced in ¼ inch slices*
vegetable non-stick cooking spray

In a medium bowl, combine soy sauce, vinegar, oregano, thyme, garlic, olive oil, pepper , and salt, and mix with a wire whisk. Put all vegetables in a 2 qt. Ziploc bag and add the liquid mixture. Marinate at room temperature for 20 to 30 minutes. Drain the vegetables and reserve the liquid for basting pouring into a small bowl or spray bottle.

Coat the vegetable basket* or grid* with cooking spray, add veggies, and place basket or grid on grill over medium-hot heat (450° to 550°). Close the lid of the barbecue, and cook for 5 minutes.

Baste or spray the vegetables with the remaining soy-vinegar mixture and turn the vegetables, grilling an additional 5 minutes or until tender.

Serves 8

If you don't have a vegetable basket just cut the vegetables in large enough pieces that they won't slip through the grill into the flames.

CHARCOAL GRILLED SHIITAKES

8 oz Shiitake mushrooms
1 tablespoon olive oil
1 tablespoon crushed garlic
1 teaspoon minced rosemary
⅛ teaspoon sea salt
⅛ teaspoon black pepper
1 teaspoon maple syrup
1 teaspoon walnut oil

Using a fine brush, clean the mushrooms. Wipe them with paper towels. Remove and discard the stems.

Toss the mushrooms with the olive oil, garlic, rosemary, salt, pepper, maple syrup, and walnut oil in large bowl or Ziploc bag until ingredients are evenly mixed and then marinate the mushrooms for 10-15 minutes.

Drain off and discard the marinade. Grill the mushroom caps over medium coals or gas (400° to 500°) until browned, about 5 minutes.

Serves 4

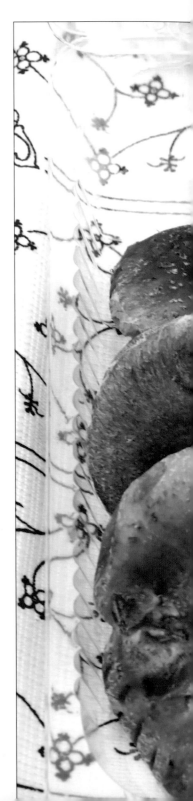

GRANDMA LEAH'S GRAPE SALAD

Tara Bennett, Ridgefield, WA

A recipe from her grandmother Leah, which is perfect with hot, spicy barbecued meats, fish or poultry. At first this dish looks a bit odd, but it tastes wonderful.

1 large bunch of green grapes, washed and thoroughly dried
¼ cup brown sugar
1 pint sour cream
½ teaspoon cinnamon
2 cantaloupes, cut in half, seeded, and chilled

Wash and thoroughly dry the grapes. Mix the sour cream, cinnamon and sugar in a large bowl, until well combined, then add the grapes and carefully mix with rubber spatula.

Serve in cantaloupe halves which have been chilled.

Serves 4

GRILLED WILD MUSHROOM SAUSAGE

2 small chicken breasts, skinned and de-boned
2 lg. eggs
salt and pepper to taste
¼ cup heavy cream, chilled
1 cup cremini mushrooms
1 cup portabella mushrooms
1 cup morel mushrooms
1 cup button mushrooms
1 cup porcini mushrooms
1 tablespoon finely chopped sweet onion
1 teaspoon tarragon
½ teaspoon summer savory
½ teaspoon chives
½ teaspoon cilantro
white pepper
pinch of sea salt
1 tablespoon chopped shallots
1 bunch fresh parsley, chopped
1 tablespoon butter
1 tablespoon olive oil

Put the chicken breasts in a food processor and process until smooth. Add the eggs, then salt and pepper, and process briefly to combine ingredients, then add some cream, pulse, add more cream, pulse, until all the cream is incorporated and the mixture is smooth. Place the mixture in the refrigerator to chill.

Wash and finely chop the mushrooms. In a medium pan over high heat sauté the mushrooms with butter until brown, about 5 minutes. Add onion, herbs, and shallots. Cook until onion is translucent, about 5 minutes. Remove the mushroom mixture from the pan to a medium bowl and place in the refrigerator to chill.

Once mixture is thoroughly chilled remove mushroom and chicken mixtures from the refrigerator. Fold the mushrooms into the chicken. Spread a large piece of plastic wrap on a table. Spoon the mixture into a 1 ½-2-inch wide strip in the middle of the plastic wrap (or pipe it into strip with a pastry bag). Roll the plastic into a log, squeezing the sausage material so that it forms a tight sausage.

Repeat the process until all of the mixture has been used. It should make 1 or 2 foot-long sausage rolls. Tie the ends of the plastic with a string. Gently lower the roll(s) into simmering (NOT BOILING) water in a large pot. Poach the sausage rolls for 10-12 minutes. Remove the rolls from the water with tongs or two slotted spoons.

Dip the plastic wrapped meat in ice water to stop it from cooking, then put in refrigerate the sausages in a wide flat pan until ready to grill.

Preheat the grill to medium hot fire (450° to 550°) and oil or spray the grill. Remove the sausage from the plastic wrap, brush it with olive oil and barbecue it whole, turning often, until browned on all sides, about 8-10 minutes.

Remove from grill and place on a heated platter and serve with morel gravy (below), sprinkling the fresh parsley on top.

Serves 4

MOREL MUSHROOM GRAVY

¼ cup water

⅛ cup brown sugar

¼ cup rice wine vinegar

1 tablespoon balsamic vinegar

3 tablespoons butter

1 ¼ pounds fresh morels, washed and trimmed

¼ cup minced shallots

½ teaspoon chopped parsley

2 cups chicken stock

2 cups white wine, fruity

In a large saucepan over high heat, boil the water with the sugar, without stirring, until golden caramel color, about 15-20 minutes. Remove the pan from the heat and slowly drizzle the rice wine and balsamic vinegar into the sugar water. Return pan to the stove, over medium heat for 2-3 minutes, stir the mixture until caramel is absorbed.

Heat the butter in a cast iron pan over high heat on grill (500° to 600°) until the butter bubbles. Move pan to a cooler part of the grill (medium heat), or turn down the gas, then add the washed and trimmed morels and shallots, stirring over until the liquid from the mushrooms evaporates, and the shallots are golden brown, about 5 minutes. Remove mixture to a bowl..

Add the wine and stock to the cast iron pan and stir, cooking until the liquid reduces to approximately 1 cup. Remove from the heat and stir in the caramel mixture, then add the morel-shallot mixture. Stir once or twice and let the gravy sit for 3-4 minutes. Taste it and add salt & pepper as desired.

Serve with mushroom sausage, chicken breasts, or beef tenderloin.

ONION-FIRED STEAKS

2 large Walla Walla (or other sweet) onions, cut in ½″ slices
McCormick's Honey-Mustard Herb Marinade
1 tablespoon Worcestershire sauce
kosher salt
fresh ground pepper
pinch of paprika

Brush both sides of the onion slices with the marinade and grill alongside ribs, steaks or roasts on a hot grill (500° to 650°).

Brush the onions with sauce several times while cooking until the onions begin to char on each side, about 4 to 5 minutes. Remove onions from the grill with a spatula and put them on plates with steaks. Sprinkle salt, pepper, and paprika on each slice.

Serves 4-6

OZ ONION PUDDING

Try serving this with grilled steaks or roasts and use the Morel Mushroom Gravy (page 137) to pour over the onion pudding.

8 tablespoons butter
1 tablespoon olive oil
8 cups onions, thinly sliced
¼ cup dry vermouth
1 clove garlic, crushed
6 cups. French bread, cut into chunks
2 cups grated emmenthaler or Swiss cheese
3 eggs
2 cups half-and-half
sea salt
freshly ground black pepper

Preheat grill or smoker to approximately 400° to 500° degrees.

In non-stick frying pan on stove melt 4 tablespoon butter with olive oil, over high heat. Add onions, cover, turn burner to low, and simmer for 15 minutes.

Uncover the pan, raise the burner heat to medium, and cook the mixture, stirring occasionally, until the onions caramelize and turn brown, about 20 minutes. Pour in the vermouth and continue heating until the liquid evaporates, stirring the whole time, about 10-15 minutes. Right now the smell in your kitchen will be heavenly!

Spray the sides and bottoms of a cast iron pan thoroughly with the garlic (or unflavored if you will) cooking spray.

Remove the onion mixture form the heat and transfer onions to a large bowl.

Add the bread and stir well. Spread the mix in the cast iron pan. Melt the remaining butter in a small saucepan over high heat, remove from heat and pour over the bread-onion mixture in the cast iron pan. Sprinkle on the cheese.

In a medium bowl beat the eggs slightly and add the half and half, then pour the mixture evenly over the bread-onion and cheese mixture. Use a spoon or spatula to lift sections of the bread-onion mix to make sure the liquid is infused throughout.

Place the pan on a barbecue grill and, using the indirect heat method, cook for 30 to 40 minutes at 400° to 500° degrees until the pudding puffed and golden. If you wish you can place a water pan under the grill, at the same level as the coals.

Remove the pan from the heat, cut the pudding into large triangle pieces and serve.

Serves 6

QUED GLAZED SQUASH

3 acorn squash or small pumpkins, halved and seeded, approx. 1 pound each
3 tablespoons extra virgin olive oil
6 tablespoon butter, melted
½ cup packed brown sugar
pinch ground nutmeg
pinch ground allspice
pinch of salt
½ cup golden raisins, or craisins
2 tablespoon chopped pecans

Scoop out the seeds from the squash or pumpkins. Place each half, cut-side up, on a piece of heavy foil. Brush the cut sides of the halves with oil. In a medium bowl combine melted butter, brown sugar, nutmeg, allspice, and salt, stir until well blended, and pour into shells. Sprinkle the raisins (or craisins) over halves. Wrap securely in foil, keeping the open side up. Cook on an uncovered barbecue directly over medium-hot coals (400° to 500°) for 40 to 50 minutes, or till squash or pumpkins are tender when pierced. Remove from the heat.

Carefully remove foil using oven mitts or tongs and using a pastry brush spread the butter-sugar-spice liquid which has pooled in the hollow of the squash up over the sides and top surface of the squash which will probably appear dry. Sprinkle with the pecans and cook on the grill at the same heat for another 1-2 minutes.

Serves 6

SNOW GOOSE BEANS

If you wish for less of an explosive effect, or more easily digestible beans, throw 2-3 full stalks of celery in the beans while they simmer in the water. Discard the celery stalks when the beans are cooked, before you add to the sausage, tomato sauce, etc.

1 pound dried kidney or red beans
½ pound pork sausage, from butcher, not commercially packaged
6 slices smoked bacon, cut in ½ inch pieces
½ cup brown sugar
2 cups chopped apples
4 medium onions, sliced
2 cloves garlic, chopped
1 ½ cup tomato sauce
2 teaspoons Worcestershire sauce
1 tablespoon chopped parsley
3 teaspoon salt
½ teaspoon black pepper
1 teaspoon Mexene chili powder
2-3 celery stalks (optional)*

Wash the beans and soak them overnight in a large pot of cold water. Place pot on high heat and bring the beans and soaking water to a rolling boil, then cover, add celery stalks to pot (burying them in the mixture) and reduce heat to simmer and continue cooking for 1 ½ hours. Drain the beans and reserve, discarding the water.

Add the sausage, bacon, sugar, apples, onions, garlic, tomato and Worcestershire sauces, parsley, salt, pepper and chili powder to pot and mix thoroughly while your bring the mixture to a rolling boil over a hot grill (500° to 600°).

Remove celery stalks from beans and add the drained beans, move put to cooler side of grill and simmer, covered, over indirect heat (300° to 350°) for 2 hours, or until beans are hot, tender without being mushy, and you can't stand to wait any longer.

Serves 4-6

TONGUE TANGY COLESLAW

1 cup mayonnaise

2 oz. prepared horseradish

⅛ teaspoon Louisiana Hot Sauce

½ cup sugar

1 teaspoon cider vinegar

6 cups of shredded cabbage

2 medium carrots, shredded

dash paprika

Mix the mayonnaise, horseradish, hot sauce, sugar and vinegar thoroughly in a large metal or glass bowl and then add the cabbage and carrots. Let sit for at least 1 hour to absorb flavors. Sprinkle the cole slaw with paprika just before you serve.

Serves 4-6

AUNT RHODA'S DIRTY RICE

Rhoda Coles, Hamilton, Ontario

One of the neatest ladies to ever tease a niece or nephew. Full of life, laughter and love for every living critter. A very special lady to anyone who has ever been charmed by her impish giggle, or her cooking.

3-5 pounds chicken parts: gizzards, necks, wings, thighs, backs
1 teaspoon coarse salt
½ cup butter
1 cup chopped celery
2 cups chopped onions
1 cup chopped red bell pepper
4 garlic cloves, minced

CREOLE SPICE MIX:

½ tablespoon onion powder
½ tablespoon garlic powder
½ tablespoon dried oregano leaves
½ tablespoon dried sweet basil
½ tablespoon dried summer savory
⅛ tablespoon black pepper
⅛ tablespoon white pepper
¼ teaspoon cayenne pepper
2 cups converted rice
1 quart chicken stock, or water
2 small cooked sausages, chopped
4 tablespoons sweet paprika

Put the chicken parts in a cast iron pot filled with 4 cups water, put n hottest part of grill and bring to a boil then move pot to cool side of grill to simmer for about one-half hour, skimming off any scum that rises to the surface. Remove from heat, let cool and remove the meat from the bones, chop finely, discard bones but put the meat back in the cooking water and set aside.

Melt the butter in a heavy deep cast iron saucepan, on hot part of grill or on stovetop burner at medium setting. Add the onions, garlic, celery, and red bell pepper and cook till the onions are transparent, approximately 5 to 10 minutes. Add rice and cook on hot grill (450°-550°) until onions and rice starts to brown.

Add the chicken stock, sausages, and minced chicken to the pan and place on hottest part of grill, covering rice by more than an inch. Add the Creole seasonings and bring to a boil. Cook until the water has almost evaporated and is just bubbling on top of the rice, approximately 20 minutes, stirring often to prevent rice from sticking. Cover immediately and cook over low heat on coolest part of the grill (300° to 400°) for about 25 minutes, or until the liquid has been absorbed or evaporated.

Remove the pot from heat and let rice sit, covered, for about 10 minutes. Stir, sprinkle top with paprika and serve on heated platter.

Serves 4-6

CHIANG MAI SAFFRON-RAISIN RICE

Inspired by a delightful visit and meal at the White Lotus Restaurant in Chiang Mai, Thailand, during an assignment photographing the Songkran Water Festival for *Islands* Magazine.

4 cups of chicken or vegetable stock

¾ teaspoon saffron powder

salt & pepper to taste

1 minced garlic clove

1 tablespoon olive oil, or butter

2 cups of long grain rice, Basmati or Texmati, rinsed

2 cups golden raisins

Place raisins in a medium bowl and cover with warm water, soaking the raisins for 20 minutes. After this time has passed drain raisins into small bowl, discarding water left in bowl, and set aside.

In a large pot over high heat, bring the stock to a boil. Put the saffron powder in a little bowl and add 1 tablespoon of the hot stock, mixing until dissolved, then pour it back into the boiling stock. Add salt and pepper, garlic, oil or butter, and the rice. Mix once and then cover tightly, letting the rice cook for about 25 minutes. Please resist the urge to open the lid as every look prolongs the cooking.

When the rice is cooked it will be fluffy, there will be no liquid left in pot, and the rice will be easily stirred with a fork. Take the pot off of the heat, drain and add raisins, let sit for 2 minutes, fluff with a fork and serve.

For an extra bit of color and flavor instead of raisins use: 1 cup dried cherries and 1 cup dried apricots—both cut into raisin-sized chunks. Soak them in warm water for 20 minutes, prior to use.

Serves 6

SMOKED TOMATO-BASILICA RICE

2-3 medium vine ripe tomatoes
1 cup rice
½ cup onion, finely grated
1 tablespoon fresh basil, finely chopped
¼ stick butter, in pieces
salt & pepper to taste
¼ cup shredded parmesan cheese
1 tablespoon parsley

Cut tomatoes in half and place cut side up in a Pyrex dish or flat, shallow metal pan.

Set smoker temperature to 220° to 240° degrees and place pan with tomatoes in center of cooking grate. Close lid and slow smoke over hickory or fruit-wood smoke for 30 minutes, or until tomatoes are soft but not mushy. If using BBQ grill cook using indirect heat method, placing charcoal on one side of barbecue, pan on other side of grill above and have a small foil pan filled with soaked wood chips on bed of coals to smoke-grill tomatoes at approximately 300° to 400°, for 20 to 30 minutes.

Remove tomatoes and allow to cool slightly, then chop into small cubes and add to a rice cooker or sauce pan. Add rice, basil, onion, butter, salt, and pepper and stir, Cook according to directions for cooker. If using a pan over grill or in smoker cook approximately 5 to 10 minutes until rice is fluffy and all the liquid has been absorbed.

Sprinkle with parmesan cheese and parsley and serve.

Serves 4

CURSES . . . FOILED AGIN' TATERS

10 large potatoes, sliced ¼ inch thick
5 medium onions, sliced and broken into rings
sea salt to taste
fresh ground black pepper to taste
2 sticks butter, cut into ¼" pats
1 pound of sliced cheddar cheese
2 tablespoons olive oil (per packet)

Lay out 2-3 pieces of heavy duty aluminum foil (approx. 11" X 14"), and place a layer of potatoes in the center of the foil. Add a layer of onion on top of the potatoes, sprinkle with salt and pepper, add two butter pats, and follow with a layer of cheese on top. Continue to alternate layers till you have three layers. Drizzle with olive oil. Fold foil over the top and close with a double fold to seal completely. Make 2-3 packets like this.

Place foil packets on the grill over medium coals or heat (400° to 500°) for approximately 1 hour, turning occasionally. To check on their progress you'll have to open a packet and peek. When ready potatoes and onions will be browned on the edges and soft.

Remove from hat and serve foil packets directly onto plates for serving. Caution your guests to avoid the hot steam when packets are opened.

Serves 6-8

TUG BOAT ANNIE'S SWEET POTATO SALAD WITH MARJORAM HONEY VINAIGRETTE

Richard Westhaver, Norwell, Massachusetts

This recipe goes great with any grilled or barbecued fare. When we were growing up and had family gatherings in the summer this salad was always on the menu. My first cousin Annie worked on a tugboat in Boston Harbor for a few years while she was in college, hence the name of the recipe.

5 cups peeled and cubed sweet potatoes
2 tablespoons extra virgin olive oil
1/3 cup honey
1/3 cup red wine vinegar
2 tablespoons fresh marjoram
2 garlic cloves, minced
½ teaspoon salt
½ teaspoon fresh ground pepper
2 teaspoons brown sugar
2 tablespoons extra virgin olive oil

Place sweet potatoes in baking pan and toss with 2 tablespoons oil to evenly coat potatoes. Cook them on a vegetable grate or basket on smoker or grill at 400° degrees for 40 minutes or until tender.

Remove from heat and put in medium bowl, set aside and allow them to cool to room temperature.

Whisk together the honey, vinegar, marjoram, cloves, salt, pepper, sugar and remaining oil in a large bowl. Toss well with the sweet potatoes, until they are well covered, and serve.

Serves 4-6

DOROTHY'S SWEET POTATOES

Dorothy Browne, Indianapolis, IN

A sweet wonderful woman who could cook up a gourmet meal out of the simplest fare, and who happens to be the author's mother, God rest her gentle soul. I hated sweet potatoes until she cooked them this way . . . now I use her recipe at least once a month, year round.

2 pounds sweet potatoes, peeled and cut into
    ½-inch slices lengthwise
1/3 cup honey mustard
2 tablespoons olive oil
2 tablespoons melted butter
1 tablespoon minced fresh rosemary leaves
salt to taste
pepper to taste

In a large pot, boil 6 cups of water and drop potato slices in, and boil for 2-3 minutes, then drain and pat dry.

Combine mustard, olive oil, butter, and rosemary, in a medium bowl, mix evenly, and brush on both sides of the sweet potato slices. Reserve the rest of the mix for basting. Grill slices on oiled rack over medium-high heat (450° to 550°) for 5 minutes or until fork-tender, turning and basting often with liquid. Remove from heat, lightly salt and pepper each side.

GRILLED ONION & POTATO SKEWERS

Serve the kebabs on a bed of fresh lettuce, radicchio and sliced onion.

1 pound peeled boiling onions (about 2-inches in
    diameter)
1 pound small, new potatoes, unpeeled
salt and pepper to taste
¼ cup olive oil

BROCHETTE SAUCE:

3 tablespoons extra virgin olive oil
1 tablespoon white wine vinegar
1 tablespoon fresh coriander leaves, torn
¼ teaspoon lemon zest
1 teaspoon ground coriander
1 clove garlic, crushed
1 teaspoon wholegrain mustard
salt to taste
pepper to taste

In a large pot over high heat, boil the onions in 3 to 4 cups of water, until the outside layer is tender when pierced with a fork, approximately 10 minutes, then drain.

Put another 3-4 cups of water in pot and boil potatoes over high heat until they

are tender, approximately 10 to 15 minutes, drain, then cut them in half.

Alternate small onions and potato on skewers. Lightly brush with olive oil and sprinkle with salt and pepper.

Barbecue over the grill over medium coals or gas (450°-550°) until the vegetables are heated through, approximately 6-8 minutes.

Meanwhile combine all the dressing ingredients together in a Ziploc bag. Brush the skewered onions and potatoes once with this sauce just before removing from the grill. Pour the remaining sauce over the grilled onions and potatoes and immediately serve kebabs.

Serves 4

NEW POTATOES IN GARLIC-LEMON BUTTER

Pat & Tara Bennett, Ridgefield, WA. And their future ballerina/baseball all-star Alisa.

½ cup butter, softened
2 cloves garlic, minced
24 new potatoes, about 3 pounds, cut in half
2 lemons, cut in quarters
1 tablespoon sage
salt and pepper to taste

In a small bowl, using a wooden spoon, mash the garlic into the softened butter until well mixed. Arrange half of the potatoes in a single layer on top of two layers of heavy-duty foil. Dot potatoes evenly with half of the butter mixture, squeeze juice of one lemon onto potatoes and drop lemon quarters into mixture. Sprinkle with ½ tablespoon sage, salt, and pepper. Seal package securely with double fold. If necessary repeat with remaining potatoes to form a second package.

Roast directly on hot coals or on grill at high temperature (500° to 600°) for 40-45 minutes or until tender, turning packages frequently.

Serves 8

RBQ'S SMOKE-BAKED POTATOES

Slather these taters with butter, sour cream, chili, and/or your favorite barbecue sauce.

8 baking potatoes
1 cup bacon grease, softened, not melted

HERB MIX:

2 tablespoons ground sage
2 tablespoons granulated garlic
2 tablespoons dried parsley
2 tablespoons salt
2 tablespoons coarse grind black pepper
2 tablespoons granulated sugar
2 tablespoons paprika
Wash and dry 8 baking potatoes.

Rub soft warm bacon grease into skin of each potato, covering each completely.

Mix the herbs together in a shallow bowl and roll the potatoes in the mixture, covering completely with spices. Puncture each potato several times with an ice pick or the sharp end of a boning knife.

Place on hot grill in smoker, and smoke for 1 hour at 250° degrees, turning once. Remove potatoes and wrap each in double layer of heavy duty aluminum foil. Seal foil, place potatoes back on grill and continue cooking for another 1 to 1 ½ hours, until they are soft when poked.

Serve in foil, cautioning guests to watch for hot steam as they open foil packets.

Serves 8

UNCLE JOHN'S BEER & POTATO SALAD

John Angood, Saratoga, California

As good a cook as he is a wood carver, and he's one heck of a wood carver!

2 ½ pounds unpeeled potatoes

½ cup finely chopped yellow onion

½ pound yellow beans, cooked

4 tablespoons plus 2 teaspoons olive oil

½ cup finely chopped onion

¾ cup lager beer

3 tablespoons vinegar (malt or cider)

1 tablespoon Dijon mustard

½ teaspoon sugar

salt & pepper

2 tablespoon chopped chives

Cook potatoes in boiling salted water until knife can be easily inserted (approx. 20-25 minutes). Remove, cool, and slice into ½-inch rounds.

In glass or ceramic bowl mix potatoes with the onion and the beans. Reserve.

In a medium saucepan, over medium heat, add 2 teaspoons of olive oil, ½ cup of onion and cook until soft, approximately 15 minutes. Add lager, vinegar, mustard, and sugar and boil for 5 minutes. Pour mixture into a blender with motor running and add 4 tablespoons olive oil. Taste and adjust salt and pepper to your liking.

Pour dressing over potatoes in bowl and gently mix. Increase salt and pepper as needed.

Garnish with chives and serve warm or at room temperature.

CHAPTER 8
SAUCES, MARINADES & DRY RUBS

'Bama BBQ Sauce   161

Beer Butte Ranch Sauce   161

Black & Bleu Cheese Q Sauce   162

Bourbon Salmon Mop   163

Chardonnay Marinade   163

Cranberry-Lemon BBQue Glaze   164

Dirty Dick's Ancho Barbecue Sauce   165

Dracula's Blood Orange Sauce   166

Gail's Guava BBQ sauce   167

Horsey Sauce with a Bite   167

Jack's Whiskey BBQ Sauce   168

Jamaican Jerk Sauce   168

Key West Citrus Sauce   170

Kiwi Beer Marinade   170

Korean Bulgogi Marinade   171

Last Gaucho Beefsteak Sauce   171

Lexington "Yaller" Sauce   172

Low-Fat Italian BBQ Sauce   172

Macon Bacon BBQ Sauce   173

Mongo's Mango Marinade   173

Missy's Mustard Marinade   174

Momma's Marvelous Margarita Glaze   174

Remus's Kansas City Classic Sauce   175

TyBet's Southern Cola Barbeque Sauce   175

Vidalia Bar-Be-Cue Sauce   176

Yellow Carolina Q Sauce   176

RUB A DUB DUB, BUB!   177

Last Roundup Beef Rub   178

Baxter BB Chicken's Back
(and everywhere else too) Rub   179

Three Iddie Fishies Rub   179

BARBECUE'S HOLY GRAIL

"It's the sauce, man, it's the sauce!"

What is sauce for the goose may be sauce for the gander but is not necessarily sauce for the chicken, the duck, the turkey or the guinea hen. Alice B. Toklas

Ah, the essence of barbecue. The glorious thickened liquid (sometimes not-so-thickened) that we gleefully baste, mop, and slop with. The delicious mixture we dip, dab and dribble over our meat. And the fragrant and flavorful concoctions we brush on, marinate with, and slather over our fowl. Oh yeah, fish get their own stuff to swim in too, while they're being broiled that is!

Sauce. To be specific: barbecue sauces. At the grocery store they come in all shapes and sizes. You have your garlic BBQ sauce, your honey-garlic BBQ sauce, your teriyaki-garlic BBQ sauce, and even your garlic-garlic BBQ sauce.

Colorful, ergonomically and aesthetically designed bottles of magic elixir that we buy by the gallon to give our BBQ'ed creations that final touch of majesty.

In fact on America's supermarket shelves you have more than 2,000 commercially bottles sauces available to take home. That's about 1,996 tomato, vinegar, and sugar-based sauces, most using (you guessed it) garlic, and almost all are seasoned with salt and pepper.

The other four use the same ingredients but add special items to make them "different." Different ingredients like Hawaiian lotus-position blossom honey, Tasmanian pink marjoram, freeze-dried Ethiopian cassava root, and Lower Congo River essence of desiccated shrimp.

By far the greatest majority of store-bought BBQ sauces are pretty much the same. You start out with your tomato sauce, add sugar, add salt, add sugar, add pepper, add sugar, add garlic, add sugar, and, if you're really daring, add red pepper.

But how, you ask plaintively, do you find the kind of yellow sauce that you dripped on your new shirt in Columbus, Ga., when you went on the picnic with Uncle Harold and Aunt Rhoda, or that black stuff they dipped their lamb in when you ate over at cousins Jimmy and Lorraine's in Paducah, Ky. last May?

Well folks, this may come as a shock, but since you bought this book, or someone brung it to ya, perhaps you already know the answer. You can make your own sauce! Right chere in your own kitchen. Zounds, what a concept.

You can, of course use tomato sauce, sugar, salt, sugar, pepper, sugar, etc., or you can go out and invent something that suits your own tastes. Zounds again! Actually zounds like a good idea.

We, the fine folks at this here publisher's place, have set about to offer up a whole passle of sauces you can do by yourself. Sauces which share the rich heritage of the places they came from: Georgia mustard sauce, Kentucky black mutton sauce, Kansas City style sauce, and even Carolina vinegar sauce. Plus we're gonna add a few new sauces keyed to "newly discovered" barbecue regions.

First we'll talk about the regional sauces that have sprung up during the short history of American BBQ. Going from East (or rather South) to West:

Carolina Sauces- Well here we have our first problem. Because there are actually several sauces which can be found in the two Carolinas. East of Raleigh you have your vinegar, black pepper, ground cayenne kinda vinegar sauce. This sauce is slopped on the meat while it's cookin' then served up tableside to pour on whatever you wish to pour it on. A BBQ sauce that's as simple as it is thin.

But over t'other side of the state you have your Piedmont variety of vinegar sauce. They do it up a tad bit different. They take the vinegar, pepper, red pepper and throw them in a pot, but then they add ketchup, or Worcestershire sauce or molasses. In some places they even add a bit of sugar to sweeten the pot. Now you have a red-colored thin sauce.

But then in South Carolina they do it up different again. Around the city of Columbia they whip a mustardy kinda sauce to serve on their meat, leaving out the tomato so now you have a thin watery yellow sauce.

Georgia Sauce- While we're talking about yellow, mustard-based sauces we might as well talk about the Georgian variety. Similar to South Carolina the folks hereabouts think that mustard and pork (ham) go pretty well together so they stir up a batch using ketchup, vinegar, brown sugar and mustard to make a thicker yellow sauce. You can't beat this on a slice of fresh ham or a thick piece of pork shoulder.

Alabama Sauce- Alabama's contribution to the barbecue world is a vinegary white sauce thickened with eggs or mayonnaise. It can be almost a creamy yellow color, is not heavy, and is chilled and put on food right before serving. Heating it would break down the eggs. Excellent marinade for chicken, Cornish hen and quail, and it doubles as a salad dressing!

Kentucky Sauce- Because somehow a whole lotta sheep and lambs ended up hereabouts they have a special barbecue sauce for those kinda critters. They do a "black" sauce, which is indeed black, peppery, and very thin. It's actually a clear vinegar sauce to which they add molasses and sometimes a dash or two of Worcestershire sauce.

In Owensboro, at their mutton festival, they use buckets and full-sized mops to slather it on whole sheep carcasses that are being roasted overnight on 100-foot long barbecues smack-dab in the middle of several downtown streets.

Memphis Sauce- On the shores of the Mississippi River, in the city which hosts the World's Largest Cooking event (so sayeth Guinness Book) they practice a different sort of sauce preparation. They take the molasses from Kentucky, vinegar from the Carolinas, Tabasco from the Bayou, and mix it with lots of tomato sauce and maybe a glug or two of ketchup. The resulting very brown-red sauce is sorta sweet, sorta spicy, and not too thick.

Texas Sauce- Deep in the heart of you-know-where they like a thick tomato sauce for their beloved brisket. Texas sauce tends to be very thick, the thickest of all the regional style sauces, mainly because it contains chopped onions. They also throw bacon grease, and/or butter, and hot peppers and hotter chilies into the fray. Sugar is left out. No sissy sweeteners for these cowpokes.

Kansas City Sauce- There's a good reason KC is known as the "meltin' pot" of barbecue sauces. They use everybody else's to stir up their sauce. They use tomato sauce, vinegar, salt, molasses, mustard, chilies or red pepper, sugar (brown or white) and stir it into a thick (not as thick as the Texan's however) sauce.

Most commercially bottled sauces are basically Kansas City style sauces as barbecuers nationwide have expressed their love of this thick, sweet, tangy, red style of BBQ sauce.

Kansas City also hosts the only "barbecue sauce only" contest in the US. Originally called the "Diddy-Wa-Diddy Sauce Contest" it's now been re-named (God knows why) the National Barbecue Sauce Contest.

Over 400 commercially bottled sauces are submitted every year to be judged by a panel of 25 judges. Sauces are graded like wine from 1-7, with a one being terrible. Sauces are graded on color, texture, aroma and bouquet, individual taste, and taste on barbecued pork and chicken. The top sauce receives no monetary award, merely the honor of being named the "Best Barbecue Sauce in America."

Traditionally the sauces that we have just described have been the regional sauces of the country—but with the popularity of barbecue from sea to shining sauce we'd like to add a few more regional sauce peculiarities for you to consider.

California Sauce- Californians tend to do things differently so they have several ways of barbecuing that they've picked up from the Hispanic culture below them, or the Pacific Rim cultures west of the state. So far west it's actually the east, the far east at that!

Cooking Tri-tip, a triangular chunk of bottom sirloin that most of the country ignores, they use a simple marinade, mop and sauce comprised of virgin olive oil, balsamic or cider vinegar, and finely chopped fresh garlic which is brushed on the meat on the grill using long rosemary branches tied together like a short broom.

For barbecuing just about anything else they often borrow from the Asian and Pacific cuisine's to use soy, teriyaki, oyster, fish, and hoisin sauces in combination with flavored vinegar's, honeys and turbinado sugars, and fruit juices (apple, apricot, pineapple, mango, etc.) to make light and flavorful basting, marinating, and serving sauces. Sometimes the same sauce is used all 3 ways.

New Mexico Sauce- It's really hot in New Mexico! Not only the weather in the summer when it can be a scorching 120° out but at local barbecues when sun-glazed pitmasters trot out New Mexico style barbecue sauces to fire up the culinary senses. Cayenne, Ancho chile powder, and Pasilla chile powder are the holy triumvirate of this regional style. Many of the sauces start out like Texas or Kansas City or Memphis style sauces, but then the chile powder, raw chilis and red pepper make an appearance and it's "***Katie, pass the ice water***." (See Scoville pepper rating below)

Hawaii Sauce- Similar to California, but more of a "sweet and sour" kind of sauce is popular here. Islanders use pineapple, mango, and papaya juice, both as a tenderizer—leave a steak in papaya juice overnight and it's good-bye, steak—and as a sauce base. By adding soy and fresh and ground ginger, Asian five-spice powder, lemon juice, rice vinegar and molasses, they come up with delicious fresh fruity flavored sauces. Great on poultry and chicken. However, there is NO BBQ sauce that tastes good on poi.

Pacific Northwest Sauce- Two things influence sauces up in the Pacific NW. First the abundance of fresh (really really fresh, like right out of the Columbia River onto a grill) salmon. The second is the abundance of really, really fresh berries: primarily blueberries, raspberries, and marionberries.

Addressing the fruit sauces first, there are several commercial bottling companies who make a fantastic line of fruit barbecue sauces. With the predominance of roadside stands selling "just-picked" berries it's easy for anyone to grab a handful, put them in a saucepan with some spices (garlic, salt, pepper, paprika, savory, cumin, etc.), and whip up sauces which are heavenly on chicken, turkey, and just about any fish filets or steaks.

And, as long as we're talking about fish, nowhere in the country do people have as much opportunities to buy right-from-the-river (or ocean) salmon. And since most commercial barbecue sauces, or most tomato-based sauces would overpower the subtle taste of the salmon, the folks from Gold Beach, Or. to Birch Bay, Wa. have cleverly developed some marinades and sauces especially for this marine treasure.

Similar to the neighbors to the south of them in the Golden State they use soy, lemon and lime, ginger, garlic, dried mushrooms, and fresh herbs like basil, cilantro, and savory to flavor the tender flesh of their Copper River, Coho, Sockeye, Pink, Silver, and King salmon.

Well I hope you've enjoyed your tour of the saucier side of America. We've tried to share the regional specialties that you should try, we've tried to encourage you to experiment, innovate, and cast away all fears as you formulate your own barbeculinary concoctions, and we've tried to get you guys to go boldly where no man has gone—into the Round Table of barbecue sauces.

Buy ye not just the bottled sauces from your local market, rely ye not soley on the Sauce of the Month Club, nor your Mother's ketchup, mustard, and cayenne pepper recipe, be brave, get thyself to a bowl, cast in tomatoes, and fruits, and spices, and beer, and oils, and sweetners, and verily we say you'll come up with your own Merlin's brew of Que.

"Hey, Guenivere, pass the Holy Grail of Sauce will ya Babe? This guinea fowl is like drysville!"

SAUCE-Y FACTS

Almost nine out of ten (88%) grill owners use barbecue sauce when they grill.

The vast majority (84%) of those who use BBQ sauce when they grill use it as a basting sauce during cooking.

About half (52%) use barbecue sauce as a marinade before cooking. Two out of five (40%) use it as a condiment after the meal is cooked.

Hickory flavor is by far the most popular commercially bottled sauce (61%).

Other sauces used regularly include honey (36%), mesquite (35%), and tomato-based (34%). Soy sauce based is far less popular (9%).

Statistics provided by the Hearth, Patio & Barbecue Association bi-annual consumer study.

HOW HOT IS DAT PEPPA?

Scoville Units, Chile Varieties and Commercial Products

100,000-500,000

Habanero, Scotch Bonnet, South American *chinenses*, African birdseye. *My mouth has died. I have no tongue or teeth or throat left. The flames coming from me would start the Space Shuttle rocket, melt one of the pyramids, and cook bacon and eggs for the entire African continent. Please pass me a fire extinguisher.*

50,000-100,000

Santaka, Chiltepin, Rocoto, Chinese *kwangsi*. *Please I'll plead guilty to any crime you want me to, only don't make me taste any more. The hell with the Chinese water torture, they should have used drops of this and saved about a jillion gallons of water.*

30,000-50,000

Piquin, Cayenne Long, Tabasco, Thai *prik khee nu*, Pakistan *dundicut. You gotta be kidding! People willingly eat this stuff. My mouth feels like the jet engine of an F-14 as it kicks in the afterburner. Momma mia my lips have melted!*

15,000-30,000

De Arbol, crushed red pepper, habanero hot sauce. *Hot, really, really hot. Please pass a gallon of milk, 2 quarts of ice cream, and some cold towels.*

5,000-15,000

Early Jalapeño, Aj Amarillo, Serrano; Tabasco sauce. *A bit of fiery unpleasantness for most of us, the edges of my tongue are browning like sautéed liver in a non-stick frying pan. A fifth of Pepto-Bismol please?*

2,500-5,000

TAM Mild Jalapeño, Mirasol, Cayenne Large Red Thick, Louisiana Hot Sauce. *Taste some and you can melt a glass full of ice, or clear the frost from your rear view mirror on a February morning in Anchorage.*

1,500-2,500

Sandia, Cascabel, Yellow Wax Hot. *Yes, there is heat here all right, not blazing heat, just a mild incendiary burn to the gums. A tiny blister or two perhaps.*

1,000-1,500

Ancho, Pasilla, Española Improved, Old Bay Seasoning. *Now we're talking! A bit of a flame erupts, sorta like a pilot light in a gas fireplace.*

500-1000

NuMex Big Jim, NuMex 6-4, chili powder. *Starting to get a tiny tingle when my gums touch this level of chilis. Sorta nice and warming, sorta.*

100-500

NuMex R-Naky, Mexi-Bell, Cherry-canned green chiles, Hungarian hot paprika. *Wouldn't even melt an ice cube in your mouth.*

10-100

Pickled pepperoncini. *If you think hard you'll taste something kinda lukewarm. I've had spicier oatmeal.*

0

Mild Bells, Pimiento, Sweet Banana, US paprika. *Your six-month old baby wouldn't even burp after a taste.*

Reprinted with permission from Fiery Foods Website (fieryfoods.com). Comments by R. Browne.

'BAMA BBQ SAUCE

David Donahoo, Prattville, Alabama

1 teaspoon crushed garlic

¾ cup white vinegar

6 oz tomato paste

½ cup dark molasses

¼ cup A-1 sauce

¼ cup beer

2 tablespoon orange marmalade

½ teaspoon ginger

¼ teaspoon nutmeg

¼ teaspoon celery seed

¼ teaspoon dried oregano

⅛ teaspoon cayenne pepper

1 ½ teaspoon sea salt

½ teaspoon black pepper

1 tablespoon liquid smoke

In a medium sized saucepan, combine all ingredients except the liquid smoke. Bring to a boil, over high heat, stirring occasionally. Reduce heat to low and simmer gently, uncovered, for 20 minutes, stirring occasionally. Remove from heat. Add liquid smoke. Stir for 2-3 minutes. Let cool and use on meat, poultry, game or vegetables.

Makes 2 to 2 ½ cups

BEER BUTTE RANCH SAUCE

Inspired by the delicious sauce served alongside the blackest, moistest piece of brisket I ever had—at the 2000 Houston Rodeo & Barbecue competition.

½ cup white vinegar

½ pound bacon grease

½ pound butter

1 tablespoon freshly ground black pepper

1 tablespoon cayenne

3 onions, chopped

¼ cup Worcestershire sauce

3 cups ketchup

1 tablespoon salt

1 tablespoon celery salt

1 tablespoon garlic salt

In a large saucepan, over low heat on stovetop burner, combine all ingredients and simmer for at least 45 minutes. Makes sauce for a 20 pound brisket or a whole mess o' beef or pork ribs.

Makes 4 ½ to 5 cups

BLACK & BLEU CHEESE Q SAUCE

1 tablespoon butter
1 tablespoon flour
¾ cup cream
½ cup crumbled bleu cheese
½ teaspoon salt
½ teaspoon coarsely ground black pepper

In a medium saucepan, melt the butter over medium heat, then stir in the flour until blended. Gradually stir in cream and cook until thickened, about 5 minutes. Remove from the heat and stir in the remaining ingredients. If not thickened enough, you can gradually add more flour or cornstarch (1 tablespoon at a time) until desired consistency is reached. Oh 'tis wonderful on grilled steaks, grilled chicken breasts, or even hamburger. This sauce doesn't keep well so make it up just before you use it.

Makes ¾ to 1 cup

BOURBON SALMON MOP

½ cup olive oil

4 tablespoons good bourbon

4 tablespoons rice vinegar

1 teaspoon onion powder

1 teaspoon dill

1 teaspoon brown sugar

pinch of sea salt

pinch of white pepper

In a large bowl mix the ingredients and stir until thoroughly blended. After mixing pour into a container and seal, refrigerate until ready to use. If olive oil has thickened when you are ready to use pour liquid into medium saucepan and heat until just warmed through and olive oil is fully liquid again. Can be used as a marinade, baste or sauce. Especially good on salmon, and other fish, but tastes pretty durn good on chicken and pork too!

Makes ½ to ¾ cup

CHARDONNAY MARINADE

½ cup soy sauce

½ cup Chardonnay

½ cup water

1 bunch green onions coarsely chopped

5 cloves fresh garlic, coarsely chopped and crushed

1 small ginger root, peeled and diced

3 tablespoons cane syrup

fresh ground pepper

pinch salt

½ teaspoon sesame oil

Mix all ingredients in a medium glass or stainless steel bowl. Place in sealable container and set aside until you wish to use this. A great marinade for beef, pork or lamb. Can also be used to baste meat while cooking.

Makes 1 ½ to 2 cups

CRANBERRY-LEMON BBQUE GLAZE

8 oz can cranberry sauce

⅛ teaspoon dried, crushed rosemary

¼ cup finely chopped dried cranberries

½ cup cranberry juice

2 tablespoons lemon juice

½ teaspoon finely chopped lemon peel

¼ cup honey

In a saucepan, over medium heat, combine all the ingredients and stir constantly while bringing to a boil. Keep over medium heat until the sauce reduces by ⅓. Remove from heat let it cool. Use the sauce to baste turkey, chicken, lamb or pork, several times during the last 5 minutes on the grill.

Makes 1 to 1 ½ cups

DIRTY DICK'S ANCHO BARBECUE SAUCE

Richard Westhaver (a.k.a. Dirty Dick)

6 ancho chilies

1 ½ cups cranberry juice

3 shallots, minced

3 garlic cloves, minced

2 tablespoon butter

4 cups ketchup

1 tablespoon paprika

1 tablespoon chili powder

1 tablespoon dry mustard

1 tablespoon Worcestershire sauce

¼ cup red wine vinegar

¼ cup brown sugar

¼ cup honey

Before handling chilis it's a good idea to put on rubber gloves, unless you want your skin to burn, that is! Remove the stems from the chilis and discard them. Split the chilis with a sharp knife and put in a medium bowl. Pour in the hot cranberry juice and let it sit for one hour. Puree in a blender.

In a small saucepan, over medium heat; sauté the shallots and garlic until tender, approximately 5 minutes, then pour in the cranberry-chili puree and turn the heat up to high. Bring mixture to a boil, then reduce heat to low and simmer for an hour.

This sauce is super on beef, pork, venison or wild boar. It's also great on wild turkey, but perhaps a bit spicy for the domestic variety of old Tom. Some Yankees up in New England put this sauce on their grilled lobster.

Makes 6 ½ to 7 cups

DRACULA'S BLOOD ORANGE SAUCE

1 10 ¾ oz can tomato soup

1 cup tomato sauce

2 tablespoon soy sauce

1 tablespoon Worcestershire sauce

½ cup light molasses

2 tablespoon finely chopped orange peel

½ cup blood orange juice, about 2-3 oranges juiced

1 ½ tbs. dry mustard

2 teaspoon paprika

½ cup packed dark brown sugar

¼ cup peanut oil

½ teaspoon garlic powder

1 tablespoon seasoned salt

½ teaspoon ground black pepper

Optional:

1 teaspoon Louisiana Hot Sauce

1 teaspoon cayenne pepper

3-4 drops red food coloring (optional)

In a medium saucepan over high heat combine all the ingredients and bring to a boil. Immediately reduce heat to low,, and simmer uncovered for 20 minutes. Use this sauce to baste beef or poultry in the last 15 minutes of grilling. If you're using the sauce to cover chicken wings add 1 teaspoon Louisiana Hot Sauce or 1 teaspoon cayenne pepper.

For a dramatic effect add the red food coloring at the last moment, stir into the sauce and enjoy the reactions of your guests.

Makes 4 to 4 ½ cups

GAIL'S GUAVA BBQ SAUCE

Gail Miller, Nome, Alaska

10 oz. guava jelly

2 teaspoon dry mustard powder

¼ cup lemon juice

4 tablespoon white vinegar

1 teaspoon cumin

2 shallots, minced

2 green onions, green part only, minced

¼ cup dry sherry

3 tablespoon tomato paste

2 tablespoon brown sugar

1 lemon, sliced thinly

Combine all ingredients in a medium saucepan, stir, and bring to a boil over medium heat. Immediately reduce heat to low and simmer for 30 minutes. Remove the sauce from the heat and cool.

With a brush, baste pork ribs or fish (salmon and halibut work especially well) several times during the last ten minutes of cooking only. Serve extra on the side with freshly sliced lemons floating on the surface.

Makes 1 to 1 ½ cups

HORSEY SAUCE WITH A BITE

1 cup mayonnaise

¼ cup water

2 oz. horseradish

2 tablespoons Louisiana Hot sauce

1 tablespoon spicy mustard

2 tablespoons white sugar

Pinch black pepper

Pinch salt

In a medium bowl mix the ingredients together with a spoon and let the sauce sit in the refrigerator for about 30 minutes. It's super on brisket or BBQ'd roast pork which have been pulled or chopped for sandwiches. Also this adds a super taste when served alongside roast beef cooked on the barbecue.

Makes 1 ½ cups

JACK'S WHISKEY BBQ SAUCE

Adapted from a recipe seen at the Jack Daniel's World Invitational Barbecue contest in Lynchburg, TN.

½ pint Jack Daniel's whiskey
1 can tomato soup
1 tablespoon Worcestershire sauce
pinch of garlic powder
2 tablespoons brown sugar
1 teaspoon ground white pepper
dash of Louisiana Hot Sauce

Mix all ingredients in a medium saucepan, over medium heat, stirring constantly for 5 minutes. Remove from heat and pour into a medium bowl to cool. When cooled put in a sealable glass or plastic bottle.

Use this sauce on anything you barbecue, but it's especially good on grilled leg of lamb and grilled lamb riblets.

Makes 2 to 2 ½ cups

JAMAICAN JERK SAUCE

Recipe loaned to me by a woman at a Jerk Restaurant near Montego Bay, Jamaica. She wrote it down on the back of a brown paper bag, then put my take-away order in the bag and wished me "Good eatin' Mon!" She did not have amounts of the various spices, "I do it by what feels good," she related, "so just makes up yo' own." Have a fire extinguisher ready . . . .this is hot stuff!

½ cup allspice berries
½ cup packed brown sugar
6-8 garlic cloves
4-6 Scotch bonnet peppers *
1 tablespoon ground thyme
1-2 bunches green onions
1 teaspoon cinnamon
½ teaspoon nutmeg
salt and pepper to taste
4 tablespoon soy sauce

Put all ingredients in a food processor or blender and liquefy. Pour sauce into a glass jar or plastic container, cover, and keep refrigerated. The sauce will keep forever if refrigerated ! Do not store in metal container as the peppers can eat into the metal and cause contamination.

Use it on chicken, lamb, pork, beef, venison, rabbit or you guessed it: anything that you cook that in any way resembles meat or poultry. This sauce would be overwhelming for most fish dishes, though.

* Please, please be very careful when handling Scotch bonnet peppers (the hottest peppers on the planet). Use rubber or plastic gloves, whenever you handle peppers, and if these are not available, wash your hands THOROUGHLY after handling. One mistaken rubbing of an eye and you will never forget the experience!

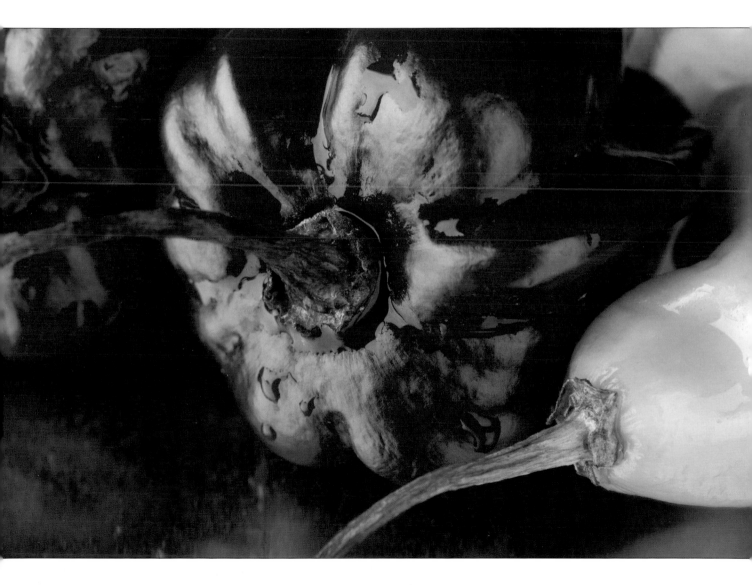

KEY WEST CITRUS SAUCE

This is wonderful on just about any grilled, or smoked, fish and equally as tasty on BBQ chicken or other poultry.

3 cups ketchup
2 cups tightly packed dark brown sugar
1 tablespoon dry mustard
½ cup lime juice
½ cup onion juice
¾ cup mango juice
¾ cup orange juice
¾ cup pineapple juice
1 tablespoon black pepper
pinch of salt
pinch of cumin
4-5 tablespoons cornstarch

Combine all ingredients in a large glass or ceramic bowl, mixing well with a spoon until fully blended. Pour the sauce into a large glass or ceramic pot, add 2 tablespoons of cornstarch and cook over low heat until mixture thickens, about 5 minutes. If sauce is still too thin slowly add more cornstarch, 1 tablespoon at a time, stirring, until you reach desired the thickness. Take the sauce off the heat and cool it, uncovered. When the sauce is cool, pour it into sealable jars or plastic containers. Can be used as a marinade, basting sauce, or warm it and serve on the table with the entree.

Makes 9 to 10 cups

KIWI BEER MARINADE

Marcus Knight, Auckland, New Zealand

The "Kiwi" refers to the origin of the recipe, as New Zealanders like to be called Kiwi's after their national bird. No kiwi fruit is used in this recipe.

1 can of beer
1 small can tomato soup
1 tablespoon sweet chili sauce
2 tablespoons soy sauce
1 tablespoon Worcestershire sauce
3 cloves garlic, crushed
1 teaspoon brown sugar
½ teaspoon savory
½ teaspoon oregano
½ teaspoon basil
dash of red wine
½ teaspoon sea salt
½ teaspoon lemon or citrus pepper

Mix all the ingredients in a medium glass or metal bowl. Put any meat or poultry you wish to marinate in a Ziploc bag and add marinade, seal bag and refrigerate overnight.

Drain meat or poultry and cook on your favorite barbecue. Enjoy the finished results with a cold New Zealand Steinlager beer.

Makes 2 to 2 ½ cups

KOREAN BULGOGI MARINADE

Recipe learned by watching a cook in the kitchen of the Grand Hyatt Hotel on lovely, tropical, Cheju Do island in Korea.

1 cup soy sauce
1 cup brown sugar
3-4 cloves garlic, minced
1 inch ginger root, minced
2 tablespoons sesame oil
1 bunch green onions, finely chopped

In a small saucepan, over low heat, combine the soy sauce, sugar, garlic, and ginger, and stir until sugar is dissolved. Remove from heat and add the remaining ingredients.

This is a super marinade or basting sauce for Tri-tip, beef for sandwiches, and beef ribs. You can use this as a marinade, baste or serving sauce. But since there is sugar in this sauce you can only use it to baste during the last five minutes the meat is on the barbecue or the sugar will burn.

Makes 2 cups

LAST GAUCHO BEEFSTEAK SAUCE

Claus Meyer, Rio de Janiero, Brazil
In Argentina and Brazil, this sauce is served at the side of juicy grilled steaks.

1 cup chopped Italian parsley
½ cup olive oil
¼ cup red wine vinegar
1 tablespoon garlic, chopped
1 teaspoon oregano
1 teaspoon red pepper flakes
½ teaspoon coarse salt
Optional:
1 tablespoon chopped fresh rosemary
1 teaspoon chopped fresh thyme

In a medium bowl mix the ingredients well and let them marinate in the refrigerator for at least a day. You may add thyme and rosemary if you like, but in very small amounts.

Remove the mixture form the refrigerator. In a medium saucepan over high heat boil the liquid for 10 minutes. Serve the steak sauce in a sauce boat alongside medium rare steaks.

Makes 1 ¾ cups

LEXINGTON "YALLER" SAUCE

This is near to being the ONLY kind of sauce served in some parts of North Carolina. Incredible on a sandwich of pulled pork shoulder served on hamburger buns. Add a little of the mustard-based cole slaw and you're in hog heaven, North Carolina style.

¾ cup yellow mustard
¾ cup red wine vinegar
½ teaspoon Worcestershire sauce
2 tablespoons butter
1 ½ teaspoons salt
¼ cup brown sugar
1 teaspoon ground black pepper
½ teaspoon Louisiana hot sauce

In a medium saucepan, combine ingredients, stirring to blend. Over low heat, simmer 30 minutes, stirring until thoroughly blended Let stand at room temperature for 1 hour before using.

Makes 2 cups

LOW-FAT ITALIAN BBQ SAUCE

This sauce is super on chicken, fish or grilled sausages.

2 tablespoons finely chopped onion
2 garlic finely chopped garlic cloves
1 pound cored and seeded Italian plum tomatoes
1 tablespoon Worcestershire sauce
2 tablespoons tomato paste
2 tablespoons red wine vinegar
1 teaspoon mustard powder
¼ teaspoon thyme
2 ½ tablespoons molasses
1 teaspoon chili powder
½ teaspoon safflower oil
1 bay leaf

In a medium saucepan, over medium heat, sauté the garlic and onion in safflower oil for 3-4 minutes until garlic starts to brown. Put the tomatoes into a food processor and blend until smooth. Add the remaining ingredients, then pour the mixture into the pan with the garlic, and onion. Simmer, uncovered, on very low heat for 15-20 minutes. Remove from the pan, pour into a medium bowl and allow to cool to room temperature. Discard the bay leaf and bottle the sauce in glass or plastic containers.

Makes

MACON BACON BBQ SAUCE

Billy Bob Mallard, Macon, Georgia

6 slices smoked bacon, uncooked
½ cup minced onion
½ cup minced green pepper
1 10 oz can tomato soup
½ cup water
¼ cup A-1 steak sauce
2 teaspoons sugar
1 tablespoon cider vinegar
½ teaspoon salt

In a medium frying pan, over high heat, fry bacon until it's crisp, drain and reserve. Remove all but 3 tablespoons of bacon fat from the pan. Sauté onion and green pepper in the remaining fat, over medium heat, until tender. Stir in the remaining ingredients, except crisp bacon.

Cover the pan and simmer over medium heat for 15 minutes, stirring occasionally. Crumble and add the bacon, stirring it into mixture. Use this thick, lumpy sauce liberally on spareribs, steaks, chicken, meatloaf, and hamburgers.

Makes 2 cups

MONGO'S MANGO MARINADE

2 tablespoon lime juice
2 limes
zest from one lime, finely chopped
1 cup mango chutney
1 teaspoon brown sugar
¼ cup light corn syrup
pinch of marjoram
⅛ teaspoon red pepper

Peel the limes, saving the zest from one of them. Cut the limes in half, de-seed them and put them in a food processor. Add lime juice, zest, chutney, and brown sugar. Pulse until the lime is fairly well chopped up, although it will still be chunky.

Pour this mixture into a bowl and add the corn syrup, marjoram, and red pepper, and mix well.

Pour mixture into sealable glass or plastic containers and refrigerate until ready to use as a marinade, baste or serving sauce. Absolutely superb on halibut, shark and salmon.

MISSY'S MUSTARD MARINADE

It's said this is also good as a sauce on as a sauce on vegetables: cauliflower, asparagus or boiled potatoes.

6 sprigs fresh rosemary
1 cup tarragon vinegar
6 tablespoon Dijon mustard
2 tablespoon minced garlic
pepper to taste
salt to taste
2 tablespoons olive oil

Whisk all ingredients together in a medium bowl. Use this as a marinade for beef, chicken, lamb, pork (shoulder is wonderful in this marinade), or firm fish steaks Marinate at least 6 hours or, preferably, overnight.

Makes 1 ½ cups

MOMMA'S MARVELOUS MARGARITA GLAZE

Barbara Smith, Southington, CT

Who learned this from her big sister, Kathy, under supervision of their father, Dennis.

½ cup triple sec
½ cup lime juice
½ cup tequila
½ cup honey
pinch of salt

Mix all ingredients in a medium saucepan over low heat, stirring constantly, for 4 to 5 minutes. When the glaze is thoroughly mixed, remove from the heat and cool. When cooled you can bottle or use the glaze straight from the pan to brush over chicken, fish, or shellfish.

Try basting shrimp with this, or use this as a dip for cooked chicken wings or shrimp. One more way to use is to drizzled the glaze on grilled oysters or clams, after the shells have opened.

REMUS'S KANSAS CITY CLASSIC SAUCE

Remus Powers, Kansas City, Missouri

Originator of the Diddy-Wa-Diddy Sauce contest, held during the American Royal Barbecue contest.

¼ teaspoon allspice
¼ teaspoon cinnamon
¼ teaspoon mace
¼ teaspoon black pepper
½ teaspoon curry powder, Oriental preferred
½ teaspoon chili powder
½ teaspoon paprika
¼ cup white vinegar
½ teaspoon hot pepper sauce
1 cup ketchup
⅓ cup dark molasses

Place all of the dry ingredients into a bowl. Add the vinegar and stir. the hot pepper sauce, ketchup, and molasses and stir until the mixture is thoroughly blended. This sauce may be served room temperature or heated.

Adds a wonderful zip and burst of flavor to beef brisket, pork tenderloin and lamb chops.

Makes 1 ½ cups

TYBET'S SOUTHERN COLA BARBEQUE SAUCE

Tyler and Betsy Smith, Southington, Connect-icut

1 can cola (12 oz.) DO NOT USE DIET SODAS
1 ½ cups ketchup
1 cup finely chopped onion
¼ cup cider vinegar
⅛ cup A1 steak sauce
1 teaspoon Mexene chili powder
2 teaspoon lemon granules
1 teaspoon white sugar
1 teaspoon salt
white pepper to taste

In a medium saucepan, over high heat, combine all the ingredients and bring to a boil, stirring often. Immediately reduce the heat to low and simmer, covered, stirring occasionally, for 30-45 minutes or until sauce is thickened. Remove pan from heat, let mixture cool, and then store in a tightly covered glass jar or plastic container.

Makes

VIDALIA BAR-BE-CUE SAUCE

Depending on where you live you can substitute Walla Walla or Maui onions, or any variety deemed "sweet." If sweet onions are unavailable, increase the honey by 2 teaspoons.

1 lg. finely chopped Vidalia onion (or Maui, or Walla Walla)
1 cup apple cider vinegar
½ cup apple cider
¼ cup lemon juice
⅓ cup distilled (white) vinegar
5 tablespoons prepared yellow mustard
3 teaspoons A-1 sauce
4 tablespoons honey
2 teaspoons brown sugar
3 cups ketchup
1 teaspoon mesquite seasoning salt *
1 teaspoon black pepper
¼ pound butter, or margarine

In a medium saucepan mix all ingredients together well, and simmer for 10-15 minutes, stirring often. This sauce works especially well with beef but can be used for just about any barbecue meat, poultry, or fish.

Makes 5 cups

* available online from Oregon Spice Company (www.oregonspice.com)

YELLOW CAROLINA Q SAUCE

There are as many versions of this golden colored sauce as there are of tomato-based sauces. This is a bit sweeter than the other Carolina style sauces we've offered up (see page 156). Alter the red pepper amount in this recipe according to your own taste-buds.

4 cups apple cider vinegar
¼ cup honey
¼ cup yellow mustard
4 tablespoons brown sugar
4 teaspoons sea salt
4 teaspoons crushed red pepper flakes
2 teaspoon coarse black pepper

In a large saucepan, over low heat, add all the ingredients and simmer all for 15-20 minutes, stirring constantly with a spoon. DON'T BOIL!

Remove pan from the heat, and let pan cool to room temperature. Pour mixture into a sealable glass or plastic bottle.

Fantastic with smoked ham, pork shoulder, or pork ribs. But should be tried on beef, lamb and chicken too.

Makes 5 cups

RUB A DUB DUB, BUB!

Quick rubs to delight the culinary senses, they taste good too!

The following rubs are easy to make and use. The ingredients should be mixed together well, rubbed gently into meat, fish, poultry, or game, with your hands and left to dry marinate for at least 4 hours, but preferably overnight. Then it's time to grill, smoke or charbroil to your heart's content.

WHITE KNIGHT RUB

¼ cup onion powder

¼ cup ground white pepper

1 tablespoon salt

2 tablespoons garlic powder

2 tablespoons granulated sugar

CURRIED RUB

¼ cup chili powder

1 teaspoon onion powder

1 teaspoon curry powder

1 teaspoon cumin

1 teaspoon garlic powder

1 teaspoon dry mustard

1 teaspoon white pepper

1 teaspoon oregano

2 teaspoons celery salt

1 teaspoon parsley flakes

BOBTAIL RUB

3 tablespoons paprika, mild

2 teaspoons seasoned salt

2 teaspoons freshly ground black pepper

2 teaspoons garlic powder

1 teaspoon cayenne, not too hot

1 teaspoon summer savory

1 teaspoon dry mustard

½ teaspoon chili powder

1 teaspoon thyme

1 teaspoon coriander

2 teaspoons green peppercorns

1 teaspoon allspice

Brandy's Rubbing powder

1 teaspoon garlic powder

1 tablespoon honey granules

1 teaspoon green onion powder

½ teaspoon ground thyme

1 tablespoon lemon granules

1 tablespoon Worcestershire powder *

1 teaspoon white sugar

* available on-line from Oregon Spice Company (www.oregonspice.com)

ROMANOV RUB

1 garlic clove, crushed

10 allspice berries, crushed

½ teaspoon finely chopped rosemary leaves

2 tablespoons olive oil

Casablanca Rub

2 tablespoons paprika

1 teaspoon salt

1 teaspoon sugar

½ teaspoon coarsely ground black pepper

½ teaspoon ground ginger

½ teaspoon ground cardamom

½ teaspoon ground cumin

½ teaspoon ground fenugreek

½ teaspoon ground cloves

¼ teaspoon ground cinnamon

¼ teaspoon ground allspice

¼ teaspoon cayenne pepper

RED RIVER RUB

1 teaspoon cayenne pepper

1 teaspoon curry powder

1 teaspoon turmeric

1 teaspoon ground ginger

1 teaspoon ground cumin

1 tablespoon Mexene chili powder

1 tablespoon paprika

dash of nutmeg

LAST ROUNDUP BEEF RUB

Caleb Pirtle III, Dallas, Texas

½ teaspoon lemon pepper

¼ teaspoon ground rosemary

4 teaspoons garlic powder

4 teaspoons onion powder

1 tablespoon Worcestershire powder *

1 teaspoon paprika

1 teaspoon beef bouillon granules

2 teaspoons Montreal Steak Seasoning

2 teaspoons salt

2 tablespoons black pepper, coarsely ground

Combine all the ingredients in a large bowl, mixing well. Use immediately or store tightly sealed in glass, or plastic, container. Shake before each use to re-mix the spices.

Makes 8 ounces

* available on-line from Oregon Spice Company (www.oregonspice.com)

BAXTER BB CHICKEN'S BACK (AND EVERYWHERE ELSE TOO) RUB

Marsha and Russ Matta, from somewhere on their sailboat, somewhere on the Columbia River

1 tablespoon garlic powder
1 tablespoon green onion powder
1 tablespoon honey granules
1 teaspoon white pepper
1 tablespoon mild curry powder
1 tablespoon brown sugar powder
1 tablespoon soy sauce powder
1 teaspoon Montreal Chicken seasoning

In a small bowl mix all the ingredients well with a spoon. Pour into a glass jar which has a shaker top and use to sprinkle on barbecued or roast chicken. Keep in a cool, dry place so spices don't form a useless cake.

Makes 8 ounces

THREE IDDIE FISHIES RUB

Anne & Terry Callon, Jalisco, Mexico

1 tablespoon onion powder
1 tablespoon white sugar
1 tablespoon summer savory
1 teaspoon McCormick Imitation Butter Flavor Salt
1 teaspoon green tea leaves
1 teaspoon finely ground black pepper
1 tablespoon lemon granules
1 tablespoon ginger powder

In a small bowl mix all the ingredients well with a spoon. Pour into a glass jar which has a shaker top and use to sprinkle on barbecued, broiled or pan-fried fish. Keep in a cool, dry place so spices don't form a useless cake.

Makes 8 ounces

CHAPTER 9
VEGETARIAN BBQ

BBQued Seitan Burgers   184

Dave's Seitan Grilling Sauce   185

Fantasia's BBQ Tofu Cakes   185

Golden Rosemary Polenta   186

Grilled & Breaded Tofu (Seitan)   187

Grilled Lemon-Lime Tempeh   188

Ole Ole Infree's Tempeh Satay   189

Rick's Grilled Ratta-Tooey   190

Smokin' Tofu-ed BBQ Beans   192

Tantalizing Tandoori Tofu Brochettes   193

Tofu Steaks with Pineapple/Mango Salsa   194

NAME DE LA FLAME

Barbecue Team Names We Love

3 Fat Guys & A Smoker
3rd Degree Burn
A Hobby Gone Awry
Adribbers
Airpork Crew
Always Rubbin Somethin
Any Pork in a Storm
Aporkalypse Now
Armed & Hammered
Artrageous Cookers
Asleep at the Grill
Badges, Brews & BBQ's
Bama Butt Burners
Barbeque Republic
Barefoot in the Pork
Barn Burners
Basty Boys

Baxter's Beer-Butt Cookin'
Team
Becky & the Blind Puppy
Beefy Cowboys
Beer Nutz
Beer, Meat, and Rebar
Beverly Pigbvillies
Big Bad Wolf & 3 Little Pigs
Big Bee Que
Big Momma & Uncle Fats
Bite My Butt
Blazin Bacon
Blood, Sweat, & Que
Boars R US
Bob-A-Que
Bovine & Swine BBQ
Brisket Cases

Brunt Ends
Bubbaque Boys
Buck & Wing Cooking Team
Bucken-Far-B-Que
Bum Steers
Buns & Roses
Burning Desires
Burning Sensation
Burnt Offerings
Butt Naked Barbecue
Byte My Ribs
C Mor Butts
Can't Quit Smokin
Car Dogs BBQ
Cayenne Social Club
Char Czar
Chicken Chokin Smokin

Cochran Juris Porkers

Cowboy Yacht Club

Crispy Critters

Damnifino

Dead Meat BBQ

Denver Dine-O-Might

Dirty Dick & the Legless Wonders

Dizzy Pig BBQ

Don't Burn the Beer

Dr. Frankenswine

Dr. I Can't Stop Smoking

Drag N' Smoke

Dueling Bubbas

Dyin' To Smoke

Exhausted Rooster Club

Fat Chance BBQ

Fat, Drunk, & Stupid

First Pig & Loining Bank

Gar B Que

Gas Hawgs

Genuswine

Gettin Piggy With It

Girth Wind and Fire

Got Pig?

Grand Masters of Cooking Disasters

Great Grill O Fire

Green Eggs & Hog

Grillas

Grilligan's Island

Grillin N Chillin

Half Fast Cookers

Ham Hocks N' Dirty Socks

Harrah's Porker Chips

Heartburn BBQ

Heavenly Piglets

Hidin From Our Wives

Highway Ribbery

Hocus Smokus

Hog Rock Cafe

Hog Tied

Hogaholics

Hogapalooza

Hogasm

Hoggie & The Blowpigs

Hogwizer

Holy Cow Cookers

Hook & Crooks

I Smell Smoke

In Porcus Veritas

Inlaws & Outlaws

Iowa Hawgeyes

Jacques Strappe & Supporters

Jamakin Ba Ba Q

Joint Chiefs of Smoke

Junk Yard Hogs

Kill It, Chill It, Grill It

Let's Kick Some Ash

Mac Daddy Meat

Macon Bacon Cookers

Master Basters

Me and My Pig

Meat Me In KC

Meateorites

Meatloafers

Mis-B-Havin'

Modern Porkfolio Theory

Moon Swiners

Moose & Lobster Preservation Society

Natural Born Grillers

Not Ready for Swine Time Porkers

Nude BBQ

Oink, Cackle, & Moo

Oink, Inc.

Operation Rolling Smoke

Orthopigs

Oscar & The Grouches

Outhouse BBQ

P. H. A. T. Chance

Pepper Mike & The Firebreathers

Peyton Place Motley Crew

Pig Newtons

Pig Pounda Kappa

Pig'n & Swig'n

Piggin' N Grinnin'

Piggy Licious

Pigs-R-Us

Pirates of the Car-Rib-Bean

Pits & Ashes

Pok N' Da Ribs

Poke in Da Eye

Pork Authority

Pork Floyd BBQ Team

Pork Me Tender

Porkbarrel Legislators

VEGETARIAN BBQ

Porkcrastinators

Porkey & Beans

Porkin Ain't Easy

Porkitects

Porkosaurus

Porkstruction

Porn N Bones

Portfolio of Pork

Pot Bellied Cookers

Prime Swine International

Pyropigmaniacs

Que N' Brew

Rib Ticklers

Ribs, For Her Pleasure

Roadkill BBQ Company

Shut Up & Cook

Smok'n in the Boys Room

Smokelicious

Smokin Bovine

Sow Luau

Sweet Swine O' Mine

Swine & Dine

Swine Flew

Swine Tingling BBQ

Swinefeld

Swiney Ribbers

Team Stupid

Ten That Grilled Elvis

The Grate Pretenders

The Hogfather

The Meat Loafers

The Missing Links

The Pit & The Pigulum

The Sowpranos

The Sprice Grills

Three Brisketeers

Three Carps & A Tarp

TNT BBQ Co.

Tom & John's Orgasmic Slabs

Top Gun Brisketeers

Totally Boar'd

Transporkers

Turn & Burn

Tush Hawgs

Two Jokers With A Smoker

We B Smokin

We "Auto" Be Grillin'

We B Q' N

Westport Weinies

Whole Hog Café

You Choke It We Smoke It

BBQUED SEITAN BURGERS

For a non-vegetarian I was shocked at how good these are. They take a while to make but the flavors are wonderful together and they're as healthy as you can get. Garnish these with tomato, avocado, red onion or dill pickle slices

12 oz. seitan
1 tablespoon olive oil
4 medium shallots, minced
½ pound button mushrooms, chopped
1 large Portobello mushroom, chopped
1 teaspoon sea salt
1 teaspoon dried chives
1 teaspoon dried summer savory
1 teaspoon ground ginger
⅛ teaspoon red pepper flakes
½ cup whole-wheat bread flour
½ cup yellow cornmeal
2 teaspoons Mexene chili powder
½ teaspoon granulated garlic
1 teaspoon ground cumin
¼ teaspoon black pepper
¼ cup dark cane syrup
¼ cup favorite BBQ sauce
1 tablespoon concentrated lime juice
6-8 hamburger buns

Drain seitan, squeezing to remove excess liquid, then roughly chop, this amount should make 2 cups. Process the seitan in a food blender until it resembles large-grind hamburger, which should be accomplished in several short pulses.

In a cast iron skillet, heat the oil over medium heat. Add the shallots and cook, stirring often, until softened, about 3-4 minutes. Add the chopped button and Portabello mushrooms, ½ teaspoon salt, chives, savory, ginger, and red pepper and cook for 4-5 minutes stirring often, until heated through and well mixed. Transfer the ingredients to a large bowl and let the mixture cool. Add the ground seitan and mix well with your hands or with a wooden spoon.

In a large bowl, mix together the flour, cornmeal, chili powder, granulated garlic, cumin, remaining ½ teaspoon salt, and pepper. Slowly stir the flour mixture into seitan mixture until well combined. Using a ½ cup each, form mixture into round and firm patties, you'll get 6 to 8.. In a small bowl mix BBQ sauce, cane syrup and lime juice and set aside.

Place seitan patties on a pre-oiled grill over medium-high heat (450° to 550°), brushing liberally and often with BBQ sauce-cane syrup-lime sauce. Cook 5-6 minutes, turn once, brush fresh side with sauce, then cook another 4-5 minutes.

Brush hamburger buns with olive oil, separate, and grill for 1 to 2 minutes to brown the buns.

Present the seitan patties on grilled buns with remaining sauce on the side.

Serves 6-8

DAVE'S SEITAN GRILLING SAUCE

Dave Olson, a photojournalist at *The Columbian* newspaper in Vancouver, Washington, is a gentle, caring man who first showed me that "vegetarian" foods can be delicious, as well as "good for you." This is one of his recipes.

1 ½ cups thick tomato sauce
3 tablespoons honey
1 tablespoon molasses
1 tablespoon olive oil
2 tablespoons soy sauce
1 tablespoon paprika
1 tablespoon chili powder
1 tablespoon mustard
1 teaspoon garlic powder
1 teaspoon oregano

Combine all the ingredients in a large bowl and mix well. Cover and let mixture stand for at least 1 hour before using. Refrigerate in a tightly sealed bottle if not using right away.

Use as a marinade for grilled tofu, seitan or tempeh.

Makes 1 ½ cups

FANTASIA'S BBQ TOFU CAKES

Fantasia, Maui, HI

An earth mother and blithe spirit who bubbles love for mother earth, and every living thing on the face of the planet.

1 tablespoon arrowroot powder
½ cup water
¼ cup barley miso
½ cup Mirin
¼ cup plum sauce
1 tablespoon brown sugar
2 tablespoons hone
12 small Japanese eggplants, or American
   variety
4 Atsu-Age cakes (firm thick deep-fried tofu),
   available at health food stores
8 whole shiitake mushrooms, fresh
1 bunch green onions

In a small saucepan, over medium heat on a grill or stovetop burner, whisk together arrowroot and water. Cook for 2 to 3 minutes stirring constantly and add miso, Mirin, plum sauce, brown sugar, and honey for 5 minutes until thickened. Remove from the heat, pour into a medium bowl and let cool. Reserve.

Slice each eggplant in half lengthwise (if American variety used slice in ½-inch thick rounds) and trim ends from the green onions. Clean mushrooms.

Brush grill with sesame oil to prevent sticking. Cook the Atsu-Age tofu cakes over medium-hot coals (450° to 550°) 7-8 minutes each side until the edges start to crisp and turn brown. While tofu grills, place whole green onions, shiitake mushrooms and eggplant (cut-side down) on the grill and cook for 5 minutes. Turn and baste with miso sauce. Continue cooking 5-8 minutes until eggplant can be pierced easily with a fork.

Serve the tofu cakes with the grilled vegetables on top and drizzle both with the remaining miso-plum sauce.

Serves 4-6

GOLDEN ROSEMARY POLENTA

24-oz. log prepared polenta
2 teaspoon extra-virgin olive oil
garlic salt to taste
lemon pepper to taste
2 tablespoons chopped rosemary

Prepare a hot charcoal fire or preheat gas grill on high.

Cut the polenta into 12 ½-inch thick slices. Place the slices on a baking sheet. Brush both sides of the polenta rounds with oil and season lightly with garlic salt, lemon pepper, and sprinkle with chopped rosemary leaves. Lightly oil the grill rack and cook polenta slices over high heat (500° to 600°) until nicely browned, 3 to 5 minutes per side.

Remove from heat and serve on a heated platter.

Serves 4-6

GRILLED & BREADED TOFU (SEITAN)

Marinade/Sauce:

⅓ cup soy sauce

¼ cup maple syrup

½ teaspoon minced garlic

2 cups water

1 pound of extra firm tofu or seitan, cut into
    ½-inch thick steaks

1 cup whole wheat flour

1 cup soy milk

2 cups bread crumbs

1 teaspoon granulated garlic

1 tablespoon dried parsley

1 tablespoon dried thyme

1 tablespoon ground cumin

1 tablespoon orange peel granules

pinch of red pepper

In a medium bowl whisk together the marinade ingredients and set aside. Soak the tofu steaks in the marinade mixture for 2 to 3 hours.

Place the flour, soy milk, and bread crumbs in three separate flat Pyrex dishes. Add the garlic, parsley, thyme, cumin, and orange peel to the bread crumb dish and mix well. Dredge the tofu or seitan first in the flour, then the soy milk, and then coat heavily with the herb bread crumbs. Place the breaded tofu or seitan onto a grill which has been sprayed with olive oil or non stick spray, over medium hot coals or medium gas flame (400° to 500°), leaving space between each piece.

In a medium bowl heat the marinade over medium for 3-5 minutes, and add a pinch of the red pepper flakes to the mixture, lower heat to lowest setting and keep warm.

Grill the breaded tofu or seitan for 3-5 minutes on each side, until browned and crispy-looking. Serve with the sauce for dipping.

Serves 4-6

GRILLED LEMON-LIME TEMPEH

MARINADE:

⅛ cup freshly squeezed lime
¼ cup freshly squeezed lemon juice
¼ cup olive oil
¼ teaspoon summer savory
¼ teaspoon thyme
1 tablespoon raspberry leaves *
⅛ teaspoon black pepper
16 ounces tempeh
1 large sweet onion, sliced
sliced tomatoes for garnish
fresh lettuce leaves for garnish
4-6 hamburger rolls (whole wheat)
Heat grill to high, about 400° degrees.

In a small bowl, combine the lime and lemon juice, olive oil, savory, oregano, raspberry leaves, and pepper, mix well and set aside. Cut the tempeh into 1-inch strips and place in a metal or bamboo steamer or over boiling water. Steam for 15-18 minutes, until heated through. Remove and drain the tempeh, then place it in a 2-4 qt. flat casserole dish or Pyrex baking dish. Pour the marinade over the tempeh add the onions and marinate in the refrigerator for 4-6 hours.

Grill the tempeh and onions over a medium hot (400° to 500°) BBQ grill you've sprayed or coated with oil, basting the tempeh frequently with the marinade. Grill each side until it's heated through and appears a light brown.

Serve the tempeh slices and onions on the hamburger rolls. Garnish with onion slices, lettuce, and sliced tomatoes. Have your favorite BBQ sauce ready on the side for those who wish to add it to their grilled sandwiches.

Serves 4-6

* Raspberry leaves are available on-line through Oregon Spice Company (www.oregonspice.com)

OLE OLE INFREE'S TEMPEH SATAY

Dave Olson, Vancouver, Washington, and Paheo, Hawaii

One of the earth's most special people. A gentle man who truly is himself and who opened my eyes about lots of things including some incredible vegetarian recipes.

MARINADE:

½ cup grated coconut

¼ cup orange juice

1 tablespoon honey

¼ cup tarmari (whole wheat soy sauce)

⅛ teaspoon cayenne pepper

4 tempeh cutlets

PEANUT SAUCE:

¼ cup smooth peanut butter

¼ cup finely chopped roasted peanuts

3 tbs. tarmari

1 tablespoon Mirin or sherry

½ teaspoon rice vinegar

⅛ teaspoon garlic powder

1 tbs. honey

1 cup nonfat yogurt, plain

⅛ teaspoon cayenne pepper

1 16 oz. can pineapple chunks

To make the marinade, puree ¼ cup of the coconut with the orange juice, honey, tamari and cayenne in a blender until smooth, 2-3 minutes. Pour the marinade into a shallow baking dish. Cut the tempeh into 1-inch cubes and add it to marinade. Set aside for 30 minutes.

In a small saucepan, blend together the peanut sauce ingredients with a wire whisk, and warm sauce on low heat, for 7-8 minutes. Do not let boil.

Thread the tempeh cubes and pineapple chunks onto bamboo skewers that have been soaked in hot water for 20 minutes.

Grill the tempeh/pineapple skewers on a grill over medium-hot coals 3 to 5 minutes on each side, or until cubes start to get brown edges. Brush the kebabs with marinade 2 to 3 times during cooking. When kebabs are browned on all sides they are done. Remove from heat and set on a platter. Sprinkle with the remaining coconut.

Serve immediately with warm peanut sauce.

Serves 4

RICK'S GRILLED RATTA-TOOEY

1 medium eggplant, about 1 pound

2 medium onions, Walla Wall, Vidalia or Maui preferred

1 medium summer squash or zucchini

1 large golden or red bell pepper

2 tablespoons olive oil

1 large ripe tomato, seeded and diced

¼ cup chopped black olives

2 tablespoons chopped fresh basil

2 tablespoons chopped fresh cilantro

1 teaspoon fines herbes

1 teaspoon oregano

2 tablespoons red wine vinegar

sea or coarse salt to taste

freshly ground pepper to taste

¼ pound asiago cheese

Cut the eggplant into ½-inch-thick slices. Salt them on both sides and place them in a colander for 30 minutes, then rinse and drain. You may cut off the peel if you wish.

Peel the onions and cut them in ½ inch slices. Quarter the summer squash or zucchini lengthwise. Cut the bell pepper into ½-inch pieces lengthwise.

Prepare a hot grill (500° to 600°). Brush the vegetables lightly with the olive oil. Grill the eggplant on both sides until nicely browned and quite tender, about 12-15 minutes total. Grill the onions, bell pepper, and zucchini on both sides until they're tender and marked with brown, about 10 minutes total. (You may want to use a vegetable basket or grid to prevent veggies from sliding into the fire.) Remove the veggies from the grill, place in a medium bowl and let cool.

When all the vegetables are cool enough to handle, chop them into fairly large chunks and combine them in a serving bowl.

Stir in the tomato, olives, basil, cilantro, fines herbes, olive oil, and vinegar, and toss well. Season to taste with salt and pepper. If desired, sprinkle the top with crumbled asiago cheese. Serve at room temperature with grilled garlic bread or foccacia bread.

Serves 4-6

SMOKIN' TOFU-ED BBQ BEANS

3 ½ cups cooked Great Northern or navy beans

1 ½ cups cooked soybeans

1 cup chopped sweet onion

1 cup chopped bell pepper, yellow or red

2 cloves garlic, minced

1 8 oz. can tomato sauce

2 tablespoons molasses

3 tablespoons brown sugar

1 tablespoon cider vinegar

1 teaspoon prepared mustard

1 teaspoon ground ginger

¼ teaspoon cinnamon

¼ teaspoon allspice

¼ teaspoon black pepper

1 teaspoon Beano (optional—to reduce the
    inherent gas in the beans)

2 tablespoons light molasses

2 tablespoons clover honey

Drain the navy and soybeans well. Combine them with all the remaining ingredients, except the molasses and honey, in a Dutch oven or flameproof cast iron pot. Cover and bake them over indirect heat for 1 ½ hours in a hot smoker or gas barbecue (325°-350°), or until mixture is bubbling and beans are just becoming soft. Remove the cover, stir the bean mixture, and cook for about 30 minutes longer.

Mix the honey and molasses together and drizzle the mixture over the beans before serving

Serves 8

TANTALIZING TANDOORI TOFU BROCHETTES

1 pound extra firm tofu, drained

MARINADE:

3 stalks green onion

1 tablespoon minced fresh ginger

3 garlic cloves

1 tablespoon brown sugar

1 tablespoon soy sauce

1 generous pinch saffron

½ cups soy yogurt

2 tablespoons chili powder

2 tablespoons paprika

salt to taste

pepper to taste

Brochettes:

4 small red onions, halved

½ pound crimini mushrooms

1 pint cherry tomatoes

1 green pepper, sliced

Gently press the tofu to remove excess moisture. Slice the tofu into bite-sized chunks. Set aside.

Place the green onions and ginger in a food processor and process briefly. With the machine running, drop in garlic cloves, one at a time. Process for 30 seconds. Add remaining ingredients. Process for 1 minute and set aside. The marinade will be somewhat chunky.

Spoon the onion, mushroom, green pepper and tofu into a Ziploc bag and pour in marinade. Refrigerate overnight.

Heat the grill to medium high (400° to 500°), oil the grill or spray it with non-stick spray. Remove the tofu and vegetables from the refrigerator and thread onto bamboo or metal skewers.. Skewer vegetables and tofu alternately. Place the brochettes on the hot grill, and brush with the remaining marinade. Cover the barbecue tightly and allow it to heat for 5 minutes. Turn the kabobs once and cook for another 3-5 minutes. You may need to keep repeating this cycle.

Serves 4-6

TOFU STEAKS WITH PINEAPPLE/MANGO SALSA

1 bunch fresh cilantro

⅔ cup white vegetable stock (below)

¼ cup lemon juice

1 tablespoon crushed red pepper

¼ cup minced fresh ginger

1 tablespoon brown sugar

1 teaspoon blackstrap molasses

5 garlic cloves

black pepper, to taste

1 small fresh pineapple

2 mangos

1 ¼ pound firm tofu, drained, cut lengthwise into four 1-inch thick "steaks"

Chop the cilantro to make ½ cup and set aside 1 tablespoon of it for salsa. In a medium-sized baking dish, combine the chopped cilantro and the stock, lemon juice, red pepper, ginger, sugar, molasses, garlic, and black pepper. Stir and add the tofu. Marinate it for 2 hours at room temperature.

Peel the pineapple and mangos, then finely chop, discard pineapple skin and core and mango skin and pit. In a medium serving bowl combine the fruit and 1 tablespoon of the reserved chopped cilantro. Set it aside at room temperature to let the flavors combine.

Prepare the outdoor grill for medium heat Drain tofu, reserving marinade. Lightly oil grill and place tofu on grill over Grill the tofu until lightly browned, 4-5 minutes, brushing frequently with the marinade and turning once. Serve the tofu steaks with the pineapple and mango mixture.

Serves 4-6

CHAPTER 10
WILD GAME

Alice Springs Emu Steaks   203

Fred's Apple/Cherry-Stuffed Pheasant   204

Barbecued Ostrich Filet Mignon * with Ginger &
Lime   205

BBQ'd Venison Loin Chops   206

Apricot Mango Chutney   208

B&M's New Mexico Smoked
Wild Boar Ham   209

Breast of Wild Goose with
Lingonberry Sauce   211

Grilled Loin of Venison with Wild Mushroom
Ragout   212

Mushroom Ragout   213

Maple Pecan Stuffed Rabbit, Eh?   213

Ol' Bill's Teriyaki Elk Steaks   214

Teriyaki Buffalo Ribeyes   215

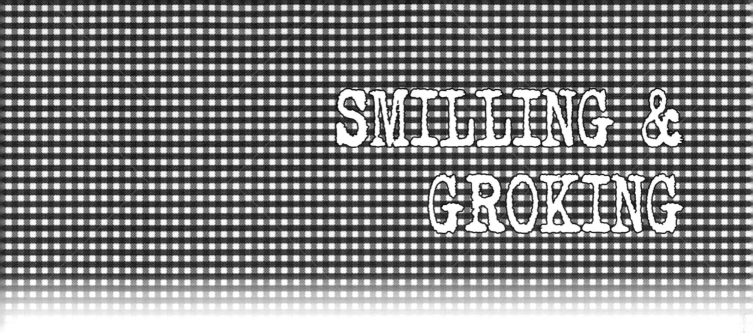

SMILLING & GROKING

BARBECUE'S NEWEST COOKING STYLE

More and more people are combining the techniques of grilling and smoking food in their backyard barbecues. The benefits of grilling include quicker cooking times and a charred ("barbecued") look to the meat, while smoking imparts a smoky flavor and moistness, albeit in a longer amount of time. Sometimes substantially longer. We are offering up a new style: **Smilling**, or, if you prefer, **Groking**. Combining the best of both BBQ worlds.

Groking (or Smilling) is making use of the best characteristics of the two main styles of barbecue cooking.

We use the quicker-heating characteristics of grilling. Putting food over direct heat cooks it much quicker than either over indirect heat or in a smoker, where the food is mainly heated by the hot smoke from an adjacent firebox. The food cooks quicker and has a more "barbecued" look to it because of the grill marks caused by the very hot grill surface coming in contact with the food.

And we use the flavor-producing characteristics of smoking. Foods smoked over fragrant fruit and hardwoods have a super, well, "smoke" taste that enhances just about anything you place on a BBQ and they are often more moist than grilled foods because the lower and slower cooking temperatures allow the natural juices to stay deep inside the food, instead of coming to the surface as often happens in grilling. That's why, when grilling, you should let the meat "rest" after it's cooked, so the juices can go back inside the meat from the hot surface where they've been driven.

We've found the best way to combine the two heating/cooking methods is to begin on the grill. We can use either direct grilling, where the food is right over the hot coals, briquettes, charcoal chunks or gas flame, or the indirect heat method described in the first chapter of the book (see page XXX).

Either does the trick, and both produce delicious, tender and flavored meat, fish and poultry.

For this chapter let's direct grill. And let's say we have a large roast to cook, perhaps a pork roast. First you should prepare your smoke package. For this I like to take a large piece of heavy duty aluminum foil (a square piece about 2 feet by 2 feet) and lay it flat on a table. Then take 1 or 2 handfuls of your favorite wood chips, pellets, or chunks of fruit wood, oak, hickory, pecan, maple, or mesquite, etc.) and mound the dry wood in the center of the sheet of foil.

Now to be honest there are two schools of thought on this process. Some insist that the wood needs to be soaked in water to produce more, better, or more consistent smoke. But others of us, including moi, think that wood has a more natural smoke if put in the packets dry. Unless you've poked holes all the way through the foil the wood shouldn't catch fire. It will merely smolder along sending clouds of yummy smoke up to and through the food you're cooking. So it's up to you: the wet method or the dry method, your choice.

Now fold over one side to the other on both sides, and the top and bottom, of the foil until you have a foil packet. Take a pencil or sharp knife and poke 3-4 small holes into the **TOP** of the foil only.

Do not go entirely through the package. Now you have your smoke packet all ready.

Prepare the fire by heating the briquettes, coals, mesquite chunks, or gas flame until they are hot enough for your roast. When ready, and just before you put the grill over the coals or flame, place the smoke packet directly on the coals, or a gas jet. Place the grill on top of the barbecue, place the meat, fish, or poultry on the grill, and close the lid.

Almost immediately the wood chunks in the foil begin to smolder and add their fragrant smoke to the food that's being grilled over the heat. Ta—da! You're Groking! Or is it Smilling? Whatever you want to call it it's as easy as that.

When the pellets, chunks or chips are all burned-up the smoke will stop. And a packet this size will provide plenty of flavorful smoke for just about any size roast, bird or fish you want to cook on the grill. If you find you want more smoke, well, just repeat the packet preparation. Then lift the grill carefully, and add a new packet to the bed of coals or gas jets. You might want to reach in with a long pair of tongs and remove the old foil packet first, but that really isn't necessary.

Now we'll share some sage words of wisdom from one of the top experts in the field as what woods to use in this process, and, of course in normal grilling and smoking as well.

WOODS TO USE IN GRILL-SMOKING

by Dave DeWitt, Editor, Fiery Foods magazine
This super article on how to, and how not to, use woods in grilling and smoking is re-printed with permission from Fiery Foods Magazine. Check out

the magazine or their website (www.fiery-foods.com) for great articles on both styles of barbecue cooking, recipes, and lots of information on cooking with hot peppers & chilies: www.fiery-foods.com

Two of the classic arts of grilling and barbecuing are knowing which woods to use and how to use them. Before I got a gas grill, all I had was a smoker, and I used the main chamber of it to grill meats over wood. It was by far the most challenging cooking I have ever done, because the distance from the coals was fixed, and I had to estimate when the fire was the hottest so the meat would cook before the fire burned out. It is difficult to add wood during the grilling process because it takes so long for it to burn down to coals. Here are some hints:

THE TREE WITH THE LEGUMINOUS SMOKE

You either love mesquite or hate it, depending on whether or not you're a farmer, hunter, cook, rancher, or woodworker. Farmers and ranchers hate the tree, of course, because it chokes out needed grazing grass, and, as a result of its extensive root system, is nearly impossible to remove from pastures.

A clump of mesquite trees provides shade, humidity, and food for such animals as doves, deer, javelina, and rabbits, which is why hunters like the tree. The mesquite beans, which are sugar-rich, provide food for both animals and man, and it once provided up to forty percent of the food in the diet of Native Americans in Texas. The wood of the tree is variously shaded, which is why woodworkers love it for making sculptures, gunstocks, parquet floors, and other hardwood products.

Cooks love mesquite because its wood produces a very hot flame which is great for grilling steaks. Most mesquite trees these days are being cut down for wood chips and to make charcoal, but there's such an abundance of trees that there is no threat to mesquite.

Travelers all over the United States will have little trouble finding mesquite-grilled foods. But a hint to the home cook—the wood is used for grilling only because the smoke is considered to be too acrid for the lengthy smoking or barbecuing of meats. For that, pecan or hickory wood is suggested. And if you're grilling with mesquite, be sure to use aged wood because the green wood is too oily.

OTHER WOODS

Do I really have to state in print not to use construction lumber scraps in your smoker or barbecue? Well, here I go. Most of these scraps are resinous pine or fir; some are treated or contain glue, like plywood. All are useless for cooking or smoking purposes. And, under no circumstances should you grill or smoke over woods such as cottonwood, willow, pine, or poplar. Stick to the woods listed below and you'll produce great heat and fragrant smoke. And when you consider smoking foods, think of the wood as a spice to add flavor instead of just being a fuel.

The woods that work best for grilling and smoking are hardwoods, particularly (for some unknown reason) the woods of certain fruit and nut trees. We should point out that any of these woods can be used to smoke any meat—we are just commenting on what meats these woods are commonly linked with.

Some woods are available locally only where they grow, such as alder and pecan. But most woods are available by mail order or at your nearest barbecue supply store. In most cases, the hard remnants of fruits or nuts of the hardwood trees can also be used in the smoking process. Specifically, we mean peach pits and nut shells, but not acorns.

Alder imparts a light flavor that works well with fish and poultry. It is native to the northwestern United States, and is the traditional wood for smoking salmon.

Apple has a sweet, mild flavor and is used mostly with pork and game, but works with ham as well.

Cherry is also used for ham, but some cooks think that its smoke is too acrid.

Hickory is probably the most famous smoking hardwoods. It's the wood of choice in the Southern barbecue belt. It imparts a strong, hearty flavor to meats, and is used mostly to smoke pork shoulders and ribs.

Maple is a mild and mellow smoke that imparts a sweet flavor that is traditional for smoking ham but is also good with poultry, pork, and seafood.

Oak, the favorite wood of Europe, is strong but not overpowering. A very good wood for beef or lamb, it is probably the most versatile of the hard woods. Do not use acorns for smoking.

Pecan is similar to hickory but milder. It's also a southern favorite that is becoming the smoking wood of choice in the Southwest because of the extensive pecan groves in Texas, New Mexico, and Arizona. Because of its availability, it is the wood most commonly used in our smoker.

Remember that the above woods can be mixed in the smoking process to add another dimension to barbecue. Some cooks in the Southwest, where I live, mix a little of the stronger mesquite in with pecan or apple wood. Other woods used in the smoking process include **almond**, **black walnut**, **juniper** (slightly resinous), and **locust**.

MORE SMOKE-PRODUCING PLANTS

There are other wood-like flavorings to add to the heat source, but we don't recommend smoking with them for lengthy periods of time because they create smoke that is very intensely flavored. If you like the flavor of coconut, then smoke or grill fish with a little **coconut hull** added. Also, **grapevines** make a tart smoke that can overwhelm poultry or lamb. Use it sparingly. **Herbs**, such as **oregano**, **sage**, **thyme**, **marjoram**, **rosemary**, and **basil**, used both dried and fresh, can imbue the meat being smoked with their own particular flavor profiles. Since rosemary and sage have woody stems, their thick stems can be used as well as the branches and leaves. As with grapevine, a little herb—in either form—goes a long way.

Incidentally, do not burn chile pods to flavor grilled or smoked meat. The pods produce an acrid smoke—so irritating that Native Americans burned huge piles of them in an attempt to use gas warfare against the invading Conquistadors..

SOME FINAL HINTS

Match the wood to the meat.

If possible, use a thermometer to check the heat of your smoke when smoking meats, and make sure it is under 200° degrees.

Keep a squirt bottle next to the grill to instantly fight flare-ups.

Also, keep a long fork or tongs ready to remove the meat from the grill if flare-ups start. If possible, the meat should be removed as the water is being sprayed.

If using wood chips on charcoal or gas to flavor grilled foods, you may wish to soak them in water first.

Never use eucalyptus for grilling or smoking.

Stopping by some woods on a barbecue evening . . . . . .

OTHER WOODS YOU CAN USE:

ACACIA—Same family as mesquite and has a similar flavor but not quite as heavy. Burns very hot.

ALMOND—A sweet smoke flavor, light ash. Good with most meats. Try it with shrimp or lobster.

ASH—Fast-burning wood which gives off a light, gentle, distinctive flavor. Good with fish and red meats.

BIRCH—Medium-hard wood with a flavor similar to maple. Good with pork and poultry, especially turkey.

COTTONWOOD—It is very subtle in flavor. Use with other woods like hickory, oak, pecan for more flavor. Don't use green cottonwood.

CRABAPPLE—Similar to apple wood. Baby back ribs take the flavor nicely.

LILAC—Very light, subtle with a hint of floral. Good with seafood & lamb.

MULBERRY—The smell is sweet and reminds one of apple. Try it with brisket.

ORANGE, LEMON, and GRAPEFRUIT—Produce a mild smoky flavor. Excellent with beef, pork, fish, and poultry.

PEAR—A nice subtle smoke flavor. Much like apple. Excellent with chicken and pork, especially roasts.

SWEET FRUIT WOODS—APRICOT, PLUM, PEACH, NECTARINE—Great for fish, and most white meats, including chicken, turkey, and pork.

ALICE SPRINGS EMU STEAKS

MARINADE:

½ cup soy sauce

¼ cup lime juice

2 tablespoon rice wine vinegar

¼ cup orange juice

1 tablespoon brown sugar

1 tablespoon honey

1 teaspoon minced garlic

¼ cup chopped scallions

½ teaspoon fresh ground ginger

1 teaspoon olive oil

pinch of nutmeg

sea salt to taste

citrus pepper to taste

2 pounds Emu steaks *

2-3 tablespoons chilled butter

In a large bowl whisk together all marinade ingredients and pour into a Ziploc bag, add the emu steaks, and marinate them for 8-10 hours in the refrigerator.

Drain the meat, reserving the marinade, place the meat on a platter, cover with plastic wrap, and let it come to room temperature while you oil or spray the grill. Place an aluminum foil smoke packet on the coals (or medium gas flame) and when the wood chips begin to smoke, put the steaks on the grill.

In a medium saucepan, over high heat, boil the remaining marinade for ten minutes. Remove pan from heat and set aside keeping warm, over lowest heat setting. Just before serving the emu, cut the butter into small chunks, add to the sauce, and whisk into mixture until smooth.

Grill the emu over medium coals or gas fire (400° to 500°) until medium rare, approximately 2-4 minutes per side.

Place the steaks on a heated platter, cover with foil, and let meat rest for 2-3 minutes. Serve with the sauce on the side.

Serves 4

* Emu steaks, as well as other exotic meats (including alligator, caribou, frog, kangaroo, and rattlesnake) can be ordered on-line from Seattle's Finest Exotic Meats at www.exoticmeats.com

FRED'S APPLE/ CHERRY-STUFFED PHEASANT

Fred & Dottie Anderson, Battle Creek, Michigan

Gave me my first taste of pheasant one Thanksgiving and we ate so much we literally had to lie down on the living room carpet for fear we'd explode if we so much as moved a finger. I have never forgotten the taste of those heavenly birds.

STUFFING:

1 small tart apple, cored and chopped

½ cup dried cherries, soaked in hot water for 20 min.

1 small onion quartered

1 stalk of celery, sliced

1 teaspoon of rosemary

1 teaspoon poultry seasoning

½ teaspoon sage

4-5 pound pheasant, cleaned and checked for shot

2 tablespoons olive oil

1 tablespoon melted butter

salt to taste

pepper to taste

6-8 bacon slices, raw

Core and chop 1 small tart apple, place in bowl, set aside. Place cherries in another small bowl and cover with hot water. Soak for 20 minutes then drain.

Mix the apples and cherries with the rest of the stuffing ingredients together in a medium bowl, set it aside.

Mix the melted butter and olive oil in a small bowl. Rub the bird down good with butter/oil, salt and pepper the bird inside and outside well, then stuff the cavity with the stuffing mixture.

Put the bird on an oiled grill rack in a shallow pan and add ¼″ of water to keep the first juices from burning. Cook 1- 1 ½ hours on medium-high heat (450° to 550°), turning often. Check the pheasant after about 30 minutes and baste it again with the oil-butter mixture. Turn it over if the top starts to get too brown.

You can also cover with bacon slices while it cooks. Remove when finished and discard bacon

Remove the pheasant from the grill, place it on a warm platter, cover it and let it rest for 10 minutes before carving and serving.

Serves 2-4

BARBECUED OSTRICH FILET MIGNON * WITH GINGER & LIME

2 packages ostrich filet mignons * (or 2-inch
thick Emu steaks)
1 tablespoon fresh ground ginger
1 tablespoon fresh garlic
Salt & pepper to taste
2 fresh limes

In a large flat pan cover ostrich filet mignons with ginger, garlic, salt and pepper. Squeeze fresh limes over the top and let filets stand for 1 hour at room temperature. Remove filets from marinade and discard liquid.

Grill filets over medium high heat (450° to 550°) for 8 minutes (4 minutes per side) for medium rare, turning once. Let the filets stand for 5 minutes before serving.

Serves 4-6

* Ostrich steaks, filet mignons, and other cuts are readily available on the internet from companies all over the US. One interesting site: Broadleafgame. com has an unbelievable selection of exotic game meats including alligator, musk ox, rattlesnake, kangaroo, Kobe beef, Scottish Grouse, wild boar, buffalo and New Zealand venison.

BBQ'D VENISON LOIN CHOPS

with Apricot-Mango Chutney

8 venison loin chops
salt to taste
pepper to taste
Baste:
½ cup plus 1 teaspoon olive oil
2 cloves garlic, chopped
1 sprig rosemary
1 sprig thyme
2 teaspoons black peppercorns

In a small frying pan place 1 teaspoon of olive oil, then add garlic cloves and gently sauté over medium heat until they brown, about 2-3 minutes.

Salt and pepper the loin chops. Brush the chops with olive oil mixture. Place the chops on a grill heated to 400° to 500° and grill for 4-5 minutes per side until meat is cooked the way you like it, basting every time you turn the meat. Remove chops from the grill, place on heated platter and let the loin chops rest for 2 minutes before serving.

Accompany the chops with apricot-mango chutney (below).

Serves 4

APRICOT MANGO CHUTNEY

4 medium apricots, diced

3 medium mangos, peeled and diced

8 oz. sugar

2 cups white wine vinegar

1 teaspoon cardamom

1 teaspoon dried ginger

1 teaspoon salt

1 teaspoon white pepper

1 red bell pepper, finely diced

8 oz. golden raisins

½ cup red onion, finely diced

¼ cup minced shallots

Combine all ingredients in large saucepan. Stir well and simmer, uncovered, for 45 minutes, on low heat, or until fruit is soft. Remove the chutney from the heat. place in a small bowl and cool to room temperature. Pack in clean jars and refrigerate. Warm up in a small saucepan or microwave oven before serving with meat recipes. Chutney should last 3-4 days refrigerated.

Serves 4-6

B&M'S NEW MEXICO SMOKED WILD BOAR HAM

Bob and Marti Browne, Indianapolis, Indiana

This recipe was inspired first by our love of wild game, and especially the discovery of the true pork flavor of wild boar. Friends tell me it is what pork used to taste like before it was sterilized, homogenized, and modernized. It was quite a revelation to my family, who loves it! Second was our passion for the vinegar-based barbecue sauces of the Carolinas. Finally, it was our passion for the flavors of Northern New Mexico, the rich flavor of chilies used not for heat but for richness.

MARINADE:

1 tablespoon olive oil
1 small white onion finely chopped
3 cloves chopped garlic
1 can chipotle peppers in Adobo sauce
1 cup cider vinegar
1 cup dark molasses
12 oz. dark beer
2 tablespoons Pommery style mustard
1 teaspoon dried Mexican oregano
½ teaspoon fresh ground black pepper
1 cup chopped cilantro
1-2 teaspoon mild chile powder
1 tablespoon ground cumin
1 teaspoon dried epizote

1 teaspoon dried sage
1 tablespoon onion powder
5-7 pound unsmoked bone-in boar ham **
Sauce:
2 cups ketchup (or tomato sauce)
1 roasted red pepper, skinned, seeded and pureed
1 cup tequila
Juice of 1 lime
Louisiana hot sauce
Salt to taste
Optional spray:
1 cup apple cider
¼ cup balsamic vinegar
¼ cup olive oil
fresh cilantro for garnish

Heat the olive oil over low heat in a large sauté pan and then add the onions and garlic and cook till onions are translucent, abut 5-10 minutes. Add the chopped chipotle peppers in adobo sauce and cook for 2 minutes. Combine the cooked mixture with all other ingredients in a large saucepan and simmer on low heat for 20 minutes, stirring occasionally. Remove pan from heat and let the mixture cool. Place ingredients in a blender or food processor and puree until smooth

Score the fat surface of the meat in two directions and puncture the meat all over with a serving fork. Place the meat in a large plastic bag or covered container and add the marinade, refrigerate it for 1-2 days, turning several times per day.

Drain the meat and retain marinade. Place the retained marinade in a large saucepan and boil for 10 minutes. Immediately turn heat to low and add ketchup or tomato sauce, red pepper, tequila, lime juice, hot sauce, and salt as desired to taste. Stir occasionally.

Simmer covered for 60 minutes over low heat, then simmer uncovered for 30-60 minutes until the sauce has reduced by ⅓ so it is a thick syrupy liquid.

Prepare your smoker or barbecue grill with charcoal and soaked hardwood chunks (we prefer hickory and another wood such as maple, cherry or apple) until a steady temperature of 200° to 250° F is reached. Place the ham on the smoker, or , if using barbecue grill, on cool side of grill rack to cook over indirect heat.

Add a pan of water to the smoker to keep the meat moist. If your grill permits it, put the pan under the grill rack so it catches the drippings from the roast. The recirculating juices add to the flavor.

Smoke or grill the meat for approximately 10-12 hours, (again using smoker or indirect heating method) turning 3-4 times during the cooking cycle. If you wish spray cooking ham with optional spray (a mix of apple juice, balsamic vinegar and olive oil) each time before and after you turn meat.

When finished meat should be nicely browned all over, and tender when

pierced with a meat fork. Any juices should run clear.

Remove the meat from grill, put on a platter, and let it rest, covered in foil for about 20 minutes, then slice it and serve on a large heated platter. Garnish with fresh cilantro. Drizzle with sauce and serve the remaining sauce on the side.

Serves 8+

**NOTE: The ham must be unsmoked. Shoulder or butt can be substituted but wild boar has by far the best flavor. range. If frozen, make sure the ham is thawed.

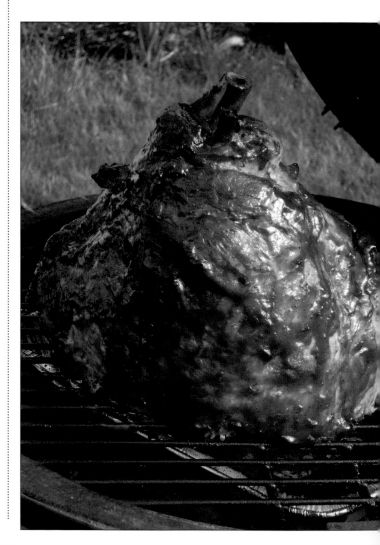

BREAST OF WILD GOOSE WITH LINGONBERRY SAUCE

MARINADE:

½ cup olive oil

½ cup water

¼ cups apple cider vinegar

2 tablespoons balsamic vinegar

3 tablespoons Worcestershire sauce

1 teaspoon garlic powder

1 teaspoon onion powder

1 full breast of wild (or domestic) goose, about 3 pounds

SAUCE:

1 12 oz. jar Lingonberry preserves

½ cup gin

Pre-heat grill to 350° to 400° degrees.

Mix up the marinade in a large Ziploc bag and add the goose breast, letting it marinate for 2 hours in refrigerator. While the goose is marinating, mix the gin and the preserves and heat them in a saucepan over medium heat, stirring often until the mixture thickens, about 5 minutes. Remove from heat, pour into a small bowl and refrigerate. Re-warm in microwave or on stove just before serving goose.

Remove the goose breast from the marinade, reserving the liquid. Place the breast on a platter, covered, for 15-20 minutes to dry.

Pour marinade into a medium saucepan, over high heat, and boil the marinade for 10 minutes. Use it to baste goose occasionally during cooking. Meat is ready when the goose breast reaches an internal temperature of 160° degrees, about 1 ½ to 2 hours. Remove the breast from the grill to a platter, and allow to rest for 15 minutes, covered in foil, before slicing.

Serve with the warm Lingonberry-gin sauce on the side.

Serves 6

GRILLED LOIN OF VENISON WITH WILD MUSHROOM RAGOUT

5-6 pound loin of venison

MARINADE:

1 cup dry red wine

2 tablespoons olive oil

2 tablespoons soy sauce

1 teaspoon garlic powder

1 teaspoon liquid smoke

juice of 1 lemon

½ teaspoon black pepper

6 slices apple smoked bacon, thick cut

BASTE:

1 cup red wine

½ cup olive oil

1 tablespoon cider vinegar

1 small bunch rosemary for garnish

1 small bunch marjoram for garnish

Remove the white, shiny muscle sheath from outside of the loin, and cut a ¾-inch deep slit down the full length of the meat. Mix the marinade in a large plastic bag, add the loin and store it overnight in the refrigerator.

Prepare a barbecue for indirect heat, cooking at medium high heat (450° to 550°) with a water pan beside the coals under the area of grill where meat will be placed. Make long slits across the loin and stuff the bacon strips in the slits. Cook meat approximately 15 to 20 minutes, until desired doneness (like prime rib, the rarer the better). Mix the baste in a medium bowl and baste the loin every 10-15 minutes during cooking.

When meat is done remove it from the grill, let it rest covered for 10 minutes, then serve on a bed of mushrooms and onions (recipe follows). Garnish with fresh sprigs of rosemary and marjoram.

Serves 4-6

MUSHROOM RAGOUT

3 pounds fresh wild mushrooms: shiitake, chanterelle, oyster, morel, and straw varieties
1 medium onion, chopped
1 stick butter
2 tablespoons olive oil
¾ cup red wine
juice of ½ lemon
pinch of marjoram

While the meat is cooking, sauté the ragout ingredients in large cast iron skillet, over medium-high, while stirring constantly, until most of the liquid is gone, about 10-15 minutes.

Serve alongside venison or other game or fowl

Serves 4-6

MAPLE PECAN STUFFED RABBIT, EH?

Bruce Jacobson, Swine Fellows Barbecue Team Brantford, Ontario, Canada

In 1999 the Swine Fellows won FIRST PLACE in "Cooking From The Home Land" competition at the Jack Daniel's World Invitational Barbecue Competition, in Lynchburg, TN., using this smoked rabbit recipe. They won the competition in 2000, 2001 and 2002 with different recipes.

1 cup pure maple syrup
1 cup finely chopped pecans
1 tablespoon mustard
1 teaspoon allspice
5 strips bacon
pinch salt and pepper
1 apple, peeled and sliced
3-pound of rabbit, deboned

Start the charcoal in the smoker or barbecue and bring the temperature to about 200°-225° degrees F.

Mix evenly the maple syrup, pecans, mustard, allspice, salt and pepper in a glass bowl and cover it . Let the mixture stand for 48 hours at room temperature. Drain in colander and reserve the liquid to a small bowl for basting. Save the pecan mixture for the stuffing.

Place the larger shoulder cuts of the rabbit together, then lay the rest of the deboned meat on top in a rectangle. Spread the pecan stuffing on top of the meat, then roll the meat into a large roll up and wrap the bacon strips around the rabbit. Use wooden skewers to hold it all together.

Using the indirect cooking method place the rabbit on the rack away from the heat. Baste with some of the reserved maple syrup liquid. Place the apple slices on the rack beside rabbit. Using one cup of water-soaked wood chips, start smoking or grill/smoking the rabbit adding one cup of wood chips every half hour for the first three hours. Continue basting the rabbit every half hour.

Cook the rabbit until the internal temperature is 165° F, about 4 to 6 hours depending on the smoker or barbecue.

When the rabbit is done, remove it from the barbecue and wrap in foil. Allow it to sit for 20 minutes before slicing. Carefully remove the wooden skewers and discard. Slice the rabbit about 1 inch thick and stack offset on a platter, place apple slices between the meat slices. Baste the rabbit and apples one more time with the maple syrup baste for presentation.

Serves 4

OL' BILL'S TERIYAKI ELK STEAKS

Bill Kelly, Woodland, Washington

This simple recipe may be expanded with veggies and mushrooms and brushed with marinade to make great shish-ka-bobs or cook just the meat as a pre-main course finger food. It works well with all sorts of dark-meat game including duck and goose. We've even had success with wild turkey (the feathered kind, as well as the bottled variety). For turkey and chicken, just marinate for 20 to 30 minutes.

1 pound elk or deer venison (round steak or shoulder cuts)
1 cup. of your favorite commercial teriyaki marinade
1 cup. brown sugar
1 teaspoon garlic salt or minced garlic (to taste)
4 ft. long willow switch

Cut the meat into 1-inch cubes. In a large bowl, dissolve the sugar in the marinade, and mix in the garlic. Add the meat and marinate, covered, for 2 to 3 hours. Place it on skewers and set skewers on a hot barbecue grill (500° to 600°) for about two minutes per side — don't overcook it.

Note: Stay close to your grill with a willow switch while cooking. Guests tend to sneak samples off skewers. Use switch sparingly, but with authority.

Serves 4-8

TERIYAKI BUFFALO RIBEYES

Bozeman Trail Wagon Train

Cooked by the wagon train cook over a hardwood fire as we made camp under the stars in the Sawtooth Mountains. Serve buffalo ribeye steaks with barbecued beans, barbecued corn on the cob, and Indian fry bread.

2 tablespoons soy sauce

1 clove garlic, minced or pressed

2 tablespoons brown sugar

1 teaspoon ground ginger

2 tablespoons lemon juice

3 tablespoons olive oil

1 tablespoon minced onion

¼ teaspoon black pepper

1 tablespoon Montreal Steak Seasoning

4 buffalo ribeye steaks, 12 oz each

Combine the soy sauce, garlic, brown sugar, ginger, lemon juice, oil, onion, pepper, and steak seasoning. Pour it over the steak, in a wide flat Pyrex dish. Cover with plastic wrap and refrigerate for 6 hours or (much, much better) till the next day.

Lift the steaks from the marinade and drain briefly. Save the marinade and boil it for 10 minutes in a small saucepan, over high heat. Place the ribeyes on barbecue and grill them for 6-8 minutes over medium-hot fire (450°-550°) for medium rare, turning once and basting with boiled reserved marinade.

Serves 4 BIG eaters, or 8 small ones

CHAPTER 11
DESSERTS

"Heddo" Baked Apples   224

Arnold's Soused Peaches   226

BBQ 'Mericun Apple Pie   227

Fijian Barbequed Pineapple   229

Flamin' Gol-durn Bananas   230

Frau Blau's Chocolate Cake
with Smoky Chocolate Frosting   232

Smoky Chocolate Frosting   234

Grilled Pears & Apples with
Mango Relish   234

Katie's 180 Cheesecake   235

Miss Abigail's Grilled Nectarines   236

RB's Barbecued Ice Cream   238

Somebunny's Chocolate Banana Boats   240

Tipsy Fruit Skewers   240

To Di For Berry, Cherry Nut Cobbler   242

Tricia's Pineapple, Raisin & Plum Upside-Down
Thing   244

The Official Barbecue Judges
Oath of Office   245

QUE'N AT THE RITZ

HOW TO KNOW IF YOU'RE IN A GOOD OR BAD BBQ JOINT

SCENE A—The front door is unpainted, broken, hanging on one hinge, and has Band-Aids covering rips in the screen. There are three bullet holes through the door jamb. Or maybe it doesn't even have a door. "Welcum to Bubba's."

SCENE B—The front door is carved from rare woods, has a polished brass handle and has a uniformed doorman standing by to open it for you. "Λ bienvenue to Chez Barbeque Magnifique."

SCENE A—You're greeted by a 5-foot 2-inch tall man who's as wide as he is tall, wearing the remaining frayed wisps of a stained tank top, a three-year old torn paper fry cooks hat, and rubber thongs. Hard to understand what he's saying because he is chomping on a 2-inch long remnant of a bad cigar.

SCENE B—The doorman introduces you to the Maitre De, Pierre, who's dressed up like Fred Astaire, including the top hat, cane and spats, and who asks if you have reservations disdainfully dissecting your net worth in one glance. You should have worn the Gucci's, or at least the DKNY. When his monacled eye finds your name he claps daintily and sashays around the desk "we have a special table set aside tonight Monsieur, in the Renaissance Room."

SCENE A—You're seated at a Formica-topped table which had to have been stolen off the Sanford & Son set, one metal leg broken but held up by an upended tomato juice can, cobwebs dangling from the underside, a sticky substance on one corner gathering a marching band of ants, and another corner chewed away with obvious teeth marks. As you sit down you slip on a puddle of either blood or bbq sauce (you hope it's the latter). Two dead flowers, and some sort of green thing droops out of a cracked beer bottle. None of the chairs could have cost more than $1.99 and none match. Not just at your table, in the entire room.

SCENE B—You're guided down a carpeted foyer into a dining room that looks like Liberace decorated it, and are seated at a table covered with white linen, Baccarat crystal, and a bouquet of perfect salmon pink and white roses. The chandelier could have been used in the Palace of Versailles, the sterling silver probably came from Buckingham Palace and the chairs are better than you have in your living room. In fact they're probably better than those at Buckingham Palace too. You drop a pen and can't find it in the two-inch thick antique Persian pile.

SCENE A—After noting the quaint ambiance of neon beer signs, 1950's tool shop calendars adorned with partially clothed "models," multicolored strands of ceiling-mounted fly paper (many of which are moving due to the heavy population of flies entrapped thereon), and a rotating floor mounted fan that alternatively emits a loud hum or a sound not unlike metal pieces being shoved through a meat grinder. The busboy tosses you a fly swatter, "just in case."

SCENE B—The five-piece orchestral group begins a selection of Strauss waltzes as you are being seated. The collection of classical and contemporary paintings, on loan from the Metropolitan Museum of Art, and which has been featured in Gourmet Magazine, is perfectly set off by the French lace curtains and Viennese velvet draperies. Your waiter, actually you discover it's your waiter's "first assistant," glides by and welcomes you as he hands your lady a perfect red rose, whispering, "Bon Appetite."

SCENE A—As you search vainly for a menu, finally asking the now belching busboy for help, you discover "there ain't one bub," as he delicately points with a hangnailed middle finger (the rest on that hand are missing) toward a chalk board of "Daily Specialz." You think you'll have the briskit of beef, ribs, fries, white bread and sauce. After all that's all there is.

SCENE B – A white gloved hand appears from nowhere and hands you a leather and velvet menu folder, engraved with the name of the restaurant in 24-karat gold leaf. Inside a parchment manuscript adorned with perfect calligraphy announces the soup, salads, entrees, vegetables, starches, and desserts. But only your menu has prices, the menu given to the ladies has small violets where the price should be. It takes you twenty minutes to read the 164 items, and you haven't even looked at the "Surprize de la Chef" page inserted in the middle.

SCENE A – The food arrives at last, plunked on a piece of butcher paper. A massive pile of pork ribs and a Volkswagen sized hunk of black-as-a-meteor beef sit steaming under the waving flypaper strands. The chef, excuse me, pitman, grabs a handful of French fries directly out of a basket still dripping with hot lard, takes half a loaf of bread from the Wonder wrapper, and throws in a half handful of pickle slices. When you ask about an accompanying sauce he mumbles "what ya kiddin, its on da table already!" You quickly retrieve the sauce from the garbage can, where you had heaved it, thinking it was a leftover, unfinished bottle of very cheap beer.

DESSERTS

SCENE B – After deciding on the Barbeque Kobe Beef (flown in that day from Nagasaki, Japan), the Smoked Pork riblets from New Zealand, the Patates Frites de Belgique and the Moet de Chandon barbecue sauce (vintage 1954) you watch as the food is delivered on Louis XIV sterling silver platters by a platoon of waitpersons. In perfect unison the plates are placed in front of each diner, and the warming lids lifted with the precision of a symphony orchestra. One tuxedoed lass runs up with a golden plate adorned with imported French cornichons and slips it on the table.

SCENE A – There is no conversation at the table now. Guttural grunts, moans, sighs, lip smacks and the sound of ripping flesh obliterates even the Grandpa Jones, Roy Acuff and Ferlin Husky records playing on the jukebox. Flying fingers grab ribs, hunks of brisket, slopping brick red sauce on white bread and using the sopping mass to fashion gooey sandwiches of beef. Rib bones fly like drumsticks at a Buddy Rich drum concert. Gurgles of beer, slurps of sauce, appropriate and inappropriate body cavity sounds bounce off he linoleum as the four crazed barbecue fanatics go at it full boar. Finally, as the food vanishes into sauce stained mouths an eerie quiet ensues. Now only faint sighs and the sound of wet naps being released from foil packages mar the otherwise quiet room. The paltry bill was paid with pocket change. The fan has finally died, Ferlin Husky has faded into the night and peace has settled at Bubba's.

SCENE B – After finding a rib and a piteous quarter-inch of fibrous meat under a two-inch thick layer of tepid, tasteless sauce and after what seemed an hour masticating an immolated chunk of beef (or was it snow tire) which was painfully, swallowed in an esophagus-stretching gulp. And after the limpid fried potatoes swimming in precious oils and vintage Belgian mayonnaise were sadly pushed aside. The feast began and saw an entire plate of pickles (excuse me cornichons) frantically gobbled up as the only really edible food items on the table. Oh yes the water was okay too, except for the damnable lemon-in-netting floating between the Greenland Glacier ice cubes. Groans, growls and gnashing of teeth followed as the itemized bill, the computation of which certainly would tax a mainframe computer, totaled slightly less than the latest contract for a fully-loaded Boeing 777, was delivered by yet another gloved hand holding yet another gilded platter. As the orchestra packed up to go, the chandelier dimmed, the rose petals fluttered to floor and our still-ravenous dinner party voted unanimously to adjourn to another local eatery. A new que joint down the street . . . Bubba's!

The moral of these stories: Fancy names, white linen and astronomical prices do not good BBQ guarantee. Rather savor and relish the wise expenditure of money, passion, and time on the quality of the Que itself. Leave the tables to Formica, the floors to Linoleum and the dinnerware to Chinette. The BBQ belongs to Bubba !

"HEDDO" BAKED APPLES

Grandma Welch, Hartford, CT

A mere wisp of a woman who delighted all with her smile, her endless cheer, her boundless love for everyone and everything, and her love of good food (as long as she didn't have to cook it).

4 large golden delicious apples, ½ lb. each
¼ cup maple syrup, the real stuff please!
¼ cup golden raisins
¼ cup brown sugar, packed
¼ cup currants
½ cup crushed graham crackers
½ teaspoon curry powder
dash of cinnamon
4 lg. pats of butter

Mound charcoal or briquettes on one side of barbecue, or turn on gas on one side of barbecue only. Temperature should be approximately 400°-500°.

Place currants in small bowl and cover with hot water, soak for 20 minutes.

Wash and core the apples, leave at least a ½ inch core hole. Mix the raisins, sugar, currants, graham crackers and curry powder well in a medium bowl, and stuff tightly into the apple cores with a small spoon.

Put ½ inch of water in a baking pan on the bottom side of the grill not covered with hot coals or lighted gas jets. Place each apple on a square of aluminum foil and top it with a butter pat. Seal the foil and place the apples on the grill above the water pan. Bake on the grill for 1 to 1 ¼ hours, or until tender.

Remove from heat, unwrap the apples, and serve immediately.

Serves 4

ARNOLD'S SOUSED PEACHES

6 peaches, firm but ripe

¾ cup Grand Marnier

1 teaspoons vanilla extract

2 Tablespoon dark brown sugar

TOPPING:

1 ¼ cups mascarpone cheese

6 shortbread cookies, crushed

½ cup Grand Marnier

12 shortbread cookies

Halve the peaches and discard the pit. Do not peel the peaches. Mix the Grand Marnier, vanilla, and the sugar together in a shallow, wide bowl and place the peaches in it flesh side down. Cover with plastic wrap, and allow them to soak for 3 to 4 hours.

Place the charcoal on one side of the barbecue, or, if using gas, turn on the burner on one side only.

Try for a grill temperature of 300° to 350°. Place the peaches on the oiled grill away from the heat. Cook them flesh side down, for 6-8 minutes, or until grill marks appear, then turn over and cook for 5-8 minutes more, until the second side has grill marks and the peaches are soft.

About 5 minutes before the peaches are done mix together the mascarpone and crushed cookies in a medium bowl, cover and refrigerate until ready to use. This is best done no earlier than 5 minutes before serving, otherwise the biscuits will be very soggy.

When peaches are done remove them from grill with large slotted spoon or spatula. Place 2 halves on each plate; place a spoonful of the mascarpone into each hollow, and pour a bit of Grand Marnier over the dessert.

Place 2 shortbread cookies on each plate and serve.

Serves 6

BBQ 'MERICUN APPLE PIE

Jerry Soucy is the founder of the Pig and Pepper Barbecue Harvest, a KCBS-sanctioned event held each October to determine the Massachusetts State Barbecue Champion. Founded in 1991, Pig and Pepper is the first, largest, and longest-running KCBS-sanctioned barbecue cookoff in New England, and has raised over $250,000 for charity. Jerry lives near Boston with his wife, two teen-aged children, and a battered old kettle grill named 'Sputnik.' When the pie is ready to serve (still warm), enhance the presentation with a garnish of bright autumn leaves or fresh berries. Serve with ice cream, or traditional extra sharp cheddar cheese the way New Englanders like it.

1 package of our favorite pie crust recipe, or a
frozen, ready-to-use brand

3 pounds peeled and sliced apples, Macouns,
Empires, or Granny Smiths

Sugar to taste

Cinnamon to taste

2 tablespoons lemon juice (optional)

Light cream for brushing the crust

2 tablespoons unsalted butter

Build a fire for indirect cooking or, if using gas, only turn on burners on one side of grill, to reach a temperature between 350° to 400°. Place the water pan on opposite side. Cover the cooker to control the fire, watching to be sure that it does not become too hot (use the oven thermometer or placing hear over grill and counting, to make sure the temperature does not go above 400°.

.Prepare your pie dough in advance, wrapping the ball of dough tightly in plastic wrap or waxed paper and keeping it refrigerated until you are ready to roll it out.

Peel and slice your apples into a large bowl, and toss with sugar and cinnamon to taste until the pieces are well coated. You can also use a squirt of fresh lemon to keep apples from turning brown or if you find the whole mix is too sweet.

On a piece of aluminum foil that has been lightly dusted with flour, roll out the pie dough into a single large circle—larger than you normally would if you were going to put this crust in a pie plate.

Mound the seasoned apples in the center of the crust, then fold the edges of the crust towards the middle of the mound. You will end up with an open inner circle of exposed apples, and the whole thing will look sort of like a tart but with more top crust. Dot the open area with small pieces of the butter, and brush the top crust with the light cream. Finish by sprinkling some additional sugar over the pie.

Slide the pie onto the grill, keeping the foil in place for ease of handling. Cover the cooker.

Add lit charcoal as required to maintain the cooker temperature at 350° to 400° for 35 to 40 minutes, or until the top crust has browned and the filling is bubbly. We used a flashlight to monitor the progress through the vent holes, to avoid raising the cover and losing the heat.

When the pie is done, transfer it onto a cutting board or other surface, sliding it off of the foil to cool. While you may be tempted to just dig right in, the filling of a pie right out of the cooker may be dangerously hot. A brief cooling period also helps the juices to settle and the filling to firm up, resulting in neater cuts and a better presentation. Wait at least 15 minutes to let the pie cool and firm up. Serve warm.

Serves 4-8

FIJIAN BARBEQUED PINEAPPLE

½ cup orange honey
½ cup butter
½ cup dark brown sugar
2 tablespoons water
½ cup dark rum
1 pineapple, cored and cut into 8 vertical wedges
Coconut ice cream

Combine the honey, butter, sugar, water, and rum in a medium saucepan. Bring to a boil, over high heat, stirring constantly. Reduce the heat to low and simmer until the sauce begins to thicken, about 10 minutes. Remove from the source of heat and allow it to cool.

Preheat the grill to medium hot fire (450° to 550°) and oil the grill. Using a long-handled pastry brush coat pineapple pieces with sauce and place them on the grill. Cook them for about 5 minutes, turning occasionally, until the edges of the pineapple brown. Surface of the pineapple should brown.

Remove the pineapple from grill, serve immediately with ice cream and the remaining sauce.

Serves 8

FLAMIN' GOL-DURN BANANAS

6 tablespoons butter

¾ cup dark brown sugar

6 bananas, very new and hard, peeled, sliced in
    half lengthwise

1 tablespoon cinnamon

1 teaspoon nutmeg

¾ cup dark rum

¼ cup banana liqueur

vanilla ice cream

Preheat the grill to a medium hot fire (400° to 500°). Melt the butter in a cast iron skillet on hot side of the grill, then add brown sugar, stirring well to dissolve the sugar. Add the bananas, sprinkle with the cinnamon and nutmeg, and sauté gently over cooler side of the grill until the fruit is golden brown on both sides, about 10 minutes.

Take the pan off the grill. and place it on a heat pad on the table or countertop. Slowly pour the rum and liqueur over the bananas. Carefully ignite the liqueur with a long match, using a large spoon to baste bananas with flaming liquor.

Serve over ice cream when the flame dies out, which should take only a few seconds.

Caution is the rule whenever liquor is to be flamed – you must ALWAYS remove the pan from the heat source when adding liquor.

Serves 6

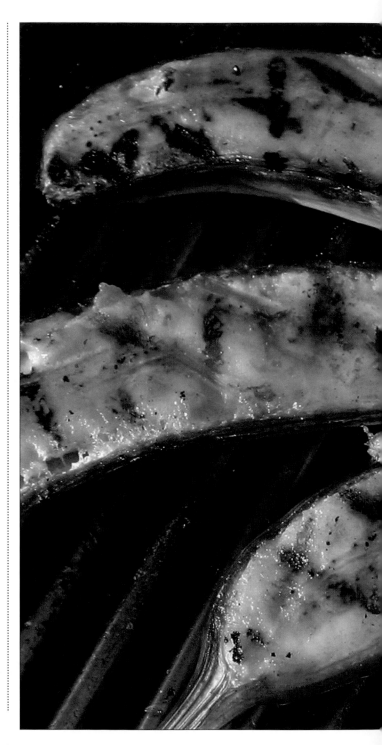

FRAU BLAU'S CHOCOLATE CAKE WITH SMOKY CHOCOLATE FROSTING

CAKE:

6 oz. plain flour

1 oz. cocoa

1 level teaspoon baking powder

5 oz. soft brown sugar

2 eggs yolks, separated

6 tablespoons salad oil

4 tablespoons cream

1 teaspoons vanilla essence

6 tablespoons dark rum

Preheat the smoker or BBQ kettle to 350° F for indirect cooking. Thoroughly grease with Crisco or butter an 8-inch round cake tin. Sift the flour, cocoa, and baking powder into a medium bowl, stir in brown sugar, add egg yolks, oil, cream, vanilla essence, and rum and beat to a smooth batter using a hand or electric mixer.

In a separate bowl whip the egg whites to soft peaks and fold into the batter with a large metal spoon. Transfer the mixture to a prepared round cake tin and bake it in a hot barbecue grill or smoker (on indirect heat) for 1 ¼ hours until the cake has fully risen, is golden, and a skewer or toothpick inserted into the middle comes out clean.

Remove the cake from the barbecue. Leave it for 10 minutes, then turn it out onto a wire cake rack. Let the cake cool completely.

SMOKY CHOCOLATE FROSTING

2 lb. semi-sweet chocolate, grated
1 pt. fresh whipping cream
6 oz. light rum

Grate the chocolate into a medium stainless steel mixing bowl. Add the cream and stir.

Place the bowl in smoker and smoke at 220° for 30 minutes. Stir the mixture every 15 minutes. For a heavier smoke flavor increase the smoking time by 15 minutes. If the chocolate mixture is not completely melted after 30 minutes, place it over a pot of boiling water and bring up to 160° degrees; whisk until smooth and add light rum, then whisk until smooth again.

When the frosting is smooth, remove the bowl from the heat with oven mitts. Let the frosting cool thoroughly. When you are ready to frost the cake beat the frosting until fluffy with a hand mixer and then smooth it over the cake.

Serves 8

GRILLED PEARS & APPLES WITH MANGO RELISH

2 large pears, ripe but firm, cut into 1" chunks
2 apples, cut into eighths
8 tablespoons preserved ginger syrup
4 tablespoons rice wine vinegar
4 tablespoons olive oil

MANGO RELISH:

2 mangoes, diced
2 tablespoons chopped shallots
¼ teaspoons powdered ginger
2 tablespoons chopped fresh mint leaves
2 teaspoons olive oil

Preheat the grill to 350° to 400°. Place bamboo skewers in a flat glass pan and cover with hot water, weight down with a full water glass or bottle.

Thread the pears and apples on the soaked wooden skewers. In a small bowl combine the ginger syrup, vinegar, and oil, and stir until well blended. Grill the skewers, brushing them frequently with ginger syrup mixture, until lightly browned and crisp, about 10 minutes.

While the pears and apples are cooking, in a small bowl, combine the relish ingredients, stir well to mix thoroughly and place in a small bowl. Serve at room temperature alongside pear/apple skewers.

Serves 4

KATIE'S 180 CHEESECAKE

Katie Lane, Austin, TX

This took 1st place in desserts at the Jack Daniels CookOff a few years ago. The cheesecake recipe is called "Katie's 180" for the perfect scores it garnered; 10's in each of the appearance, taste, and texture categories—from all six judges! Wow!

1 ½ cups vanilla wafer crumbs

6 tablespoons melted butter

1 tablespoon Gentleman Jack

1 14 oz. package caramels

1 5 oz. can evaporated milk

1 generous cup coarsely chopped nuts (I use pecans)

3 8-oz. packages softened cream cheese

3 eggs at room temperature

1 teaspoon vanilla

½ cup granulated sugar

1 can Eagle Brand Sweetened Condensed milk

½ cup melted chocolate chips

Spray the sides of a 9″ springform pan with nonstick spray and dust with ½ of the vanilla wafer crumbs. Mix the excess crumbs with the melted butter and Gentleman Jack. Stir together and press into the bottom and ½ inch up the sides of the pan. Set the pan aside.

Slowly and over low heat, melt the caramels and evaporated milk together in a medium saucepan, stirring occasionally, about 5 minutes. When the mixture is completely melted, pour it over the crust. Sprinkle the chopped nuts over the caramel mixture.

Using an electric beater, mix the cream cheese, eggs, vanilla and sugar together until smooth. Add milk and mix well. Add the melted chocolate and blend completely with mixer. Carefully pour this mixture over the top of the nuts and, using a toothpick or a sharp knife, try and get out the air bubbles.

Bake the cheesecake for 45 minutes in a 350° smoker or BBQ grill (over indirect heat with a water pan under the cheesecake). The cheesecakes should appear golden brown on top and be firm to the touch. Remove it from the heat and cool completely.

Serves 12–14

MISS ABIGAIL'S GRILLED NECTARINES

4 large nectarines, cut in half (or peaches)

1 ½ oz. butter, melted

3 tablespoons brown sugar

2 8-oz. lemon yogurt containers

dash of cinnamon

dash of nutmeg

Place the nectarines in a medium cast iron dish with cut side up and brush them with butter. Scatter half the sugar over the fruit and grill over high heat (450° to 550°) for 8-10 minutes until the sugar caramelizes.

Leaving the dish on the grill, place a large spoonful of lemon yogurt on top of each nectarine, sprinkle with the remaining sugar, cinnamon, and nutmeg, and grill for another 3 minutes.

Remove from the heat and let them stand for 3 minutes before serving.

Can be served with fresh vanilla ice cream or fruit sorbet.

Serves 4

RB'S BARBECUED ICE CREAM

(a.k.a. Grilled Alaska)

1 standard sized pound cake, frozen
1 gallon high quality ice cream, frozen hard
12-16 egg whites
1 teaspoon cream of tartar
1 cup granulated sugar
chocolate sprinkles
1 8 oz. jar chocolate fudge sauce
1 small bunch fresh mint leaves for garnish

Take 1 wooden plank, 12 "x 12" by 1" thick, and wrap it in 2 to 3 layers of heavy-duty aluminum foil.

Get a good hot fire (600° to 700° degrees plus) going in a grill or smoker. If you use charcoal or briquettes in a grill, cover the bottom of grill pan. If using a gas grill, turn on all burners to high.

Using an electric mixer or hand beater, whip the egg whites, cream of tartar, and sugar into a very stiff meringue so that when you pull the beaters away, sharp points stand up in the meringue. At the last minute add a generous amount of chocolate sprinkles and quickly fold them into the egg whites. Put the mixture in the refrigerator until ready to use.

Set foil wrapped board on counter. Working quickly, use a sharp serrated knife to cut the frozen pound cake in half horizontally, and lay one half on the foil.

Open the carton of ice cream and cut a 1-2" to ⅔" slice lengthwise off the brick of ice cream. Place slice of ice cream on the cake. If ice cream is not completely covering the bottom slice of cake cut another ½" to 3" piece and fit alongside so you have an even layer over the cake. Sprinkle more chocolate sprinkles on the ice cream and cover it with the top half of cake.

Using a flexible spatula completely cover the cake on all sides with meringue, being sure to bring the meringue all the way down to TOUCH THE FOIL all around the cake. If you leave any gaps the ice cream may melt and spoil the dessert.

Place the plank in the center of the grill or smoker and immediately close the cover. Check it after 2 minutes and as soon as you see the peaks of meringue turning brown remove the dessert from the cooker. This will only take 4 to 5 minutes with a very hot fire.

Slide the cake off the plank and onto a chilled serving platter. With a heated, serrated knife, cut vertical slices through the meringue, cake, and ice and put slices on plates onto which you have spooned a generous pool of chocolate sauce.

Garnish the sauce with fresh mint leaves, shake more sprinkles over the meringue, and serve immediately.

Serves 4-6

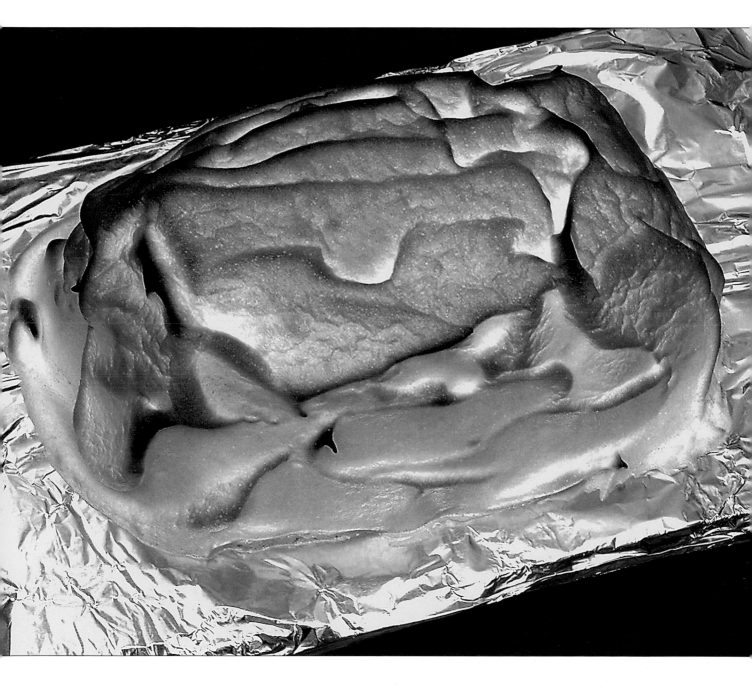

SOMEBUNNY'S CHOCOLATE BANANA BOATS

4-6 bananas, green, under-ripe are best
1-2 large milk chocolate bars

OR

1 small, 11-ounce bag milk chocolate morsels

Lay the banana on its side and with a sharp knife slit the bananas, from end to end, deep into the bananas, but not cutting through the bottom peeling.

Spread the slits wide and stuff with the pieces of chocolate. The amount you put into each banana is usually determined by the amount of chocolate or the number of people eating the treats.

Wrap the bananas in foil. Place them on the grill over medium heat (350° to 400°) for about 10 minutes or until the chocolate is melted and the bananas are partially cooked. Remove bananas from tin foil, then carefully cut away the top section of the peel, and scoop out the chocolate and fruit from the resulting banana "boat" with a spoon.

For true decadence place a large scoop of vanilla ice cream beside the banana boat and dig in.

Serves 4-6

TIPSY FRUIT SKEWERS

The best way to barbecue fruit is by making fruit kebabs. Most fruits work well, especially when slightly marinated in an alcoholic sugar syrup, so that the outside of the fruit pieces caramelizes when grilled.

½ medium pineapple, cubed
3 tart apples, cubed
3 pears, cubed
¼ small watermelon, cubed
1 pint strawberries, whole
2 mangos, cubed
6 small apricots, pitted and halved
1 medium bunch grapes, whole

MARINADE:

½ cup brown sugar
1 teaspoon butter
½ cup dark rum or fruit-flavored liqueur
-

Place bamboo skewers in a flat pan and weight down with a water glass, cover with hot water, and let soak for 20 minutes.

Wash then thoroughly dry the fruit. Thread alternative fruit pieces onto bamboo skewers.

In a medium pan over low heat gently warm the sugar and butter until all the sugar has dissolved, and the resulting syrup has thickened slightly. Allow it to cool before adding rum or the liqueur of your choice.

Brush the fruit with the marinade and put it aside for 15 to 20 minutes to enable the flavors to develop. Before barbecuing, brush the kebabs once again with the marinade.

Grill over medium heat (400° to 500°) approximately 1 to 2 minutes per side, then turn over and grill until the outside of the fruit begins to caramelize and edges brown.

Serve 4-6

TO DI FOR BERRY, CHERRY NUT COBBLER

Diana Dillard, Lakeshore, WA

Diana is a graduate of the Culinary Institute of America, former owner/executive chef at Rain City Grill in Seattle (which was voted one of the top 5 restaurants in the city), and currently teaches professional culinary arts courses at Seattle Culinary Academy at Seattle Central Community College, and is a freelance culinary consultant.

FRUIT FILLING:

1 ½ cups raspberries, fresh or frozen and thawed
1 cup blueberries, fresh or frozen and thawed
1 cup sweet cherries, pitted, fresh or frozen and thawed
¼ cup granulated sugar
1 tablespoon cornstarch
2 teaspoons fresh lemon juice
Topping:
¾ cup all-purpose flour
¼ cup brown sugar
⅛ cup powdered sugar
¼ teaspoon salt
¼ teaspoon baking powder
¼ teaspoon ground cinnamon
¼ teaspoon ground nutmeg
½ cup coarsely chopped walnuts
⅓ cup butter; melted

Pre-heat the smoker or barbecue to 350°-400° degrees for indirect heating.

Lightly butter an 8-inch cake pan. Gently rinse the berries and cherries. Drain on a paper towel lined cookie sheet to absorb the moisture.

Place the berries and cherries in a medium mixing bowl. In a separate small bowl combine the sugar and cornstarch and sprinkle over the berry mixture. Add the lemon juice and toss gently. Transfer to the prepared cake pan.

Sift together the flour, sugars, salt, baking powder, cinnamon, and nutmeg. Add the walnuts. Pour in the butter and toss the ingredients with a fork to form large crumbs. Sprinkle topping over the berry and cherry fruit filling with a large spoon.

Bake the cobbler for approximately 30 minutes or until the crumbs begin to brown and the filling juices are bubbling. Serve slightly warm or at room temperature topped with whipped cream or ice cream.

Serves 4

TRICIA'S PINEAPPLE, RAISIN & PLUM UPSIDE-DOWN THING

¼ cup stick butter

¾ cup dark brown sugar

1 can pineapple chunks, drained

½ cup golden raisins

12 dried plums, pits removed

1 box lemon (or orange) cake mix, (ie: Betty
    Crocker SuperMoist Lemon cake mix)
which requires:

1 ¼ cups water

⅓ cup vegetable oil

3 large eggs

1 container of whipping cream for garnish

1 to 2 tablespoons confectioners sugar

1 teaspoon vanilla

Mix the butter and sugar together in a bowl with a fork until it forms flake-like pieces. Spread this mixture evenly across the bottom of a foil pan.

Place the fruit on top of the butter and sugar mixture, alternating layers: pineapple, then raisins, then plums.

Follow the instruction on the box for mixing the lemon (or orange) cake and, after mixing, pour the cake batter over the pan of fruit.

Mounding the coals on one side of the barbecue, place a water pan on the other side, replace the grill rack and put the cake on the side away from the coals (indirect heat).

The temperature should be around 300° to 350° degrees. Keep the barbecue lid closed as much as possible. The cake is ready when a toothpick inserted into the middle comes out clean, usually 30-35 minutes.

Remove the cake from the heat and cool for 15 minutes. While cake is cooking use electric mixer to whip cream, adding confectioners sugar, and vanilla while whipping. Then turn the cake over on a platter and serve each piece with a large dollop of fresh whipped cream on the side.

Serves 8

THE OFFICIAL BARBECUE JUDGES OATH OF OFFICE

I do solemnly swear to objectively and subjectively evaluate each barbecue meat that is presented to my eyes—to my nose—to my hands—and to my palate.

I accept my duty as a barbecue judge, so that

Truth,

Justice,

Excellence in barbecue,

and the American way of life,

is strengthened and preserved forever!

You're on your oath!

— Remus Powers, PhB (AKA: Ardie Davis)

Our special thanks to the following corporations, for their assistance, enthusiastic support and for helping to make this book happen.

Char-Broil

McCormick Spices

BIC Corporation

Georgie Boy Manufacturing

and the folks at:

Blue Mountain Design Works

Bruce Foods Corporation

Canadian Bison Association

Cash & Carry

Chefwear

Estes Clothiers

KitchenAid

Louisiana Hot Sauce

Oregon Cedar Grill

Oregon Spice Company

OXO International

Smart & Final Stores Corporation

Sur La Table—Portland, Oregon

The Real Canadian Bacon Company

Wells Lamont

A hearty and heartfelt ThankQUE to the people who helped me in my passion to search out and share the best barbecue I could find:

Alison Bitner, Sur La Table

OAll-American Smokers, Leesburg, Ga.

Allen Erkhart & the Grill Masters Team, Americus, Ga.

Anne & Terry Callon

Ardie Davis, aka Remus Powers

Arthur Peterson, Char-Broil

Barbara Johnson

Barry Pelts, Jan Klein, Corky's Ribs & BBQ, Memphis

BBQfan1

BBQ'N Fools

Betsy Sunden, Bayer Corporation

Bill & Pam Medlock, Cow-A-Bunga

BJ Hockman, Oregon Spice Company

Bob Hastings, Rockland Area C of C

Bob & Debbie Morris

Bob, Marti, Rick and Anne Browne

Bray Vincent, Goode Co.

Brea Lang

Brette & Lindy Harte

Brian Campbell

Brian Murphy

Bruce Jacobson, Canadian Barbecue Smokers Association

Bruce & Pam Paris

Carl Triola & Family

Carlene & Mitch Phelps, barbecuenews.com

Captain BBQ

Carolyn and Gary Wells, Kansas City Barbecue Society

Charlie McMurry

Chris Sandberg

Christopher Ladner

Chuck kruger, Entertainment Resources

Colette LeGrande

Cynthia J. Smith

Damnifino Team

Dan & Sue Brodsky

Daniel Ostroff

Dave DeWitt, Fiery Foods Magazine

David Klose

David Skinner, Whirlpool Corporation

David & Mary Spriggs, newbookscheap.com

Dean Dirks

Diana & Tom Dillard

Diana Loesch, Sow Luau

Diane Hampton and Lynn Doyle, Memphis in May

Delores Spruell-Jackson

Donna Myers, Hearth, Patio & Barbecue Association

Doug Fisher

Doug & Joyce Spittler

Doug Mosley, National Barbecue News

Duane Trygg

Ed & Julie Nyland

Erin Kirk

Esther Lippman & Susanna Clyde

Fran Hall, Columbus Pig Jig

Frank Boyer, California Barbecue Assoc.

Garry Howard, The Smoke Ring

Georgie Boy: Patrick Terveer, Rich Allen, Dick Yost, Jerry Dunfee, Frank Long

Grant & June Browne

Grill to Go Team

Harry Aldrich, Oregon Cedar Grill Co.

Hayward & Eva Harris, The Rib Doctor

Heather Bryan, Oregon Spices

Helen Himple, Travel Meetings & Incentives

Jack Bettridge & family

Jack Rogers, Jim Minion, The Car Dogs, Puyallup, Wa.

Jamie Gwen, Chef, Smart & Final

Jamieson Fuller

Jason Gronlund, Chef, McIlhenny Company

Jeff Loya, Phil's BBQ

Jeff Miller, Vancouver PD

Jennie Halfant

Jennifer Alexander

Jennifer Lyons

JoAnn & Larry Laney

Joel Schroeder

John & Kathy Angood

John Davis

John Scroggins, Noble Communications

Jon & Jana Trueb, J&J BBQ, West Linn, Or.

Judith Regan, Aliza Fogelson–Regan Books

Kathleen S. Davis, Blue Mountain Design Works

Karen Adler, Pig Out Publications

Karen Gelbart, Food Network Canada

Karen Von Eisenburg, Bayer Corporation

KCTS-TV, Seattle: Jay Parikh, Randy Brinson, Glenn Dreyfuss, Greg Davis, Tim Olson, Tom Speer, Marion Smith, David Rabbinovich, Tom Niemi, Jeff Gentes, Erin Miller, Rupert Macnee

Lee McWright, Music City Pig Pals

Lisa Moore

Lou Brancaccio & family

Lynn & Jeff Shivers, IBCA

Kevin, Mary, Amber & Stephen

Kevin Flannery, NEBS

Kurt Andrews, Regan Books

Kyle Greenwood

Linda Myers, MYCOMM

Luther Echols' Club Red Team, Columbus, Ga.
Lynne Tolley, Miss Mary Bobo's
Mad Momma & The Kids
Margaret Sharp
Marianne Beckwith
Marsha & Russ Matta, & the original Baxter
Melanie Jones
Michael Coyne
Mike & Ed's Barbecue, Phenix City, Arkansas
Miss Mary Bobo, Miss Mary Bobo's Boarding House
Misty River Band
Nathan Wu & Karen Kulm
Nick Spinelli, Jr., Kraft Foods
Oliver Gomes
Patrick Faulstitch
Pat & Tara Bennett
Patti Abel, Work Kitchen Inc.
Patty Boday, Oregon Spice Company
Paul Kirk, The Baron of Barbecue
Peggy Scott
Phil Pace, Phil's BBQ
Regis Philbin
Randall Oliver, Smart & Final
Rhoda Varley & family
Rick & Barbara Smith
Rocky Danner, National Barbecue News
Rolf Zubler, World BBQ Association
Rose Arceneaux
Rubie Lloyd, ChefWear
Scott Campbell & family
Scott Ressmeyer, Country's, Columbus, Ga.
Smoke Stack Lightning

Sow Luau Team
Spats & Spoons Browne
Stephanie Wilson, KCBS
Steve Liberty, Trade Winds Motor Inn
Swine & Dine Team, Memphis, Tn.
Swine Fellows Team
Tana Shupe, Jack Daniel's World Invitational
The Browne's: Kathy, Kara, Tricia & Chris
The Parikh's: Monica, Andrew, Jacob & Rebecca
The Columbian Photogs: Milan Chuckovich, Kim Blau, Jerry Coughlan, Troy Wayrynen, Linda Lutes, Dave Olson, Janet L. Mathews, Steve Lane
Tom Ryll
Thomas Sandmeier, Swiss Barbecue Artists
Tracy Satterfield, The American Royal Tom Ryll
Tony Spear, Estes Clothing Designs
The Smiths: Barb, Jim, Abby, Anthony, Tyler & Betsy
Tia Burke, The Rivermark, Memphis, Tn.
Tiffany Collins, Houston Livestock Show
Tom & Charlie Vergos, The Rendezvous, Memphis
Tom Ryll
Tom Spear, Estes's Men's Clothing, Portland, Or.
Top Gun Brisketeers
Tracy Satterfield, American Royal
Valerie Schmid, Swiss Barbecue Artists
Virginia Peebles, Historic Columbus Foundation
Zoe Miller, Oregon Spice Company

Index

A

acacia wood, 202

Alabama Sauce, 156

Alder wood, 200

Aldrich, Harry, 45

Alice Springs Emu Steaks, 203

almond wood, 202

American Royal Barbecue contest, 37, 38, 175

Anderson, Dottie, 204

Anderson, Fred, 204

Anderson, Patty Browne, 76

Angood, John, 120, 152

apple wood, 200

Apricot Mango Chutney, 208

Armadillo Eggs, 8

Armstrong, Drew, 81

Armstrong, Jayme, 81, 83

Arnold's Soused Peaches, 222

Asparagus with Lemon Marinade, 127

ash wood, 202

Assyrian Grilled Leg of Lamb with Pomegranate Sauce, 70

Aunt Lilly's Sizzling Lobster, 40

Aunt Rhoda's Dirty Rice, 142

Aussie BBQ Lamb Leg, 71

Aw Shucks Grilled Corn, 128

B

Bacon-Wrapped Smoked Pork Tenderloin, 85

Baker, John, 77

'Bama BBQ Sauce, 161

B&M's New Mexico Smoked Wild Boar Ham, 209

Barbecue America (Browne), 3

Barbecued Ostrich Filet Mignon with Ginger & Lime, 205

Bar-B-Q Polenta Cakes & Tomato Sauce, 130

Baxter B. B. Chicken, 125

Baxter BB Chicken's Back (and Everywhere Else Too) Rub, 179

BBQ'd Venison Loin Chops, 206

BBQ 'Mericun Apple Pie, 223

BBQ Peking Duck with Cold Duck–Hoisin Sauce, 108

BBQued Seitan Burgers, 184

Beer Butt Chicken, 110

Beer Butte Ranch Sauce, 161

Beer Butt Turkey, 112

Ben (Milan Chuckovich's son), 15

Bennett, Alisa, 150

Bennett, Pat, 150

Bennett, Tara, 136, 150

Best Butt Contest, 22

Best Recycling Team, 22

Best Team Skit, 22

Big Al's Smoked Chili, 24

birch wood, 202

Black & Bleu Cheese Q Sauce, 162

Blazin' Saddles Fireside Beans, 131

BoBo's BBQ Boid, 114

Bourbon Salmon Mop, 163

Bozeman Trail Wagon Train, 215

Breast of Wild Goose with
    Lingonberry Sauce, 211

Brennan, Stephen, 62

Brides of Black Hole Chili team, 24

Brodsky, Dan, 26

Brooklyn Jerk Wings (or Thighs), 114

Brooks, Garth, 22

Browne, Bob, 60, 209

Browne, Chris, 43, 132

Browne, Dorothy, 148

Browne, Grant, 16

Browne, June, 16

Browne, Kathy, 88

Browne, Marti, 60, 209

Browne, Rick
    Barbecue America, 3
    Grilling America, 3

Browne, Terry, 103

Bruhweiler, Flash, 24

Bryant, Vicky, 118

Burden, Les, 54

C

Cabernet Sauvignon, 75

California Sauce, 157

Callon, Anne, 179

Callon, Terry, 179

Canadian BBQ Championship, 41

Cape Cod Cottage Cabbage, 132

Car Dogs' Award-Winning Salmon,
    41. See also Car Dogs Barbecue
    team

Car Dogs Barbecue team, 38, 41

Carl's Smoked Quail, 115

Carolina Sauces, 156

Carolina-Style Pulled Pork Shoulder,
    87

"Casey at the Bat" (Thayer), 126

Catfish Institute, 42

Catfish with Tangy Orange Sauce, 42

CB's Oh-You-Devil Eggs, 9

CB's Saturday Nite Grilled Veggies,
    132

Cedar-Planked Sugarcane Canadian
    Peameal Bacon, Eh?, 89

Cedar Plank Swordfish with
    Pineapple Salsa, 45

Ceremonial Black Hole Chili, 24

Charcoal Grilled Shiitakes, 134

Chardonnay Marinade, 163

Cheesey BBQ'd Roast Beef, 25

cherrywood, 200

Chiang Mai Saffron-Raisin Rice, 144

Choy, Sam, 54

Chris & Colette's Venetian Stuffed
    Calamari, 43

Chuckovich, Milan, 15

Cleanest Team Area, 22

Coles, Rhoda, 142

Columbian, 185

Cooking from the Home Land
    competition, 213

Copper River, 37, 38

cottonwood, 202

Coyne, Michael, 14

crab apple wood, 202

Cranberry-Lemon BBQue Glaze, 164

Crumbly BBQ Rainbow Trout, 46

Culinary Institute of America, 238

Curses . . . Foiled Agin' Taters, 146

D

Damnifino team, 23, 115

Dan & Ron's Tri-Tip Roast, 26

Dave's Seitan Grilling Sauce, 185

Davis, Ardie. See Powers, Remus

Davis, John, 131

Day, Sonny, 24

De-Dip De-Dip Sauce, 117

Dennis (Barbara Smith's father), 174

Denver Mint-ed Lamb Ribs, 72

DeWitt, Dave, 198

Diddy-Wa-Diddy Sauce Contest, 157,
    175

Dillard, Diana, 238

Dirty Dick. See Westhaver, Richard

Dirty Dick's Ancho Barbecue Sauce,
    165

Dixie Watermelon Salsa, 10

Donahoo, David, 161

Dorothy's Sweet Potatoes, 148

Doyle, Denise M., 100

Dracula's Blood Orange Sauce, 166

Dr. Pepper Beef Brisket, 27

Dungeness Crab Cakes with Basil
    Mayonnaise, 48

F

Fantasia (from Maui, Hawaii), 185

Fantasia's BBQ Tofu Cakes, 185

Farmer, Albert, 118

Fields, Jim, 79, 83

Fiery Foods, 160, 198

Fijian Barbequed Pineapple, 225

Flamin' Gol-durn Bananas, 226

Frau Blau's Chocolate Cake with
    Smoky Chocolate Frosting, 228

Fred's Apple/Cherry-Stuffed
    Pheasant, 204

Frickles-Fried Pickles, 11

G

Gail's Guava BBQ Sauce, 167

Georgia Sauce, 156

Gilroy Stinking Rose Mushrooms, 11

Golden Rosemary Polenta, 186

Gouvenor Beach Peanut Salad, 12

Grandma Leah's Grape Salad, 136

grapefruit wood, 202

Grilled & Breaded Tofu (Seitan), 187

Grilled Huntsman Beef Sandwiches,
    28

Grilled Lamb Loin with Zinfandel-
    Sage-Morel Sauce, 73

Grilled Lemon-Lime Tempeh, 188

Grilled Loin of Venison with Wild
    Mushroom Ragout, 212

Grilled Loin of Wild Boar with Sour
    Cherry Sauce, 88

Grilled Mussels with Spicy Fish
    Sauce, 50

Grilled Onion & Potato Skewers, 149

Grilled Pears & Apples with Mango
    Relish

Grilled Pork Chops with Peach
    Chutney, 90

Grilled Pork Shoulder, 94

Grilled Shallot-Cognac Steaks, 28

Grilled Turkey Breast with Hawaiian
    Fruit Salsa, 116

Grilled Wild Mushroom Sausage,
    136

Grilling America (Browne), 3

Groking, 197

H

Hale, Smokey, 126

Havranek, Don, 25

Hawaiian Salsa, 116

Hawaii Sauce, 158

Hearth, Patio, and Barbecue
    Association, 159

"Heddo" Baked Apples, 220

Herbed Crown Roast of Lamb, 74

hickory wood, 200

Homarus americanus, 63, 65

Honey, Do-That-Shrimp-Thing-
    Again!, 51

Honey-Mustard Grilled Rib Eye
    Steaks, 30

Horsey Sauce with a Bite, 167

Houston Rodeo and Barbecue
    competition (2000), 161

Houston Stock Show and Rodeo, 21

Huckleberry Mountain Porterhouse
    Pork Chops, 86

I

Inebriated Top Round, 31

Islands, 144

J

Jack Daniel's World Invitational
    Barbecue Competition, 168, 213

Jackson, Alan, 22

Jack's Whiskey BBQ Sauce, 168

Jacobson, Bruce, 213

Jamaican Jerk Sauce, 168

Jell-O Shooter Committee, 82

Jessen, Ron, 26

John Davis's Oregon Cedar Salmon,
    58

Just for the Halibut, 52

K

Kansas City Barbecue Society

Kansas City Barbeque Society
Cookbook, The, 77

Kansas City Barbeque Society
Cookbook, The (Kansas City
Barbecue Society), 77

Kansas City Sauce, 157

Kara Beth's Hot Damn Wings, 12

Kathy (Barbara Smith's sister), 174

Katie's 180 Cheesecake, 231

Kelly, Bill, 214

Kentucky Sauce, 156

Key West Citrus Sauce, 170

Kirk, Paul, 126

Kiwi Beer Marinade, 170

Knight, Marcus, 170

Korean Bulgogi Marinade, 171

L

Lane, Katie, 231

Last Gaucho Beefsteak Sauce, 171

Last Roundup Beef Rub, 178

Leah (Tara Bennett's grandmother),
136

LeGrand, Colette, 43

lemon wood, 202

Leroy Brown's Thai BBQ Chicken,
116

Les Burden's Awesome Shrimp &
Scallops, 54

Lexington #1 Pulled Chicken, 118

Lexington "Yaller" Sauce, 172

lilac wood, 202

Lilly (aunt), 40,

Lil Piggy's Barbecue, 66

Lobster, 63–67

Louisiana Fire Pecans, 13

Low-Fat Italian BBQ Sauce, 172

Luckenbach Ladies World
Championship Chili Cookoff
(1978), 24

Lyons, Jennifer, 62

M

Macon Bacon BBQ Sauce, 173

Maine Lobster Festival, 63, 64, 66

Maine Luau & BBQ Pit, 66

Mallard, Billy Bob, 173

Maple Pecan Stuffed Rabbit, Eh?, 213

Maple Smoked Lamb Shanks with
Whiskey Onion Marmalade, 75

maple wood, 200

Marble Falls Chili Cookoff, 24

Marinated Dinosaur Ribs, 32

Massey, Jim, 79, 83

Matta, Marsha, 179

Matta, Russ, 179

Meek, Al, 24

Memphis in May World
Championship Barbecue Contest,
38, 80, 83

Memphis Sauce, 157

mesquite trees, 199

Meyer, Claus, 171

Mikey's Melbourne Crab Damper, 14

Milan's Coconut Baby Backs, 15

Miller, Gail, 167

Minion, Jim, 38, 41. *See also* Car
Dogs Barbecue team

Miss Abigail's Grilled Nectarines,
232

Missy's Mustard Marinade, 174

Momma's Marvelous Margarita
Glaze, 174

Mongo's Mango Marinade, 173

Morel Mushroom Gravy, 137

Most Colorful Team, 22

Most Unique Pit, 22

Mozambique Fire Shrimp with Pili
Pili Sauce, 56

Mt. Adams Huckleberry Sauce, 88

mulberry wood, 202

Mushroom Ragout, 213

N

National Barbecue Sauce Contest.
See Diddy-Wa-Diddy Sauce
Contest

New Mexico Sauce, 158

New Potatoes in Garlic-Lemon
Butter, 150

North Carolina Barbecued Turkey,
118

North Carolina Pork Producer's
Association, 95

North Carolina–Style Whole Hog, 95

O

oak wood, 200

Official Barbecue Judges Oath of
Office, 241

Ol' Bill's Teriyaki Elk Steaks, 214

Ole Ole Infree's Tempeh Satay, 189

Ol' Jeremiah's Grilled Oysters with
Butter Sauce, 52

Olson, Dave, 185, 189

omega-3, 38

Onion-Fired Steaks, 138

007 Martini Oysters, 8

orange wood, 202

Oregon Cedar Grill Cedar planks,
45

Oregon Cedar Grills, 106

Oregon Spice Company, 176, 177,
178, 188

Outdoor Gourmet, 45

Oz Onion Pudding, 138

P

Pacific Northwest Regional Barbecue
Championships, 37, 41

Pacific Northwest Sauce, 158

Patten, Rodney, 33

Patty Browne's Browned Patties, 76

Peach Chutney, 92

Pecan-Walnut Crusted Pork Loin, 97

pecan wood, 200

Pig and Pepper Barbecue Harvest,
223

Pineapple Salsa, 44

Pinot Noir, 75

Pinsonneult, Matt, 73

Pirtle, Caleb, III, 178

PNWBA Championships, 37

Powers, Remus, 126, 175, 241

Q

Qued Glazed Squash, 139

R

Rain City Grill, 238

Razorback Patay, 16

RBq's Smoke-Baked potatoes, 151

RB's Barbecued Ice Cream, 234

RB's BBQ Steak Sauce, 30, 32

Real Canadian Bacon Company, 89

Redhook Ale Brewery, 37, 41

Regis & Kathie Lee Show, 110

Remus's Kansas City Classic Sauce,
175

Reserve Champion ribbon, 41

Rick's Grilled Ratta-Tooey, 190

Roast Suckling Pig, 98

Rockies (jeans), 22

Rodeo Institute for Teacher
Excellence, 21

Rodney's Tequila Porterhouse, 33

Rogers, Jack, 38, 41. *See also* Car
Dogs Barbecue team

Rub a Dub Dub, Bub!, 177

S

salmon
chinook (king), 37, 38, 41, 158
coho (silver, 37, 158
sockeye (red), 37, 38, 41, 158

Scotch-Smoked Trout or Salmon, 16

Scottsdale Spicy Smoked Tuna
Steaks, 60

Scroggins, John, 118

Seattle Culinary Academy, 238

Sherried Pork Spareribs, 100

smilling, 197

Smith, Barbara, 174

Smith, Betsy, 175

Smith, Tyler, 175

Smoked BBQ Sausage Roll, 102

Smoked Tomato-Basilica Rice, 145

Smokin' Tofu-ed BBQ Beans, 192

Smoky Chocolate Frosting, 230

Smoky Mountain Cornish Hens with
Wild Rice, 120

Smoky Wild Mushroom Tart, 18

Snow Goose Beans, 140

Somebunny's Chocolate Banana
Boats, 236

Songkran Water Festival, 144

Soucy, Jerry, 223

Southern Sugared Ribs, 102

Spats' Grilled Meatballs, 34

Spit BBQued Duck, 122

Strait, George, 22

sweet fruit woods, 203

Swine & Dine, 79–83

Swine Fellows Barbecue team, 213

T

Tailor-Made Lamb Chops, 77

Tailor, Ralph, 77

Tang-y Grill-Roast Prime Rib, 35

Tantalizing Tandoori Tofu
    Brochettes, 193

Teel, Donny, 85, 102

Tenny Lamas, 22

Teriyaki Buffalo Rib Eyes, 215

Terry's Sweet and Sour Riblets, 103

Texas Sauce, 157

Thai Lamb Kabobs, 77

Thayer, Ernest L.
    "Casey at the Bat," 126

Thirtieth Annual World's
    Championship Bar-B-Que
    Contest, 21

Three Iddie Fishies Rub, 179

Tipsy Fruit Skewers, 236

To Di for Berry, Cherry Nut Cobbler,
    238

Tofu Steaks with Pineapple/Mango
    Salsa, 194

Toklas, Alice B., 155

Tom Lee Park, 82

Tongue Tangy Coleslaw, 141

Twenty-sixth Annual World
    Championship Barbecue
    Cooking Contest, 79

Tricia's Pineapple, Raisin & Plum
    Upside-Down Thing, 240

Triola, Carl, 22, 102, 115

Tugboat Annie's Sweet Potato
    Salad with Marjoram Honey
    Vinaigrette, 147

TyBet's Southern Cola Barbeque
    Sauce, 175

U

Uncle John's Beer & Potato Salad,
    152

V

Vidalia Bar-Be-Cue Sauce, 176

Vincent, Judith, 71

W

Wallace, Donald R., 27

Welch, Dennis, 132

Welch (grandma), 220

Wells, Carolyn, 126

Westhaver, Richard, 40, 147, 165

White Lotus Restaurant, 144

Willingham, John, 126

World's Championship Bar-B-Que
    Contest, 21

Y

Yellow Carolina Q Sauce, 176

Z

007 Martini Oysters, 8

Zesty Lemon Butter, 13

Zesty Smoked Oysters, 62